The ALE TRAIL

ROGER PROTZ

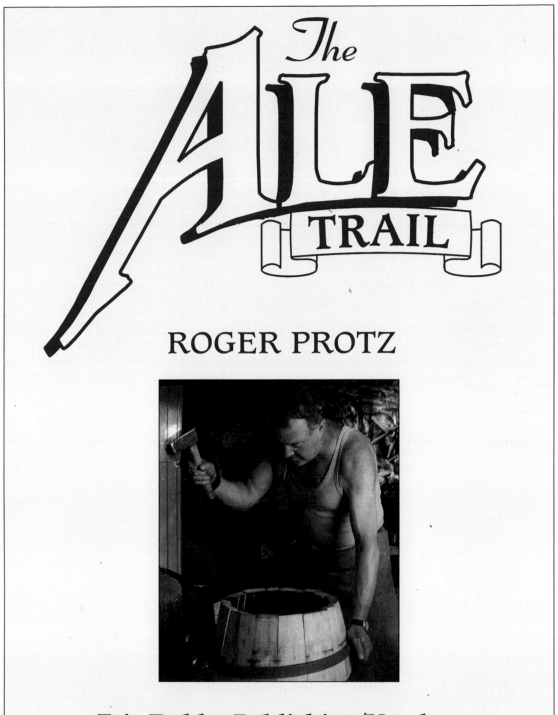

Eric Dobby Publishing/Verulam

Published by Eric Dobby Publishing Ltd,
12 Warnford Road, Orpington, Kent BR6 6LW

A catalogue record of this book is available from
the British Library.

ISBN 1-85882-041-3

Printed & bound by ORIENTAL PRESS, (DUBAI).

Designed and Typeset by Kevin O'Connor, Poole

Contents

BELOW: *Beer is truly international. Here are two versions of Scotch with no Scottish connections ... Bert Grant's Scottish Ale is from America and the Scotch is from the Silly Brewery in Belgium.*

Dedicated to the members of the Campaign for Real Ale, without whom there wouldn't be much to write about

Thanks to countless people who have helped with the writing and research for this book. In particular: Great Britain, John Emerson, Michael Cook, Nick Redman of the Whitbread Archive, Mark Dorber, Dr Keith Thomas, Graham Wheeler, Charles McMaster, Alistair Hook, Dr Fiona Wood of the Brewers' and Licensed Retailers' Association, Barrie Pepper and Peter Coulson, chairman and secretary of the British Guild of Beer Writers, Denis Cox, Denis Palmer, Francessa Becket, Barry Bremner, Khadija Buckland, David Jones of Courage, John Reynolds of Guinness, Dan Thomasson and Doug Pratt at Eldridge Pope, Jim Kerr and Tony Rowsell at Castle Eden, Elaine Magnani at Vaux; in Ireland, Jim Cradock at Smithwicks and Peter Walsh at Guinness; in Belgium, Michael Weber and Paul Arnott at Chimay, Karel VanDamme at Rodenbach; in the Netherlands, Annemiek Louwers of Heineken, Guy Thornton, and Brother Tarcissius at Schaapskoi; in France, Judith Richard of the Regional Tourist Board, Nord-Pas de Calais; in Germany, Regina Gerschermann of Spaten, Gabi Otto of Schneider; in the United States, Tom Dalldorf of Celebrator, Mark Carpenter at Anchor Brewing, John Forbes at BridgePort Brewing, Fred Bowman at Portland Brewing Co, Bert and Sherry Grant in Yakima, Charles and Rosanna Finkel, and Kelly Miess at Pike Place, J.D. Rossit at Redhook, Mark Johnston at Marin County Brewing, Steve Hindy at Brooklyn Brewery, Daniel Bradford of All About Beer, Rob Haiber of the Info Devels, Tony Forder of Ale Street News; in Canada, Paul Hadfield at Spinnakers, Michael Williams at Swan's, members of the Victoria branch of CAMRA, Drew Ferguson, chairman of CAMRA Canada, good companion and a man of infinite jest. Special thanks to Michael Jackson and Benjamin Myers for lending photographs from their private collections, proving that beer writers are a good fellowship.

And, as always, my special thanks to my wife Diana for allowing further peregrinations and occasional tantrums.

BELOW: *The Belgians have a long-standing love of Scots beer and now brew examples of the style themselves.*

He that buys land
  buys many stones,
He that buys flesh
  buys many bones,
He that buys eggs
  buys many shells,
He that buys good ale
  buys nothing else.

John Ray 1627-1705

BELOW: *Nothing else but the best barley. The floor maltings at Munton and Fison in Suffolk.*

Introduction

Ale is the born-again beer. At the end of a century that saw the apparently unstoppable rise of lager brewing, ale is now the beer of the moment. In Germany, where lagering on a commercial scale was first developed, the beers on everyone's lips are members of the ale family: wheat, Kölsch and Alt. In the United States, a beer market dominated for decades by thin, bland and undistinguished versions of lager, several hundred micros have bloomed, many specialising in ales of the highest quality and brewed with great dedication to their true styles. The micro brewers of the United States have created such interest in ale that even the giants of the industry are now experimenting with amber beers and stouts brewed with top-fermenting yeasts imported from England. In the Low Countries, Belgium in particular, ales hidden for most of the century by mass-marketed versions of Pilsner are witnessing substantial growth. Trappist beers, wheat beers, fruit beers, sour beers and 'wild yeast' beers are the talking point and drinking experience in thousands of bars and cafés. France, for long considered a closed shop where beer is concerned, has discovered ales of great integrity and complexity in its most northerly regions. In Britain and Ireland, where ales and stouts never went away but were threatened by the advance of Euro-lager, top-fermenting beers are once again in the ascendancy. The apotheosis of ale, its cask-conditioned form, has bucked every marketing trend to show substantial growth thanks to the energy and devotion of the ever-growing Campaign for Real Ale. Even in Australia, ales that were laughed to derision just a decade ago are now cult brands.

This book attempts to tell the story of ale from its ancient roots in the Old World to the modern day, unravelling in the process the history, the legends and the myths of its myriad styles and versions. It explains how ale is brewed and the ingredients that are used. I make no apology for drawing in the main on the experience of the British Isles: because ale brewing has never been vanquished in those islands, it has the best, well-documented records.

The Ale Trail is not an anti-lager book. I have enormous respect for the master brewers who produce dazzling interpretations of the style throughout the world. On the contrary, the book is a celebration of good beer. It teases out the origins of the world's oldest style and attempts to give it equal status alongside modern lager brewing. I hope lovers of

BELOW: *Breweries separated by half the world. Marin from California and St Martinus from the Netherlands — but both use an animal motif.*

good beer, whether ale or lager, will find stimulation in these pages and a better understanding of the skill and artistry that goes into brewing.

Roger Protz

BELOW: *Rolling out the barrels. Youngs of London still deliver by horse-drawn dray.*

Part One
The History

Chapter One
The time machine

RUBBING THE LAMP

When Bavarians, the most prodigious of all beer drinkers, refer to their daily tipple as 'liquid bread' they are delving deep into history, uncovering the ancient origins of the drink. For beer is as old as time. It is rooted deep in the social habits and cultures of many countries and had a key role to play in creating civilised societies, turning people from nomads into settlers. Making beer on a large scale demanded a well-organised agricultural industry. It forced people to turn from scavenging and hunting to farming. They grew and harvested grain according to the strict rotation of the seasons, taking the produce of the fields to make staple food and drink.

Nobody knows for certain whether bread came before beer. One theory is that before the art of malting was discovered, cakes were made from barley and wheat, soaked in water and then left to ferment with

LEFT: *Model of an Ancient Egyptian brewery.*

10

ABOVE: *Ancient Egyptian stone tablet carved with the brewer performing his craft.*

yeasts saved from previous brews. Another contrary view is that, by accident, barley or wheat being made into bread was dampened to make a pliable dough and it fermented spontaneously with air-borne yeasts while it was left to stand in the open. Either way the people of North Africa and the Middle East discovered a drink that, in the words of Professor Solomon Katz of the University of Pennsylvania, made them feel 'exhilarated, wonderful and blissful'. No wonder, then, that in this state of bliss they stopped wandering and settled down to brew.

Barley may well have been the means to a beery end. It is the finest cereal for brewing but does not make good bread. The Babylonians and Ancient Egyptians grew emmer, a type of wheat, as well as barley, and emmer would have made a better bread. By trial and error, hit and miss, barley became the vehicle for producing beer. Bread cakes may have been made solely for brewing purposes and not for eating. What is incontestable is that beer became an essential element of people's diet at a time when water was insanitary and undrinkable. Beer contained proteins and vitamins that helped keep the population of the old world healthy. And barley could be stored whereas grapes and other fruit used in wine making were almost instantly perishable and lacked the protein value of beer. Alan Eames, the American beer writer and anthropologist, says: 'Protected by alcohol, beer had a palatability lasting far longer than any other food stuff. A vitamin-rich porridge, daily beer drinking increased both health and longevity, reducing disease and malnutrition. Additionally, the self-medicating properties of alcohol-rich beer eased the daily stresses and tensions of day-to-day life in a hostile world. As time passed, those who drank deeply and daily thrived as the search for new sources of grain from which to make beer continued. It was this appetite for beer-making material that led to crop cultivation, settlement and agriculture.

'Ten thousand years ago, for example, barley was domesticated and worshipped as a god in the highlands of the southern Levant. Thus was beer the driving force that led nomadic mankind into village life. With the creation of writing — stylus on wet clay tablet — beer, its history and mystery, became a large part of ancient man's literary repertoire:

"I feel wonderful, drinking beer/in a blissful mood/ with joy in my heart and a happy liver".

'These words of a Sumerian poet circa 3000 BC were penned at a time when goddesses, not gods, were firmly established as the protectors and providers of beer. Ama-Gestin, the Earth Mother, and Ninkasis, the lady who fills the mouth, were the goddesses of beer of the ancient world.'

Evidence of brewing in the ancient world came from the clay tablets mentioned by Alan Eames. The tablets, with cuneiform — wedge-shaped — inscriptions on them were discovered in the 1840s at Nineveh and Nimrud by Austen Henry Lanyard, an Englishman who came across ruins in Assyria while he was making an overland journey to Ceylon. He found a massive buried library that shed light on the old world. The library contained 25,000 broken tablets. Lanyard took them to the British Museum in London where translation was started by Henry Rawlinson who had discovered the key to deciphering cuneiform through the 'Record of Darius' on the Behistun rock near the city of Kermanshah in Iran.

Many of the tablets showed that beer or 'kash' — which gave us the modern slang word for money — was used as currency or a form of barter. Stonemasons who worked on the great buildings for the Pharaohs were paid with vessels of beer. Shin T Kang, another translator of cuneiform tablets, says: 'Together with bread, onions, fish and seed-seasoning, beer was one of the more important items in the Ancient Mesopotamian diet. The Sumerians seemed to have made a fermented beer by combining barley and water and adding flavourings such as malt. Beer was used as part of the rations of government officials and messengers and was widely expended in offerings to gods and goddesses, such as for the goddess Angina, at the field-offering [for deceased people] and much was consumed at the palace. For all these purposes, beer was collected from the people, either as a form of taxation or a religious gift'.

If Babylonia, Mesopotamia and other areas of North Africa and the Middle East seem unlikely places to find the origins of brewing, they were far warmer and wetter regions than they are today. Following the last Ice Age, there was a general rise in world temperature. Between 4000 and 2000 BC the world was two to three degrees Celsius warmer than now and it rained a great deal. A profoundly important agricultural revolution around 6000 BC led to the domestication of cereals. Cereals

BELOW: *Babylonian drinkers toast the goddess of brewing.*

12

ABOVE: *The brewing process depicted on an Egyptian wall painting.*

such as barley and wheat are developments of tall grass and now their seeds could be husbanded and used systematically for sewing and harvesting.

The next important step in the history of brewing was the malting of barley. While a beer of sorts can be made from unmalted barley by fermenting the tiny amounts of sugar that are present naturally in the grain, the alcohol produced would be no more than a light flavouring. Malting, which involves germinating the grain and then drying and heating it, allows the starches to be transformed into sugar in the form of glucose and dextrose. This rich form of natural sugar not only allows a powerful fermentation to take place but also produces vitamins and proteins essential for a healthy diet.

Thanks to the work of archeologists and historians we now have a fascinating picture of what became a major industry. In 'Beer and Brewing Techniques in Ancient Mesopotamia', published in 1950, Hartmann and Oppenheim record that the role of the brewer in Ancient Egypt was sufficiently important for him or her to have a special hieroglyph, 'fty'. (Brewing in the ancient world was almost always the work of women.) The hieroglyph shows a craftsman bent over a container straining a cereal mash through a basket-shaped sieve. It seems that the brewers also added spices for flavouring. The spices were boiled with the sugary solution. Long before the hop plant became a vital ingredient in brewing, the ancients developed boiling of the sugary wort to kill bacteria and extract the bitterness and flavours of spices. Brewing techniques were even more advanced in Mesopotamia. Hartmann and Oppenheim refer to plaques and cylinders that 'bear witness to the existence of a specific technique of brewing which yielded a beer to be drunk only by means of a reed or tube, to prevent the hulls of the barley from spoiling the pleasure of the drinker'. This barley was malted. The authors discuss the 'preparation of malt won from barley' which they say is the 'all-important process in the Mesopotamian brewery of the second and third millenia. Malting belongs to an important technological stage in the development of methods for the preparation of vegetable foodstuff'. Malt was considered so important to the Mesopotamians that it was given as part of the wages to workmen. Hartmann and Oppenheim say that malt was made by drying but heat was not used. But they also describe different types of Mesopotamian beer, including 'dark beer'. This suggests that the malt must have been baked or scorched in order to produce a darker colour. They also mention 'beer with a head' which indicates that early sightings of the Yorkshire Tetley drinker were recorded several thousand years BC.

Fermentation was spontaneous. The same vessels were used from one brew to the next. Yeast would have built up in cracks and crevices and went to work on each batch of sugary liquid. As well as yeast, there would have been some lactic acid bacteria present that would have added a tart but pleasantly refreshing flavour to the finished beer. Many thousands of years later, a sour and lactic taste was an important element in the flavour of the first porter beers. The 'sour beers' of West Flanders in Belgium, stored in unlined oak vessels, also have a deliberate lactic flavour. A more advanced method of fermentation was to keep the sediment from one brew and use it to start the next. Modern brewers use more sophisticated methods to store and culture their yeasts, and separate good strains from bad ones, but essentially they are using a system founded by the Mesopotamians.

A German study of brewing in Babylon and Egypt, published in 1926, showed the Babylonians using raw, unmalted emmer [wheat] and malted barley. Beer bread was made into cakes and baked either light or dark brown, depending on the colour of beer required. Heated water was poured over the cakes to make a mash. The mash was filtered and left to ferment spontaneously. It was then transferred to smaller vessels that were half buried in cool cellars where a secondary fermentation took place. The Egyptians used more varieties of barley and emmer than the Babylonians and they malted both cereals. They baked their malt cakes a dark brown and made no light-coloured beers. Plants, including mandrake with a powerful leek-like flavour, and salt were added to the sugary solution, further signs that even the earliest brewers were keen to balance the sweetness of the malt with bitterness from herbs and plants.

Brewing was a major industry in Egypt. The brewery of the Pharaoh Rameses gave 10,000 hectolitres of free beer a year to the temple administrators. And a class system in drinking emerged. While the working population drank young beer fresh and cloudy from the fermenting vessels, the ruling class preferred mature beer that had been stored for some time and clarified with fuller's earth.

The origins of brewing are well-documented but the gap in time seemed unbridgable as far knowing what the first beers tasted like. But that gap has now been filled as a result of the remarkable work carried

LEFT: *Plants used in Old World brewing to balance the sweetness of the grain.*

out by Fritz Maytag, owner of the Anchor Brewery in San Francisco. Maytag is honoured in the United States as the father of the modern 'micro-brewing' revolution that has created scores of small breweries producing ales and lagers of enormous quality. But historians as well as beer drinkers are indebted to Maytag for his experiments in recreating a beer from Babylonia which he dedicated to Ninkasi, the goddess of beer, a name that also appears as Ninkasis or Ninkaasis. When I interviewed Maytag, the drama of creating a Babylonian beer was clear from the fervour of his voice and even a tremor of excitement on the tape.

'In ancient Sumeria [southern Babylon] beer was made from bread. We know a great deal about ancient Sumeria because of the clay tablets that have been dug up. They contain very detailed records. They're the accountants' records of a society. They're very precise and detailed.

'Beer was terribly important to that society and we have recipes for brewing five thousand years ago. They're by far the earliest record for any food. There's a professor in the United States [Solomon Katz] who quite seriously proposes that man settled down and started farming to grow barley not to bake bread but to brew beer. What he means is that although bread is a wonderful food and would have needed barley, beer is a food also. In some ways beer is a better food or a supplemental food, with the yeast and the amino acids and the nutrients in it.

RIGHT: *Innovator and recreator ... Fritz Maytag, owner of the Anchor Brewery in San Francisco, who brewed a beer based on a Sumerian recipe.*

'The professor says the effect of the alcohol would have seemed to the ancient Sumerians almost like a spiritual experience and this would have been an overwhelming force that would have caused them to stop roaming and hunting and settle down in the valleys and grow their grain. I said we should see, based upon the records, if we could try and brew some beer. The professor put us in touch with scholars all around the US and the world and we put together a list of questions from all the documents we could find about how they brewed a beer from bread.

'We had to rent a bakery during the day because bakers bake at night. We found a wonderful small bakery willing to rent to us. We moved our team in and we made five thousand little bappir loaves from recipes as best as we could define it as if we were brewing in 3000 BC. In this bread there is raw barley flour, for barley was overwhelmingly the grain of the ancient world. Barley is an amazing grain. It will grow from the Arctic Circle to the Tropic of Cancer. It can withstand drought and rain. It is the early grain because it is the toughest grain. It's magic stuff.

'There's a little bit of roasted barley because the husk on the barley is difficult to get off and we know from the ancient Sumerian records that roasted barley was common. And that makes sense because when you roast it you make the husk friable and it falls away, leaving the kernel much easier to eat. We used a tiny little bit of malted barley because we knew they had malted barley and we had made the fundamental decision that our bread should use the kinds of things we knew they had and, most important, the bread should taste good.

'But barley cannot be baked into bread with a dry centre unless you make almost a paper-thin pancake. We asked the experts and we suddenly figured out that this type of bread is twice baked. The Italian word for biscuit, biscotto, means "twice baked".

'Baking a bread once and then cutting it into pieces and baking it again in order to dry it out completely is an ancient tradition. And so we learned to our satisfaction that the ancient Sumerians made their bappir with a twice-baked bread. We made a big thick pie in the oven in the bakery. We made about one thousand of these. We let them cool and cut them into strips and about an hour later we baked them again. By the end of the day we had a little over five thousand of these little loaves. A few days later we put them into the mash tun in our brewery along with some malted barley which you need for the enzymes to make the sugar and we made a beer with no hops because we knew from the experts that there were no hops in Sumeria.

'The fact there were no hops made us a little nervous but we knew they had dates and we knew from a song from ancient Sumeria, that was one of our key sources, that they used a sweet material. The song is a hymn to the Goddess of Brewing. Her name was Ninkasi. So using this hymn to Ninkasi, which dated from 1800 BC, we saw that she added sweetness twice to the beer. We knew the Sumerians had honey and had dates. So we put honey in the bread and then we put dates in the beer because we thought that might give the beer a little flavour — not

ABOVE: *Ninkasi beer, brewed by Fritz Maytag using a bakery to make bappir loaves of brewing bread.*
(Photo: Mike Benner)

quite like hops, but a spicy flavour.

'It wasn't a wonderful beer but it was an interesting beer and one of its more interesting qualities was a slightly aromatic bouquet of dates. We put all this bappir bread in the mash tun and we started cooking it and I can tell you it was a very eerie feeling, as though we were rubbing the magic lamp.

'We were calling up the ancient words of brewing. We had called up the Goddess of Beer, Ninkasi, and we did it with a sense of respect for recreating the ancient art of brewing.

'The great moment was when we drank it at a banquet out of large bottles with tubes. We know that the top people in ancient Sumeria drank beer through golden tubes and we thought we'll have to drink it the way they drank it and so we put it into gigantic glass jugs and drank it out of tubes. We toasted the Goddess Ninkasi and then we drank the beer. It was a wonderful moment.'

I had the same eerie feeling as Fritz Maytag when I opened a bottle of Ninkasi Sumerian Beer. It was the same cold, trickle-down-the-back sensation that great age engenders, the feeling I get every time I pass the Stonehenge neolithic circles in Wiltshire in southern England. The beer was approximately five per cent alcohol by volume and was a cloudy, orange-red colour. I drank it through a straw from a glass jug and then more conventionally from a beer glass. Straight from the refrigerator the beer had a powerful aroma of honey and dates. The palate was surprisingly quenching and the finish was dry. As the beer warmed up the sweetness of the honey and dates became more apparent but it remained deeply refreshing despite the lack of hops.

The most remarkable fact was that it tasted like beer. The centuries peeled away as I drank it. I knew what the first beers, produced thousands of years ago, tasted like. As Fritz Maytag said, it was like rubbing the lamp.

THE GENIE SPREADS THE WORD

The Arabs, Koran in one hand, sword in the other, put an end to brewing as they over-ran North Africa in the eighth century AD. But the lamp had been rubbed. The genie was out. The great sea-faring traders, the Phoenicians, had taken cereals to other countries and the art of brewing quickly established itself in Northern Europe, beginning in Bohemia and Bavaria, working its way up to the North Sea and the Baltic coast and crossing to the British Isles. As the world's climate changed, a line was drawn across Europe. In the Mediterranean lands, wine was the preferred drink as grapes flourished in the hot climate. In the harsher climes of what are now Germany, northern Spain, northern France, the British Isles and Scandinavia, grapes struggled to ripen but cereals, barley and wheat in particular, were undaunted by cold and damp. Beer — along with cider and mead — became the people's staple drink and a vital part of their diet.

As the Romans marched across Europe they encountered beer for the first time. Tacitus reported that the tribes of Germany drank a liquor made from barley or wheat. Pliny wrote: 'The nations of the west have their own intoxicant from grain soaked in water; there are many ways of making it in Gaul [France] or Spain and under different names, though the principle is the same. The Spanish have taught us that these liquors keep well.' The keeping qualities were aided by the art of cooperage. While the Greeks and Romans stored wine in clay pots, the people of the north, including the Celts, had developed the skill of making casks from curved staves of wood for storing both wet and dry goods. In 21AD Strabo recorded seeing wooden pithoi [vats] in Northern Europe. 'The Celts are fine coopers,' he wrote, 'for their casks are larger than houses.'

The Romans were impressed more by the hardware than the software. The Emperor Julian was so disgusted by his first taste of British ale that he was forced to reach for the papyrus:

On Wine Made from Barley
Who made you and from what?
By the true Bacchus I know you not
He smells of nectar
But you smell of goat.

But the notion that the conquering Romans never touched the juice of the barley is false. Recent excavations of Roman sites in Britain have uncovered maltings. A Roman maltings was found in the car park of a pub in St Albans, Hertfordshire, in 1994. St Albans is on the site of the Roman city of Verulamium. Supplies of wine from the homeland

LEFT: *An 18th century English country brewery.*

undoubtedly ran out from time to time and, *faute de mieux*, the Romans turned to brewing instead. The spear-carriers of the Roman forces may have been less hostile to drinking beer than their aristocratic commanders. And at a time when cholera and typhoid were rampant, beer with its vital vitamins kept scrofulous diseases at bay.

As Pliny noted, the tribes of Northern Europe had many different names for beer. In Britain the Celts brewed a beer called curmi. When the Danes and Saxons came roistering into Britain after the departure of the Romans, they brought not only a great beer drinking culture but also the name öl, from which the term ale is derived. For centuries, the term ale meant an alcoholic drink made from malt but without hops. The expression bier or beer came much later when brewers in Germany and the Low Countries began to brew with hops and Dutch traders brought hop plants to the county of Kent in south-east England. Ironically, the British could have used hops from Roman times, for their conquerors ate them as a delicacy, rather like asparagus. Whether the Romans brought hops with them or, more likely, found them growing wild in Britain is not known. But the natives ignored the hop and flavoured their curmi and, later, their ale with other plants, including

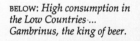
BELOW: *High consumption in the Low Countries ... Gambrinus, the king of beer.*

bog myrtle, rosemary and yarrow. The Germans and Scandinavians added a kind of bouquet garni to their ales, a mixture of different plants known as gruit. The habit of adding plants and spices to ale may have influenced the early distillers of gin, schnapps and other spirits made from grain. I have seen spices added in a muslin bag during the copper boil in modern breweries when strong winter ales were being brewed: old habits die hard.

Brewing in the early centuries AD was a domestic process. It was as natural for the woman of the house to make ale as it was to make bread. After all, she was using ingredients common to both practices. A rudimentary market economy singled out the women — ale wives or brewsters — who produced the best ale in a community to make their products available to a wider audience. When a new brew was ready they would place an 'ale stake', a long pole covered in evergreens, through a window to attract customers. The ale house was born. In Britain pubs called the Bush recall that first recorded inn sign, the ale stake.

When the Normans conquered England in the eleventh century they found brewing so deeply ingrained in the local way of life that they did not attempt to impose their own preference for wine or, more likely, cider. The Normans' Domesday Book, a survey of the life and habits of the English, found forty-three *cerevisiarii* (brewers) who could be fined four shillings or ducked in the village pond if they made bad ale. The improvements in brewing techniques can be seen in the report of a visit to France by the cleric Thomas à Becket. Becket later became Archbishop of Canterbury and was famously murdered in his cathedral but as a

ABOVE: *A Victorian fermenting room in S.A. Brain's Cardiff brewery. The 'parachutes' skim off the yeast head.*

young priest he had brewed ale for the monks of St Albans Abbey, twenty miles north of London. On a diplomatic mission to France in 1158 Becket took two chariot-loads of ale 'decocted from choice fat grain as a gift for the French who wondered at such an invention — a drink most wholesome, clear of all dregs, rivalling wine in colour and surpassing it in flavour'.

The fact that Thomas à Becket was both a priest and a brewer shows the extent to which the church had achieved a dominant role in brewing. The spread of Christianity had dampened down some of the wilder excesses of drinking in Anglo-Saxon times. The church attempted to both regulate brewing and to corner the market in its production. Monasteries offered accommodation to travellers and built brewhouses to supply them with ale. Monastic brewhouses were vast. The malthouse at Fountains Abbey in Yorkshire measured sixty square feet and the brewery produced sixty barrels of strong ale every ten days. The Domesday Book recorded that the monks of St Paul's Cathedral in London brewed 67,814 gallons of ale a year, equivalent to 1,884 barrels. They used barley, wheat and oats.

Monastic brewing was not confined to England. In the early Middle Ages there were between four and five hundred monasteries brewing in Germany. The Benedictines were the principle brewers though other orders followed their example.

Monastic brewing was remarkably sophisticated and extensive. Plans of the Abbey of St Gall in Switzerland in the ninth century show a malthouse, kiln, millroom for grinding malt and three brewhouses and storage cellars. The maltings were large enough to allow four separate 'couches' of grain to be processed at a time. The monks brewed from barley, oats and wheat. When the grain started to germinate it was transferred to a kiln, a square structure with a central chimney round which were fixed wickerwork platforms covered with rough material. The germinated grain was spread on the material and the heat of the kiln turned grain into malt. The kiln would have been fired by wood.

The malt was pounded to produce a powder known as grist. The grist was transferred to one of the brewhouses. Each brewhouse had a copper vessel heated by an open fire. Most vessels in ancient breweries were made of wood but copper technology dates from Graeco-Roman times and the metal was well-suited to brewing as it could withstand and retain fierce heat. While modern coppers are large cylindrical vessels like diving bells, the ones used in monasteries were simple open pans under which a fire could be lit.

More detailed information about medieval brewing comes from a description written in 1927 by the brewing scientist H. Lloyd Hind of the Queen's College brewery at Oxford University. The brewery survived until World War Two and had changed little since it was built in 1340. The only modern innovations were a thermometer and a copper coil in one cooler. The mash tun, the vessel in which grist is mixed with water, was made of memel oak. It had two outlets pipes covered with metal strainers to keep back the grain. The modern method of spraying or 'sparging' the spent grains with hot water to wash out any remaining sugars was unknown when the brewery was built. The sweet liquid, called wort, flowed to an under-back below the mash tun and was then pumped by hand to an open copper boiled by heat from a furnace. Hops would not have been used when the brewery started production but boiling was an essential part of the process as it killed any infections in the wort. After the copper boil the wort was cooled in large open pans made from deal and then, at 66 degrees Fahrenheit, 18 degrees Celsius, transferred to a wooden vessel called a round where it was mixed with yeast. As soon as a vigorous fermentation started, the liquid was taken in a 'tun dish', a sort of large ladle, to casks in a cellar. The casks were arranged above a trough, which collected the yeast, leaving bright beer behind. This system, with some modifications, survives today in the 'Burton Union' system in Burton-on-Trent in the English Midlands. Once fermentation was finished, the casks were sealed and the ale left to mature. The strength of the ale was 1070 degrees gravity, approximately seven per cent alcohol by volume, twice the strength of an average English beer today. A Chancellor's Ale, double the strength and equivalent to a rich red wine, was also brewed.

Records show that in eighth century England monks had a ration of eight pints of weak ale a day. Centuries later, Shakespeare referred to a

BELOW: *Inns at the Southwark entrance to London in Elizabethan times. The inns brewed their own ale and were close to the London hop market.*

similar drink — 'I will make it a felony to drink small beer' (Henry VI, Part Two). Until the introduction of sparging in the eighteenth or nineteenth century, it was common practice to make several ales from one mash of malt, each brew becoming successively weaker. Children as well as monks drank small beer of three per cent alcohol or less. As late as the seventeenth century the staff of the Civic Orphanage in Amsterdam gave the orphans a pint each of small beer a day. Milk was considered unhealthy. As well as infecting drinkers with tuberculosis, untreated milk, according to the Dutch, also lead to 'spongy brains'.

Monks called their strongest and finest ale *prima melior* and served it to distinguished visitors. A second brew, *secunda*, was given to lay workers in the monastery while the brothers and impoverished pilgrims had to make do with a weak *tertia*. As in Ancient Egypt, the best beer was reserved for the establishment. The monks marked their casks with crosses to indicate the strength of the brews: the crosses may also have been a blessing from the god-fearing brewers to prevent infections.

The importance of ale drinking in medieval times cannot be underestimated. Even at the time of the Renaissance in the late fifteenth century, the life of working people was harsh and their diet appalling. Images of endless feasts and bawdy behaviour give a false impression, as such behaviour was confined to the feudal land owners. For peasants in the country and working people in the towns, meat was a rarity and cheese was often too expensive to afford. The country people raised fowls, pigs and cattle but sold them or bartered them. Save for the occasional egg or chicken, they lived on a dull diet of thin vegetable soup and bread. Ale, for children as well as adults, made from the cereals in the surrounding fields, rich in essential vitamins, was as much the staff of life as bread.

One of the most detailed studies of medieval monastic brewing in France was written by Urion and Eyer in 1969. In 'La Technique de la Fabrication de la Cervoise et de la Bière au Moyen Age à la Renaissance' they report that while medieval brewers used barley, oats, rye and wheat, barley was the preferred grain as it was easier to malt. (In fact, little 'extract' [sugar] is derived from oats or rye while huskless wheat tends to block all the pipes in a brewhouse.) Grain was laid out in a cool cellar and then moistened with water to start germination. Monastic brewhouses were usually sited next to rivers: records of the Clairvaux Abbey say that the river ground the corn, worked the sieves that separated flour from bran, provided water for brewing, cloth-making and tannery and finally carried away the abbey's refuse. In some breweries the grain was spread on the ground overnight in secluded spots away from the wind so that the morning dew would moisten it. The malt was turned by hand to aerate it and when it started to sprout it was moved to a stone-built kiln and laid out on a thin floor covered with hair cloth above a hearth. The progress of the transformation of barley into malt was marked by chewing it until it was friable in the mouth.

French ale was known as *cervoise* from the Latin *cerevisia*. The brewers wanted soft water and tested it for the required softness by adding soap until it foamed. Malt along with some unmalted cereal was ground and placed in a mashing vessel and mixed with heated water. The mash was stirred with a *fourquet* — mashing fork — and further additions of water were made at increasingly higher temperatures until the mash was hot enough for saccharification, the transformation of starch into sugar, to take place. The brewer knew when this temperature had been reached by placing his fork in the middle of the vat until the water began to simmer near the handle. Heating was then stopped. The wort was cooled, run into tuns and mixed with yeast. When fermentation was finished the *cervoise* stood in the tuns for several more days while a secondary fermentation turned remaining sugars into alcohol and the ale cleared. The strength of the finished ale was surprisingly modest, between four and six per cent alcohol by volume.

ABOVE: *'A beerhouse with feasting customers'* ... *painting by Adriaen van Ostade* (Amsterdams Historisch Museum)

Urion and Eyer also describe the brewing of *bière* at a later date when hops were used. By now mash tuns had a slotted base so that the spent grain acted as a filter as the wort passed through to an under-back. Interestingly, hops were also added to the mash tun as part of the filtering process. Hops, the brewers felt, helped produce a better extract from the malt and also acted as a preservative. The wort was pumped back into the mash tun and filtered a second time to wash out any remaining sugars. The wort was then boiled with hops in a copper — a short boil for a light-coloured beer, a longer boil lasting several hours for a dark beer — and fermented in tuns in the same fashion as *cervoise*.

Little is recorded about yeast in any of the descriptions of medieval brewing. The reason is simple: yeast was a mystery and remained so until Louis Pasteur unlocked its secrets in the nineteenth century. The English called it 'Godisgood' and clearly thought that the violence of fermentation and the creation of alcohol were the work of the Almighty. It seems certain, however, that brewers learned to avoid as far as possible spontaneous fermentation from wild yeasts in the air. Consistency of product meant that yeast was collected from one brew, stored and used for the next one. Storage was often rudimentary and amounted to no more than allowing deposits of yeast to remain inside the vats from one brew to the next.

When beer writer Michael Jackson visited Norway in the early 1990s he discovered a method of brewing ale in the rural western region of the country — the old Norseland — that was the closest we are likely to get to medieval times. In the remote rural region of Voss most of the farmers make their own beer. When a new brew is underway, the smoke and rich odours tell everyone in the neighbourhood that beer is being made and they go to the farmhouse to help out and then sample the finished brew. Jackson went out with farmer Svein Rivenes to collect juniper

RIGHT: *Louis Pasteur with microscope. The French scientist visited several British breweries to advise on yeast cultivation and the avoidance of bacterial infection in beer.*

branches. Rivenes sawed sufficient branches to fill the 700-litre bath-shaped tank in his cabin that acts as both the hot liquor vessel and the brew kettle. He feels, just as the medieval monks recorded by Urion and Eyer felt about the hops in their *bière*, that the juniper branches, complete with berries, helped him achieve a better extract from his malt as well as warding off infections.

His water source — a stream tumbling down the hillside outside his cabin — has a double use. It is his brewing liquor and he also immerses sacks of barley in the stream where the grain starts to germinate. A neighbour has turned his garage into a kiln, powered by a domestic fan heater, and there barley is turned into malt. In the brewing process, when hot liquor has been added to the malt, the mash is filtered over more juniper branches to filter it. The berries give flavour to the wort — just as they do to gin and other distilled spirits — but Rivenes also adds hops when the wort is boiled. The yeast used in the Voss area has been handed down from generation to generation and Rivenes thinks it may date back to Viking times. The farmer-brewers in Norseland start fermentation with a 'totem stick' that carries yeast cells from one brew to the next.

The beer brewed by Svein Rivenes was, according to Michael Jackson, around nine or ten per cent alcohol and had a rich malt character, with a syrupy body, a pronounced juniper character and was clean and appetising. Jackson brought a sample of the yeast back to Britain where he handed it to Dr Keith Thomas of the Brewers' Laboratory (Brew Lab) at the University of Sunderland in North-east England. Thomas trains both commercial brewers and home-brewers and is an acknowledged expert on yeast and cleaning up old strains in order to brew with them. The Viking yeast was classified as a traditional ale yeast, *Saccharomyces cerevisiae*, but was different in several ways to a modern ale yeast. It had different taste characteristics. It was multi-strain whereas most modern ale yeasts are single or two-strain. Modern yeasts have been carefully cultured to attack different types of sugar in the wort and, where a beer is cask conditioned, to encourage a powerful secondary fermentation. A multi-strain yeast is less predictable in its behaviour and some of the strains may impede a successful fermentation. Thomas is carrying out further investigations, including DNA tests, to analyse it fully, determine the number of strains and to attempt to measure its age. In the meantime, he did what any sensible brewing analyst and historian would do: brewed some beer with it.

The result, Original Norvik Ale, differed in many ways to the ale Michael Jackson drank in Voss. It was four per cent alcohol by volume, had no juniper berries, was made only from pale malt and was hopped in the conventional manner. It is unlikely that a genuine Viking ale was brewed from pale malt: until the industrial revolution and commercial coal mining, malt was kilned over wood fires and was brown and often scorched and smoky in character, though the habit in Scandinavia of drying malt in saunas may have made it paler. Thanks to Keith Thomas's

BELOW: *Dr Keith Thomas of the Brewers' Laboratory at the University of Sunderland, North East England, has played a leading role in recreating old beer styles.*

brilliant work with the yeast, Norvik Ale did give a fascinating glimpse of what a beer from all those centuries ago might have tasted like. It was an attractive copper colour and had a deep malty and almost toffeeish aroma backed by resiny hops and a hint of almost winey fruitiness. It was bitter and hoppy in the mouth with some tart fruit and the finish was hoppy and dry with a sherry-like fruitiness.

In the Dutch town of Groningen, Nico Derks, who runs the tiny St Martinus micro-brewery, produced an ale in 1994 based on a 1340s recipe. The beer was available at a museum in Assen that staged an exhibition on medieval brewing. Derks used malted barley, oats and wheat as well as unmalted versions of all three cereals, with crystal malt for colour. The malted grains made up seventy per cent of the mash. He was forced by Dutch law to use hops, which did not appear in the original recipe. Gruit was used then. Derks used two German hop varieties, Northern Brewer and Perle, in generous amounts. The finished beer was 8.8 per cent alcohol by volume. It was called Cluyn,

RIGHT: *Brewing in the 13th century in the northern Netherlands.*

pronounced 'clown', a strong ale brewed in the fourteenth century for drinking at weddings in the far north of the Netherlands. The ale was naturally conditioned in the bottle, had a hazy copper colour and a complex aroma of orange jelly fruit and herbs. There was sour fruit in the mouth with a determined hop bitterness and the finish was dry with rich and ripe fruit. Even though neither hops nor crystal malt were used at the time, the recreation was memorable and the vinous character of the beer suggested, as with the Norvik Ale, that the wine and beer divide of modern times was less clear cut in the Middle Ages. The people made alcohol from the ingredients to hand. In the north they used cereals but the finished drink, with its vigorous fermentation and fruity esters, was not dissimilar to the wines of the time, some of which are thought to have included herbs.

In the north of Finland, a brewer named Pekka Kaariainen has recreated for commercial sale the juniper-flavoured sahti, a centuries-old beer produced in remote rural communities. In Lammi, one hundred miles north of Helsinki, Kaariainen blends malted barley and rye which he mashes over juniper. An extract of hops is added and the wort is sterilised but not boiled and then fermented. The finished beer has a herbal, winey aroma, is fruity in the mouth (damsons or plums) with more fruit and spices in the finish.

Brewing historian and home-brewing expert Graham Wheeler made a beer for me for this book based upon a recipe dating from the early sixteenth century. It is the earliest British recipe Wheeler has found and comes from Richard Arnold's book Customs of London, published in 1503. The original recipe gave the ingredients as ten quarters of malt, two quarters of wheat, two quarters of oats and forty pounds of hops to make sixty barrels of beer. Wheeler brewed a beer as close to the recipe as possible, though some guesswork was involved. He assumed the malt was cured over wood fire. He achieved this by taking pale malt and heating it on a garden barbeque using wood in place of charcoal. He used malted wheat though it was not clear from the original whether it was malted or not. For oats he turned to the famous breakfast cereal Quaker Oats. He used Goldings hops which would not have been available at the time.

BELOW: *Home-brewing expert Graham Wheeler sampling his recreation of a 16th century smoked ale.*

The full recipe appears in Wheeler's book 'Home Brewing — the CAMRA Guide'. It had an original gravity of 1065 degrees and the finished beer achieved 6.7 per cent alcohol by volume. I carried out a comparative tasting with the famous Schlenkerla Rauchbier (smoked beer) from Bamberg in Franconia, Germany. It has been brewed since 1678 and its own malt is cured over a fire of beechwood logs. It was almost certainly brewed as an ale in the seventeenth century but is now made by bottom fermentation in the lager style. But even though it has a more modest strength of 4.8 per cent alcohol it is the nearest equivalent to a medieval smoked ale. Wheeler's ale, which he calls Arnold's Single Beer, was a hazy bronze colour (beers using wheat and oats are notoriously difficult to clear) and had a pronounced smoked wood and herbal aroma. The smoky character dominated the palate with Goldings adding a resiny note while the finish was intensely dry and bitter with dark fruit notes. The Rauchbier had an attractive clear copper colour and a less aggressive smoked aroma balanced by sweet, clean malt and aromatic hops. It was quenching in the mouth with a finish that became dry and hoppy with a light smoky character. In spite of the smoked malt, the Rauchbier was a typical lager, cleaner and more refreshing, while Arnold's Single Beer had all the rounded, fruity character of an ale, overlain by the intense smokiness.

HOPPING OVER THE GREAT DIVIDE

Lager beer is a child of the industrial revolution. It was only when icemaking machines were manufactured in the nineteenth century that lager beer could be made on a commercial scale. But storing beer at low temperatures — lager is the German word for storage and the English word larder comes from the same root — started many centuries earlier. In Germany and other central European countries brewing was difficult, if not impossible, during the long, hot summers. Soaring temperatures affected fermentation and worts became infected. Brewers discovered that if they stored beer in ice-filled caves or cellars it would say in drinkable condition for several months and would provide sufficient supplies to last the summer. They noticed that when beer was stored at low temperatures, the yeast would settle at the bottom of the vessel while a secondary fermentation took place. This was in sharp contrast to the short and violent ale fermentation where the yeast formed a thick crusty head on top of the wort. Lager brewing and cold fermentation started empirically and true lager yeasts were only cultured with the aid of the scientific advances of the industrial revolution. But cold fermented beer was mentioned in a report of Munich town council in Bavaria in 1420 while a report from the city of Nabburg said: 'One brews the warm or top fermentation; but first in 1474 one attempted to brew by the cold bottom fermentation and so preserve part of the brew for the summer.'

And so the great beery divide began to take place. But even in Germany, thought of as the quintessential lager brewing nation, topfermenting ales, either wheat beers or brown beers, remained the dominant style until commercial refrigeration developed. Both ales and the new lagered beers were united, however, by the fast-spreading use of hops.

Ever since beer was first made, brewers struggled to find an ingredient to balance the sweetness of malt. No one knows when hops were first used in brewing though records show they were grown in Babylon around 200 AD and were being used in beer production from the eighth century. They were probably chosen at random at first, just another plant or herb to balance the malt. But brewers quickly discovered the almost magical qualities of the hop that set it apart from other plants. Not only do the hop resins include acids and tannins that give an enticing

29

aroma to beer and a quenching bitterness but those resins also prevent bacterial infection. Boiling wort with hops, especially when water was insanitary, became a vital stage of the brewing process. As Eyer and Urion noted in their study of French medieval brewing, hops were also used during the mashing process.

Knowledge of the hop's role in brewing was taken to the Caucasus and later into parts of Germany by the Slavs during the great migration of people that followed the break-up of the Roman empire. Hop gardens were recorded in the Hallertau region of Bavaria in 736 AD: the Hallertau today is the world's greatest hop growing area. In 1079 the Abbess Hildegarde of St Ruprechtsberg near Bingen referred to the use of hops in beer. Hop cultivation was also reported in Prague, already emerging as an important brewing centre.

In every country the hop had to fight a war of attrition with the old methods of brewing. Entrenched business interests, usually controlled by the church, resisted the plant. In Cologne, the archbishop had

LEFT: *"The Brewer" by Jan Luyken (1649-1712).*

ABOVE: *A 17th century Dutch family enjoying their beer with fine food and music. Jan Miense Molenaer, "Vrolijk Gezelschap" from the Museum Boymans van Beuningen, Rotterdam*

cornered the gruit market through a decree called the Grutrecht and he attempted to outlaw the use of hops. In Russia Archduke Vassili II forbade their use. In Holland as early as the fourteenth century the Dutch had a craving for hopped Hamburg beer in preference to local beer based on gruit. They imported thousands of barrels of hopped beer every year brewed in Hamburg and Bremen. The Dutch began to brew hopped beer and challenged the controllers of the gruit market, who attempted to impose punitive taxes on hops. The taxes raised on hops imported into Amsterdam were one reason why a great mercantile city was built out of marshland. Throughout mainland Europe the monopolistic controllers of the gruit market were under attack from drinkers and brewers. Settlements were finally reached when the religious powers agreed to accept rents in lieu of giving up their rights to supply gruit.

There was fierce resistance to hops when they finally made an appearance in England in the fifteenth century. They were banned in the city of Norwich, even though many Flemish weavers had settled there and preferred hopped beer to ale. In 1519 the use of the 'wicked and pernicious weed' was prohibited in Shrewsbury. King Henry VIII, who had put an abrupt end to the church's grip on brewing when he dissolved the monasteries, instructed his court brewer to use neither hops nor brimstone in the royal ale. But the hop had started to put down powerful roots even in England. Dutch merchants who traded in the counties of Kent and Sussex near the channel ports introduced the hop plant and hop cultivation to the area. The first hop gardens were laid out in Kent in 1520 where early land enclosures encouraged large-scale farming. The soil was rich and there was an abundance of wood for making hop poles and charcoal to dry the picked hops. Growing hops became a profitable business as a rhyme of the time suggests:

> A nobleman of Cailes
> A Knight of Wales
> A Laird of the North Countree,
> A Yeoman of Kent with his yearly rent,
> Could buy them out all three.

And it was the easier pickings from hopped beer that determined its ultimate victory over unhopped ale. At a royal banquet in Windsor Park in 1528 fifteen gallons of ale and fifteen gallons of beer were ordered for the guests. The beer cost twenty pence, the ale two shillings and sixpence. The difference in price is significant. The better keeping qualities of hopped beer meant that less malt had to be used. Traditionally ale was brewed to a high strength as the greater the alcohol the

LEFT: *The famous hop fields of Poperinge in Belgium.*

longer the life of the ale. In *A Perfite Platforme for a Hoppe Garden* first published in 1574 Reynold Scot stressed the advantages of hopped beer: 'Whereas you cannot make above 8-9 gallons of indifferent ale from 1 bushel of malt, you may draw 18-20 gallons of very good beer. If your ale may endure a fortnight, your beer through the benefit of the hop, shall continue a month, and what grace it yieldeth to the taste, all men may judge that have sense in their mouths. And if controversy be betwixt Beer and Ale, which of them shall have the place of pre-eminence, it sufficeth for the glory and commendation of the Beer that, here in our own country, ale giveth place unto it and that most part of our country-men do abhor and abandon ale as a loathsome drink.' Scot's book ran to three editions. With the aid of woodcuts he described in detail the way to prepare the soil and to erect poles for the hops to climb up. As continental growers had found, it was essential to train the stems or bines upwards to ensure maximum exposure to the sun and ease of picking. Scot also designed an oast house where hops could be dried and stored.

The use of other plants in brewing did not immediately disappear. In 1588 Jacob Theodor von Bergzabern, describing contemporary brewing practice in Europe, noted that hops were used in the copper boil but added: 'The English sometimes add to the brewed beer, to make it more pleasant, sugar, cinnamon, cloves and other good spices in a small bag. The Flemings mix it with honey or sugar and precious spices and so make a drink like claret or hippocras. Others mix in honey, sugar and syrup, which not only makes the beer pleasant to drink, but also gives it a fine brown colour.' He added that brewers had learned from 'the Flemings and the Netherlanders' that adding laurel, ivy or Dutch myrtle to beer strengthens it, preserves it and stops it going sour. As late as 1750 London brewers were still using bog myrtle as a flavouring and even today Belgian wheat beer brewers use spices and orange peel as well as hops. But hops transformed brewing. The demand for the cleaner and more refreshing hopped beer throughout Europe encouraged ale house owners to set up as commercial brewers. By the middle of the sixteenth century there were twenty-six 'common' brewers in London, most of them based in the area of Southwark close to the hop markets. In Hamburg, according to Professor J R Hale in his 'Renaissance Europe 1480-1528', the brewers were among the wealthiest men in the city and were the backbone of the new bourgeois class that sounded the death-knell of feudalism. Dutch brewers and coopers became enormously powerful. In 1618 in Haarlem, twenty-one of the twenty-four city councillors were brewers. And it was the common brewers of London, capital of the nation that killed its king in order to embrace the capitalist system, who were to dominate the market in a new style of ale called porter that created the modern brewing industry and was briefly the wonder of the world.

Chapter Two
Porter, the Universal Cordial

It is a good story and it has been told many times, how Ralph Harwood, owner of the Bell Brewhouse in Shoreditch in East London, brewed an ale called Entire Butt in 1722 and in so doing spawned a beer style called porter that changed the world of beer. Legends die hard and the enterprising Mr Harwood undoubtedly brewed an ale that had an important role to play in the development of brewing. A contemporary verse by a writer named Gutteridge paid homage to the 'inventor' of porter:

> Harwood my townsman, he invented first
> Porter to rival wine and quench the thirst
> Porter which spreads itself half the world o'er,
> Whose reputation rises more and more.
> As long as porter shall preserve its fame
> Let all with gratitude our Parish name.

But Harwood was not the first porter brewer. He attempted, clearly with some success, to replicate a type of beer that had become popular in London but which was expensive to make and retail. Harwood set out to make a similar beer that was cheaper, was controlled by publican-brewers and was therefore more profitable to them. Entire Butt and porter were not identical though in succeeding generations they were to overlap, intermingle and finally come to mean the same thing.

The origins of porter lie outside London and are connected to changes in brewing technology and punitive taxes on raw ingredients. Three major publications in the eighteenth century describe in detail how beer was brewed and the various types available. Professor Richard Bradley's 'A Guide to Gentleman Farmers and Housekeepers for Brewing the Finest Malt Liqueurs' and the 'Dictionnaire Oeconomique or the Family Dictionary' of 1727 show that brewing remained largely a seasonal activity, as he gives recipes for March and October beers. It was still the habit to produce several beers from one mash: Bradley says typical beers had original gravities of 1080-1100 degrees (between eight and eleven per cent alcohol by volume) for strong ales, 1050 degrees (five per cent) for middling ale and 1025 degrees (under three per cent) for small beer. Hop rates varied with the time of year from half a pound per barrel up to two pounds per barrel for March and October beers. The

OPPOSITE PAGE: *What's in a name? ... Entire short for Entire Butt and Porter were not at first identical brews as the signs outside this pub show.*
(Photo: Whitbread Archive)

34

seasonal beers were brewed for keeping and the high hop rates kept infection at bay in the wooden vats.

Bradley makes it clear that hops were by now in universal use. He said malt from northern counties of England was superior as a result of the use of coke to fire the kilns. Great attention was given to the quality and purity of water. 'Possibly the best water in England is that at Castleton in Derbyshire, commonly called the Devil's Arse, which oozes from a great rock — ale made from Castleton water has been found to be as clear in three days after it was barrelled as the spring water itself.' Spring water, rich in minerals, later combined with pale malt to produce pale ale. In London soft well water (it is a myth that London brewers used Thames water) and brown malt produced brown ales.

'The London and Country Brewer' was first published anonymously in 1754 and ran to nine editions. It went into great detail on brewing techniques and the types of ales available at the time. The author says that brown malt remained the most popular type because it was cheaper to make in wood-fired kilns. Pale malt had appeared in the previous century but it was expensive to produce. At first pale malt had been made by coal-fired kilns but coal gave off noxious gases that were retained by the malt. It was only when coal was turned into coke that pale malt started to be made in substantial amounts. But brown malt remained the most popular variety as a result of its cheapness — coal was taxed but wood was not — and was best suited to making the brown ales popular in London, brewed with soft water. (Up until the 1960s the specialist English coloured maltsters, French and Jupp's of Stanstead Abbotts in Hertfordshire, produced brown malt in a wood-fired kiln, using hornbeam collected from the nearby Hatfield forest.)

Improvements in kilning produced a better brown malt. Wood fires tended to flare, producing charred malt, which meant the starches could not be transformed into fermentable sugars. There were frequent accidents with the malt going up in flames. French and Jupp's told me that this still happened well into the twentieth century. But by the early eighteenth century greater care was being given to kilning brown malt and producing a paler version in order to ensure saccharification in the mash tun. Nevertheless it is estimated that brown malt produced about ten per cent less sugary extract than pale malt. 'The London and Country Brewer' also refers to amber malt that gave colour and flavour to ale, but that was made by heating pale malt to a higher temperature in coke-fired kilns. Beer was still made by washing the grain several times, though the book does list an 'intire small beer' made from just one mash. This supports the view that Ralph Harwood's Entire Butt may have been popular not so much because of its quality or colour but as a result of its cheapness to produce and retail. The strongest beer listed was Stout Beer followed by Strong Brown Ale ('Stitch') and Common Brown Ale. Two points need to be stressed here: there were no dark malts as black and chocolate malts did not exist, unless by accident; and we first encounter the term 'stout'. If there were no dark malts then the

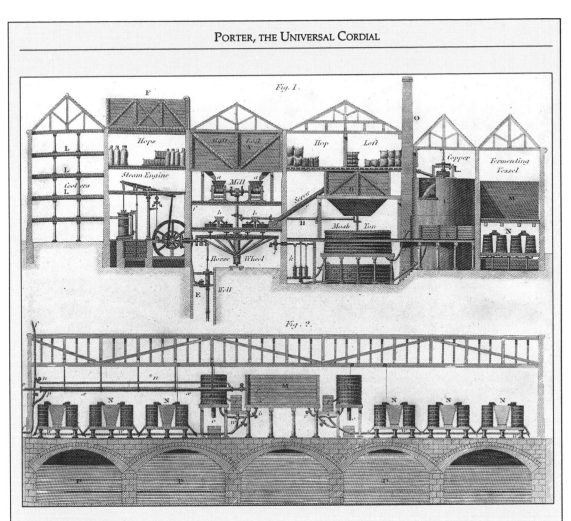

first stouts were no more than dark brown in colour, and that must hold true for both porter and entire as well.

Stout was a generic name for the strongest or stoutest ale produced by a brewery. In a Poem to Stella of 1720, the Irish satirist Jonathan Swift, living in London, wrote:

> A poet starving in a garret
> Conning old Topicks like a parrot
> Invokes his mistress and his muse,
> And stays at home for want of shoes,
> Should but his muse descending drop
> A slice of bread or mutton chop
> Or kindly when his credit's out
> Surprise him with a pint of stout.

There was no mention of porter in any of the publications listed above. Yet by 1758 H. Jackson, in his 'Essay on Bread', wrote 'Beer, commonly call'd Porter, is become almost the universal cordial of the populace, especially since the necessary period of prohibiting the Corn Distillery; the Suppression presently advanc'd the price of that common poison, gin, to near three times its former price and the consumption of beer has kept pace with such advance'. Porter sales soared. One reason, as Jackson noted, was the need to combat the evils of gin drinking which had reached epidemic proportions — 'drunk for a penny, dead drunk for twopence' — in London and other major cities. The government clamped down on gin distilling by increasing tax on its production and promoting beer drinking as a healthier alternative, exemplified in Hogarth's engravings of the depravities of Gin Lane and the rosy-cheeked wassail of Beer Street. For the first time in many years the price of beer drinking fell and consumption increased.

The impact of beer taxes and the changes this brought about were recorded graphically in 1760 by an eighty-six year-old brewer who used the pen-name of Obadiah Poundage to describe the conditions facing London brewers during the reign of William of Orange (1689-1702) and the wars with France. 'In the beginning of King William's reign ... the duty on strong beer and ale was two shillings and sixpence and small beer was made from the same grains and sold for six shillings the barrel ... But soon after our wars with France occasioned further duties on this commodity — I set them down from memory alone — ninepence per barrel more in 1693 was laid on strong ale, an additional threepence per barrel on small in 1694. The whole duty amounted to four shillings per barrel on ale and one shilling per barrel on small beer at this period ... Come we now to the Queen's [Anne: 1702-1714] time, when France disturbing us again, the Malt Tax, the Duty on Hops and that on coals took place, besides one shilling per barrel more on strong beer and ale, and fourpence per barrel more on small beer.'

Duties, according to Poundage, now stood at five shillings a barrel on strong ale and beer and one shilling and fourpence on small beer. Malt, hops and coal were all taxed but the duty on malt was higher than on hops. As a result, brewers switched to producing a brown beer, made from brown malt kilned by untaxed wood, using less malt but much more heavily hopped. According to Poundage, London drinkers missed their stronger and sweeter ale and started to mix hopped beer with ale bought from specialist 'ale drapers'. The brewers were also under attack from country brewers who supplied the wealthier citizens of London with expensive pale ale. The kilning of pale malt was banned in London and other towns and cities as a result of the fumes and fogs caused by coal burning. Until the tax on coal was lifted and the use of coke became widespread, pale ale brewing remained a country pursuit. Pale beer, in common with white bread, was twice as expensive to produce as brown beer and bread. The new type of ale was much sought after by both the rich and those with aspirations to join them. The London brewers saw their trade diminishing as the common people reduced the amount of beer they bought in taverns in order to mix it with specialist ales

ABOVE: *Imperial Russian Stout, first brewed for the Baltic trade, is still produced by the Courage group in Britain.*

acquired elsewhere, and the wealthy brought in beer from the country. In desperation, the brewers attempted to produce better quality beer by blending brown and 'stale' beer, or expensive pale ['twopenny'] ale with brown and 'stale'. 'Stale' was a well-matured brown beer that had conditioned in oak vats for up to a year and had acquired a sour, lactic character as a result of action from the Brettanomyces strain of wild yeast that lives in unlined wooden vessels.

These blended beers, with their lactic tang, were the first porters. They were expensive for the common brewers and publican-brewers in London because they lacked the space and the capital to tie up large stocks of ale that needed months to mature in casks. Wealthy entrepreneurs in London and the surrounding country districts cornered the market in 'stale' beer. They bought fresh brown ale from London brewers, matured it and then sold it back to the brewers at twice the price — a vast profit in those days. The brewers hit back by producing their own porters. According to Obadiah Poundage, whose detailed chronicle written as the result of a long career in London brewing makes him the most reliable contemporary source, wrote: 'On this footing stood the trade until about the year 1722 when the Brewers conceived there was a method to be found preferable to any of these extremes [of buying beer for blending]; that beer be well brewed, kept its proper time, became racy and mellow, that is, neither new nor stale, such as would recommend itself to the public. This they ventured to sell for one pound three shillings per barrel that the victualling might retail at threepence per quart. The labouring people, porters etc, experienced its wholesomeness and utility, they assumed to themselves the use thereof, from whence it was called Porter or Entire Butt.' The beer did not become immediately popular but sales improved when better quality malts and hops were used and isinglass finings, made from fish bladders, were introduced to clear the beer. According to Poundage, the London porters were matured for four to five months, about half the time of country beers. They were heavily hopped at the rate of three pounds to the hogshead, a fifty-four gallon cask.

So what did Ralph Harwood actually brew in the Bell Brewhouse in Shoreditch? According to the legend, Harwood and his potmen tired of trudging up and down to the cellar to mix pale, brown and stale beer from three different casks. Before either porter or entire were used as brewing terms, this mixture was nicknamed 'three threads' as it came from spiggots threaded into three casks in the pub cellar. Harwood brewed a beer to replicate the taste of three threads. It was called Entire Butt because it was a single brew dispensed from one cask or butt in the cellar, presumably using a mash of pale and brown malts. Brewing historian Graham Wheeler has suggested that Harwood may even have discovered that the maturation of his beer could be speeded up by inoculating it with a portion of sour 'stale' beer. This is how Arthur Guinness produced his porters and stouts and, before him, the great London porter brewers made every effort to speed up production: the

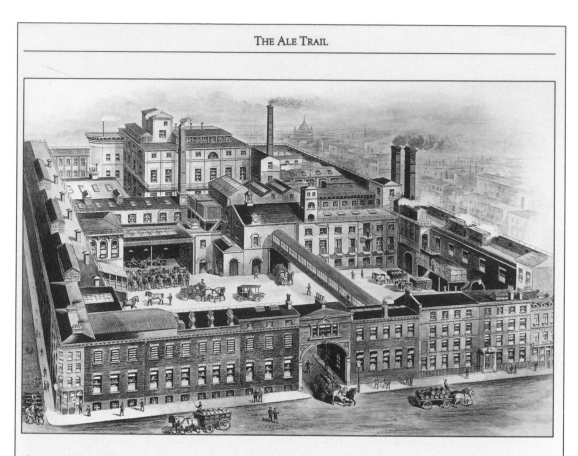

shorter the conditioning, the cheaper the beer and the greater the profit. The London brewers had reasserted their domination of the local market. But blended beers and entire butt beers existed side by side for many years, possibly decades. London pubs still bear witness to this age with fading tilework that announces they are purveyors of 'ale and porter' or 'ale and entire'.

It is commonly thought that the name porter stemmed from its popularity with street market porters. In the eighteenth and nineteenth centuries, they made up a sizeable proportion of London's working population. Graham Wheeler differs though. He argues that the origins of the name lie with the country brewers, erudite and learned men who chalked their casks with the Latin 'portare' when it was ready to be transported to London. It is a fetching idea but fails on two counts: the labourers who picked up the casks would have been illiterate and it defies belief that even aloof country scholars engaged in a profitable brewing sideline would have chalked an obscure Latin word on casks. Support for Wheeler's notion, however, comes from French-speaking Canada where porter beers take their name from the French term *à porter* — ready to be carried. Beer writer Ted Bruning has another theory: that porter is a corruption of export, as porter and stout were the first beers to be exported from London to other parts of Britain and then

ABOVE: Whitbread's Chiswell Street Porter Brewery in London. (Whitbread Archive)

to other countries. But the contemporaries must surely be right: Pound-age speaks of 'labouring people, porters etc' drinking the beer while a Frenchman, César de Saussure, writing to his family from London in November 1726, recorded: 'Would you believe it, although water is to be had in abundance in London and of fairly good quality, absolutely none is drunk? The lower classes, even the paupers, do not know what it is to quench their thirst with water. In this country nothing but beer is drunk and it is made in several qualities. Small beer is what everyone drinks when thirsty; it is used even in the best houses and costs only a penny a pot. Another kind of beer is called porter ... because the greater quantity of this beer is consumed by the working classes. It is a thick and strong beverage, and the effect it produces if drunk in excess is the same as that of wine; this porter costs threepence the pot. In London there are a number of houses where nothing but this sort of beer is sold. There are again other clear beers called ales, some of these being transparent as fine old wine. The prices of ale differ, some costing one shilling the bottle and others as much as one shilling and sixpence. It is said more grain is consumed in England for making beer than making bread.'

De Saussure's report is fascinating. It supports the theory that porter took its name from London labourers and shows just how rapidly it had come to dominate the market, with some taverns selling only that type of beer. He also mentions 'clear beers called ales'. This suggests there was already a growing demand for better quality, clarified ales: even as sales of porter took off, the seeds of the pale ale revolution of the next century were being sown.

But porter was the first mass market beer. Its success coincided with the Industrial Revolution. The cruel policy of land enclosure drove tens of thousands of rural workers into London and other towns. London's population grew at twice the rate of the rest of England and Wales, and rapidly became the greatest city in the world, the hub of a mighty empire. The new industrial working class were herded into filthy slums. The only comfort lay in the alehouse, the only solace in a cheap glass of ale.

The Industrial Revolution sounded the death knell of publican brewers. Ralph Harwood may have made an important contribution to brewing history but his Entire Butt brought about his own downfall. By Victorian times, only some four per cent of London beer came from publican-brewers. Steam engines, mechanical pumps, powered rakes for stirring the mash, hydrometers for measuring the sugars in wort and thermometers for testing temperature were beyond their means. In sharp contrast, the commercial brewers sprang to fame and fortune. The most famous of all the great porter brewers, Samuel Whitbread, was apprenticed to a London brewer and opened his own modest works in Old Street in 1742 to brew pale and amber beers. Within three years he moved to new premises in Chiswell Street in the Barbican area. Chiswell Street brewed only porter and stout. The site became one of the wonders of the new industrial world. Visitors, including King George III and

ABOVE: *An original advertisement for Whitbread Stout from Christmas 1932.* (Whitbread Archive)

OPPOSITE PAGE: *The enormous vat house on the north side of Whitbread's Chiswell Street brewery which was completed in the 1790s. From a watercolour of 1873.* (Whitbread Archive)

Queen Charlotte, hurried to the brewery to admire the steam engine installed by James Watt in 1785. By 1760 Whitbread had built a Porter Tun Room 'the unsupported roof span of which is exceeded in its majestic size only by that of Westminster Hall'. Before the Porter Tun Room opened, Whitbread rented 54 different buildings in London to store his beer. At Chiswell Street after 1760, porter was matured in enormous underground cisterns, each one containing 4,000 barrels of beer. The cisterns were cooled by internal copper pipes through which cold water was pumped to ensure the maturing beer stayed in good condition during hot weather. Brewing had ceased to be a seasonal occupation. Maturing in such bulk speeded up production, allowing Whitbread and his competitors to reduce the costs of production. In order to give the 'stale' tang drinkers demanded, brewers flattened the beer prior to vatting by running it into large, open cooling trays. Aeration of the beer speeded up acetification.

By 1812, under Sam Whitbread II, Chiswell Street was producing 122,000 barrels of porter a year. The brewery had been overtaken by Barclay Perkins (270,000), Meux Reid (188,000) and Truman Hanbury (150,000). Barclay Perkins in the early nineteenth century was larger than many modern British regional brewers. Brewers were part of the powerhouse of the new economic order. Within a century, brewing had

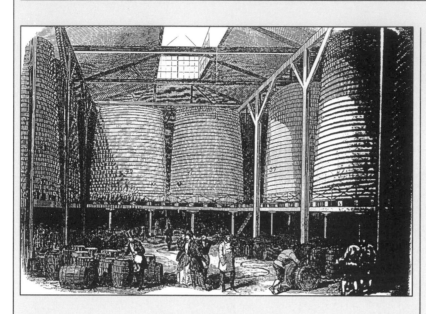

LEFT: *Porter vats of Barclay Perkins around 1850. In 1875, although the system of vatting had 'to a great extent gone out of use', the firm possessed a vast number of them ranging in size from 500 to 4,000 barrels each.*

changed out of all recognition. The capital used in the porter breweries of Barclay Perkins, Whitbread and Truman increased by two and half times in the forty years between 1760 and 1800. Massive investment replaced wooden vessels with cast iron ones as a result of metal's superior strength, longevity and heat retention.

Porter had moved beyond London. George's of Bristol, noted porter brewers, started in 1788. Arthur Guinness bought a brewery in Dublin in 1759 to make ale but had switched to porter by the end of the century. Beamish and Crawford were brewing porter in Cork by 1792. While Scottish brewers produced ales that were distinctively different to those south of the border they were alive to developments in England. The Anderston Brewery Company in Glasgow was the first to brew porter and hired Nathaniel Chivers, who had brewed in London and for Guinness in Dublin. He was paid £300 plus £25 expenses to show Anderston how to brew porter and made sure his visit to Scotland was profitable by giving identical information to rivals of Anderston, John Struthers of Gallowgate. Robert Meiklejohn of Alloa also employed a London brewer to explain the mysteries of porter brewing. The two great Scottish brewing dynasties of William Younger and Archibald Campbell Younger merged their separate businesses in order to ensure a dominant position in the porter market. Between 1750 and the end of the eighteenth century, the number of commercial breweries in a United Kingdom of Great Britain and the whole island of Ireland grew from 996 to 1,382 and the greatest of these breweries produced porter.

The porter brewers became rich and pompous. When Henry Thrale, one of the big London brewers, opened a new porter vat, one hundred

BELOW: *A Guinness poster now outlawed by fussy advertising standards legislation.* (Guinness Brewing Worldwide Ltd)

GUINNESS
IS GOOD FOR YOU

GIVES YOU STRENGTH

ABOVE: *Hops for Guinness being inspected for quality at the turn of the century.*

people sat down to dine in it. Meux built one that was sixty feet wide and twenty-three feet high. Two hundred guests dined in that one. In 1795 Meux added another vat that held the staggering amount of 20,000 barrels of beer. The almost childish, 'my vat is bigger than your vat' mentality was only halted by a terrible tragedy in 1814 when a porter vat burst at the Horse Shoe Brewery in London's Tottenham Court Road, where the Dominion Theatre now stands. The deluge swept away the brewery walls and surrounding streets of housing. Eight people were killed by 'drowning, injury, poisoning by the porter fumes or drunkenness'.

The porter brewed by the large producers continued to be a blended beer. In his 'Cyclopaedia' published in 1819, A Rees recorded that 'All the London porter is professed to be "entire butt", as indeed it was at first, but the system is now altered and it is very generally compounded of two kinds, or rather the same liquor in two different stages, the due admixture of which is palatable though neither is good alone. One is mild and the other stale porter; the former is that which has a slightly bitter flavour from having been lately brewed; the latter has been kept longer. This mixture the publican adapts to the palates of his several customers, and effects the mixture very readily by means of a machine containing small pumps worked by a handle.'

Rees is describing the early 'beer engines' that drew beer from casks in the pub cellar. 'An indifferent observer supposes that since it all comes from one spout it is entire butt beer, as the publican professes over the door,' he added. Publicans may no longer have brewed beer but they still had an important role to play in blending porter in the cellar to customers' requirement. Rees also noted that beer was sent from the brewery 'in the rough and requires fining': publicans dissolved isinglass in beer and added this to their casks to produce bright beer.

While smaller brewers attempted to make money from the burgeoning porter market with beers that were genuinely 'entire butt', the large companies continued to produce mild and stale beers for mixing in the pub. This practice continued throughout the nineteenth century even though the London porter brewers were under attack from new demands for both a sweeter mild ale and a crisper, quenching pale ale. It was only when porter sales went in to decline at the end of the century that the larger brewers began to produce a beer that was served from a single cask. But even that type of porter was still aged for a considerable time: Whitbread, for example, did not demolish the last of its porter ageing vats until 1918.

So porter and entire continued side by side. But why, if they both started life as brown beers, did they become dark and even jet black, the colour now associated with revivalist porters and Irish stouts? Once brewers were able to use a hydrometer (or saccharometer as it was first known) they could measure the advantages of using pale malt with its greater extract of fermentable sugars. Simply, they could make beer from less malt, thus lowering the costs of production, an important consideration for brewers the size of Barclay Perkins and the other large producers. In 1728, 3,501,888 quarters of malt brewed 6,433,272 barrels of beer; a century later 3,592,315 quarters of malt brewed 8,240,761 barrels. The lifting of coal tax and the widespread use of coke turned the kilning of pale malt from a speciality into a commonplace. But pale malt produced a pale beer at a time when drinkers were convinced that dark beers were stronger than lighter ones. The brewers had to offset the advantages of using pale malt for the bulk of the grist in their mash tuns with coloured malts to give the required darkness expected by porter drinkers. According to Rees, 'The greatest number of the London brewers have given up the brown malt altogether, using pale and amber malt ... From these they procure a liquor of proper strength and they give it both colour and flavour by the addition of colouring matter made from burnt sugar or by burning the sugar of the concentrated wort'. Caramel had arrived. Less scrupulous brewers used all manner of colouring agents. Between 1799 and 1813 the price of malt rose alarmingly. The brewers, anxious to keep their costs down, added the likes of molasses, Spanish liquorice, elderberry juice, coriander, capsicum and caraway seeds. Until the government clamped down on all 'adulterants', some brewers, who were not above poisoning their customers, added green vitriol — to give porter a good head — opium, tobacco, nux vomica and extract of poppies. A concentrated paste made from molasses became a popular, and harmless, way of adding colour but was placed on the banned list by the excise authorities in the early 1800s. Colour from West Indian muscovados unrefined sugar was permitted until the authorities changed their mind and banned that as well in 1816.

The brewers' problems were solved in 1817 by Daniel Wheeler with his New or Improved Method of Drying and Preparation of Malt. 'Said invention consists in the heating of malt to 400 degrees and upwards of Fahrenheits thermometer ... and so heating it that the greater part of the saccharine and amylaceous principles of the grain become changed into a substance resembling gum and extractive matter of a deep brown colour, readily soluble in hot or cold water ... A small quantity of malt thus prepared will suffice for the purpose of colouring beer or porter.' Wheeler used an iron cylinder 'similar in its construction to that now commonly used with a revolving motion for roasting Coffee.' He warned against over-roasting the grain, which would produce 'a coaly substance insoluble in water and yielding no colour'. As coffee houses had been popular for a century or more in London, the only wonder was that it had taken so long to use the technology of coffee roasting in the malting business.

Roasted malt, known as patent malt, took the industry by storm. Whitbread was using it by 1817, Barclay Perkins three years later. French and Jupp's, now in Hertfordshire, built a patent malt factory next to Whitbread in Chiswell Street in order to supply the brewery on a daily basis. As a result of roasting, patent malt is bitter and acrid to the taste and gave to porter a hint of the smokiness associated with wood-kilned brown malt and the sour tang from staling. The advent of patent malt, known today as either chocolate malt or black malt, ushered in the era of modern porters and stouts. Up until then porter had been a strong brown beer that was heavily hopped and conditioned for as long as a year. The blended porters, as distinct from entire butt, would have varied enormously in flavour as it was left to publicans to determine how much young beer and mature beer to mix in the drinker's pot. W. Tizard, writing in 1857, said with an obvious lack of enthusiasm for the subject that porter was 'sometimes blinked [not good], often tasting of empyreum [burning vegetable matter], some black, some musty, some muddy, some barmy'. From the 1820s, however, porter was a distinctive style, a ruby-black beer made from a single mash, still well matured and with an intensely bitter character from both high hop rates and patent malt.

It was at the very time that porter did become an identifiable style, as opposed to a mish-mash of beers called entire, three threads or porter, with a variety of brewing methods, ingredients, casual blending in pubs, and a plethora of aromas and flavours, that it came under sustained attack from both mild ale and pale ale as consumer tastes became more volatile. But porter remained a major element of the beer market until World War One. It would probably have remained so after the war but for restrictions placed on brewing by the government. In order to aid the war effort and conserve energy — and brewers were now using electricity rather than steam power — malting was severely restricted and strengths of beer reduced and regulated. The high kilning and roasting of malts for porter and stout were made difficult if not impossible. Pale

ale became the dominant British style as much as a result of government action as consumer preference. As the Home Rule movement in Ireland was gathering pace and support, no such restrictions were placed on brewers there. Irish porter and its cousin stout survived, blossomed and went on to conquer the world. It was only in the late 1980s that British brewers began to brew again the beer that had captured the imagination and captivated the tastes of drinkers three hundred years before.

THROUGH A GLASS DARKLY

In recent years several British brewers, prompted both by the surge in sales of Irish stouts in Britain and the rising interest in traditionally-brewed beers, started to make porters and stouts again, several of them in naturally conditioned form in cask and bottle. In a few cases, brewers researched old recipes in an attempt to recreate genuine porters. With one exception, it was impossible to go back beyond the nineteenth century as few records existed before that time and even recipes from that century were sketchy.

Dr Keith Thomas of Brewlab, already encountered with his Norvik medieval ale, has produced a porter that can claim to have a genuine nineteenth century flavour as the result of a combination of luck and remarkable laboratory skill. In 1988 deep sea divers from the City of London Polytechnic were investigating the wreck of a ship that had sunk in the English Channel in 1825 near the small coastal town of Littlehampton. They brought several bottles of porter to the surface and handed them to Thomas, who was then based in the City of London Poly before moving to Sunderland. The beer was contaminated with sea water and was undrinkable but Thomas was able to isolate a few living yeast cells in one bottle. He cultured them in a laboratory in sterile conditions and produced a strain he could brew with. He went to Whitbread and tracked down a porter recipe from 1850. Flag Porter (five per cent alcohol by volume) was first brewed — with a nice touch of history — by the Pitfield micro-brewery in Hoxton, east London, close to where Samuel Whitbread's first brewery in Old Street was based. When Pitfield closed, Flag Porter moved to Elgood's Brewery in Wisbech in the Cambridgeshire fens, which, like an original porter brewer, still uses open cooling trays or 'cool ships' to lower the temperature of the hopped wort before fermentation.

The recipe devised by Thomas and based on the 1850 Whitbread one uses pale, brown, crystal and black malts and Fuggles hops. My own research suggests that amber malt may have been used by Whitbread rather than crystal. It is interesting to note that Whitbread was still using wood-kilned brown malt in 1850, which contradicts the reports that the company had phased it out. Fuggles hops did not exist then and Thomas plans further research into hop varieties in use in the mid-nineteenth century. One of the many intriguing aspects of Flag Porter is the colour: it is a dark ruby red, not black and Thomas thinks the original may have been even paler. It has thirty-four units of bitterness: the original almost certainly had more bitterness but it was not possible to measure bitterness units in those days. The beer is enormously complex. It has a dark, tangy, slightly smoky and nutty aroma underpinned by Fuggle hop pepperiness. In the mouth there is a distinct bitter fruitiness reminiscent of blood oranges and the finish is rich in fruit, hops and bitter chocolate, becoming intensely dry. There is also a faint and fascinating herbal hint in the finish. In spite of the complexity, it is a marvellously quenching and refreshing beer and its appeal to manual workers anxious to slake their thirsts was obvious. (Information from Bottle Green: 01532 431691.)

Dr Ian Hornsey, a micro-biologist who brews at the Nethergate Brewery in Clare, Suffolk, has recreated a mid-eighteenth beer by a somewhat tortuous route. When he produced a beer called Old Growler (named after his dog) he first called it an old ale. It was based on a 1750s recipe for a London mild ale brewed by Taylor Walker. But modern drinkers expect mild to be low in strength and in 1992 the beer was relaunched under the name of porter and quickly achieved greater success, with a bottled version on sale in supermarkets and wine shops. I disagreed with Hornsey over the description of Old Growler as 'porter', as mild ale was just one of the components of the style in the 1750s. But stylistic quibbles apart, here was a potent and — in its cask-conditioned version — living recreation of a beer from more than three hundred years ago. Old Growler is brewed from Maris Otter pale malt (85.3 per cent), wheat flour (3.41 per cent), crystal malt (8.53 per cent) and black malt (2.71 per cent). It has seventy units of colour. Neither crystal nor black malt existed in 1750 and the original brew would have relied heavily on wood-kilned brown malt. Hornsey at first used a blend of Fuggles and Goldings hop pellets but has replaced them with the

BELOW: *Bob Renvoize, home brewer and jazz musician, who helped recreate an 18th century Porter for the Nethergate Brewery in Suffolk.*

modern Challenger. The beer has 27 units of bitterness. It has a fine peppery hop aroma with powerful hints of liquorice. It is intensely bitter and fruity on the palate and the finish is hoppy with dark chocolate from the malt.

My interest in the beer increased when Ian Hornsey called me one day to say he had made a special version of Old Growler with a 'secret ingredient'. He refused to say any more over the phone so I drove with keen anticipation to the ancient market town of Clare to find out more. I was met by Dr Hornsey and a home-brewer and part-time jazz musician named Bob Renvoize. Hornsey said the original Taylor Walker recipe had included coriander and bog myrtle as bittering agents along with the hops. The information showed that while brewers had switched to hops from the fifteenth century they had continued to use other plants and herbs from the days of 'gruit'. Hornsey and Renvoize decided to attempt to recreate the original beer. They didn't know what bog myrtle was — though later research discovered that the plant still grows widely in England — but a bunch of coriander was bought from a shop specialising in Asian foodstuffs. Renvoize took four and half gallons of Old Growler wort from the brewery to his home-brew plant. He added three ounces of Goldings and the bunch of coriander during the boil and then fermented it. He thought the finished beer was unsatisfactory and he planted some coriander in his garden and let it turn to seed. With the second brew he added ground coriander seeds with the hops. When the beer was ready Renvoize added some further coriander to the cask: 'I "dry coriandered it",' he laughed. The beer had a powerful herbal and medicinal aroma. It was ferociously dry in the mouth and the finish was hoppy with more herbs and spices. I described it as 'liquid snuff'. Hornsey and his colleagues at Nethergate considered the spiced Old Growler to be a one-off brew that was too bitter and spicy for commercial sale. But the interest aroused when I reported it in CAMRA's newspaper What's Brewing encouraged them to make a small batch of Old Growler with coriander for sale in a couple of pubs in Suffolk and Cambridge for the 1993 Christmas period. It was an instant success and Nethergate is likely to repeat the experiment. (Information: 01787 277244.)

Shepherd Neame of Faversham, in the heart of the Kent hop fields, is Britain's oldest working brewery, opened in 1698. The company in its early days brewed ales, porters and stouts and was one of the first to sell beer outside the narrow area around the brewery. 'Sheps', as the brewery is affectionately called, 'exported' beer to the Isle of Sheppey and across the Medway river to the county of Essex, which gives some support to the notion that the name porter was a corruption of export. The popularity of porter can be measured by the fact that a Porter Club was set up in Faversham in 1793 by local businessmen. They met for 68 years in the fifteenth-century Sun inn in West Street to discuss politics and local matters, aided by draughts of local porter.

When production director Ian Dixon set out to make a porter in 1992

RIGHT: *Head Brewer Ian Dixon with his traditional mash tuns at Shepherd Neame where he created his Original Porter with a dash of liquorice.*

he discovered from the brewery's archives that liquorice had been used in Shep's porters of the eighteenth and nineteenth centuries. Faversham was once a great sea port and was the biggest manufacturer of gunpowder in Britain. In the 1890s the port handled half a million tonnes of merchandise a year and one item regularly brought back from Spain was liquorice. Dixon fashioned a recipe of pale, crystal and chocolate malts, with dark unrefined sugar added to the copper along with Omega and Target hops and a late addition of Challengers for bitterness. Liquorice root is also added during the copper boil. Dixon drew back from also using wormwood and bog myrtle, both mentioned in the brewery archives. The porter is made in a splendid antique brewhouse with unlined teak mash tuns dating from World War One. A steam engine installed in 1698 is still on view to visitors.

I tasted Original Porter in the wood-panelled Sun with a large log fire and chimney seats. The 5.2 per cent beer, on sale in the autumn and winter, has ninety units of colour and thirty-five to forty units of bitterness. It has a big spicy and peppery hop character, overlain by bitter coffee and chocolate notes. And subtly on the aroma and palate there is a delicious hint of liquorice. (Information: 01795 532206.)

Burton Porter seems something of a misnomer, for it was the pale ales of Burton-on-Trent in the English East Midlands that helped send porter into decline in the nineteenth century. But the Burton Bridge Brewery, sited as the name suggests on the bridge over the Trent that leads into the famous brewing town, has produced one of the finest of the new breed. The small micro's beers can be tasted in the fine Victorian Bridge Inn that forms part of the venture. Bridge Porter is available in both cask and bottle-conditioned versions. It has an original gravity of 1045 degrees and is 4.5 per cent alcohol by volume. Pipkin pale malt (92 per cent of the grist), crystal (five per cent) and chocolate (three per cent) are joined in the copper by equal amounts of Challenger and Target hops. It is a deep ruby red edging towards mahogany but it is not black. The aroma is a balance of light hops, chocolate and dark fruit, there is rich biscuity malt in the mouth and the finish starts grainy and fruity until the hops take over. It is a complex and splendidly refreshing beer. Burton Bridge also produces a five per cent stout for Christmas with 72 per cent pale malt, seven per cent chocolate and 21 per cent micronised wheat. Challenger hops are used for aroma and bitterness. The beer has a gentle hops and chocolate aroma with biscuity malt in the mouth and a complex finish with a balance of bitter chocolate, hops and dark fruit. Micronised wheat is unmalted and is cooked to gelatinise it: it is also known as 'grits' and is used to counter a high nitrogen level in the malt, to give a smooth, creamy character to beer and a good, foaming head. (Information: 01283 510573.)

Another micro in the English Midlands, Titanic of Stoke-on-Trent, brews a memorable stout in the dry Irish style by using roasted barley as well as pale malt and flaked wheat. Titanic Stout is 4.5 per cent alcohol and the hops are Northdown. The aroma has roast grain, dark fruit and a big peppery hoppiness. There is a fine balance of creamy malt and hops in the mouth, followed by a dry finish with chocolate and coffee notes. The beer has an intriguing bitter-sweet appeal due to the careful balance of different grains and hops with creaminess derived from the flaked wheat. The beer is sold in cask and bottle-conditioned versions. (Information: 01782 823447.)

The porter revival was boosted in 1992 when Whitbread brewed a beer based on an 1859 Chiswell Street recipe at the group's Castle Eden brewery in County Durham in North-east England. The beer was brewed to mark Whitbread's 250th anniversary. Three Whitbread breweries — Castle Eden, Cheltenham and Sheffield — were invited to recreate a porter using the Chiswell Street recipe book. In 1859 the brewery paid tax on malt not the gravity of the wort before fermentation so there was no indication of the potential strength. But Whitbread's experts estimated that the 1859 porter would have been around 1066 degrees, approximately six per cent alcohol. The brewers were told to brew a beer with a more acceptable modern strength of between four and five per cent. Realising that today's hops have greater bitterness from higher alpha acids, the hop rate, using Fuggles and Goldings, was reduced dramatically by around a quarter. Pale, brown and black malts were used. A panel of beer writers, including Michael Jackson, Barrie Pepper (chairman of the British Guild of Beer Writers), and myself tasted the three beers and were unanimous in choosing Castle Eden's entry, produced by head brewer Tony Rowsell.

BELOW: *Perfect pint of Porter at Castle Eden.*

The beer was made available in selected pubs on a trial basis. Although it had to vie with both Guinness and Murphy's Irish stouts in Whitbread pubs it was sufficiently popular to become a regular seasonal beer, usually on sale in the spring and early summer. The beer has been refined, or 'tweaked' in brewer's language, since it first appeared, but remains a remarkable one bursting with dark malt, fruit and hop character. It is brewed from pale malt (76 per cent), brown (20 per cent), chocolate (two per cent) and black (two per cent). It has 290 units of colour and is a 'modern' porter in the sense that it has a jet black colour offset by a ruby 'edge' when held up to the light. The hops are English Goldings in the copper, with dry hopping in the cask from Styrian Goldings. The beer has thirty-six units of bitterness. The aroma is dominated by the resiny, piney Styrians with powerful hints of coffee and chocolate and a touch of liquorice. The palate is a rich blend of dark malt, hop bitterness and a figgy fruitiness. The finish becomes dry with espresso coffee and bitter chocolate notes.

The last piece of the porter jigsaw slotted into place in 1993 when the family-owned McMullen brewery of Hertford, founded in 1827, produced a porter based on a 1913 recipe. Production director Tony Skipper had also brewed with Beamish of Cork and was no stranger to dark beers. His Special Reserve Porter was 5.2 per cent alcohol and was brewed from Halcyon pale malt, ten per cent amber malt (specially made for the beer by French and Jupp's), nine per cent crystal, three per cent chocolate and nine per cent wheat malt, all the same proportions as in the original beer. The hops were Progress and Northdown with a late addition of Progress. The finished beer, fermented in magnificent high-sided oak fermenters with copper linings, had a powerful aroma of chocolate malt, resiny hops and blackcurrant fruit. There was tart malt and fruit in the mouth and the finish had a slightly oily and medicinal character — the beery version of an Islay single malt Scotch whisky. The yeast strain was Whitbread 'B', which started life in the Mackeson stout brewery in Kent and therefore had a good pedigree when it came to producing a dark and fruity beer. The porter was brewed as part of a portfolio of occasional 'Special Reserve' ales but a

RIGHT: *Mash tuns at Castle Eden.*

LEFT: *McMullen's Special Reserve Porter was launched outside that bastion of High Victorianism, the Victoria and Albert Museum.*

similar beer with a slightly higher alcohol rating is brewed for Sainsbury's stores under the name Blackfriars Porter. (Information: 01992 584911.)

McMullen recreated a beer from the time when porter was about to be eclipsed by the emergency measures of World War One and the rush to popularity of modern bitter beers.

Chapter Three
Ale's Passage to India

The pale ale revolution in England in the nineteenth century marked a decisive break with the past. Porter had been the first commercial beer but its methods of production had always been a compromise between the new technologies of the Industrial Revolution and older practices reaching back to rural, feudal times. The pale ale brewers grasped new technology with both hands and transformed not only brewing but the perceptions of beer on a world scale. Pale ale was equally as innovative as the lager beer of continental Europe. It made use of steam power, improved malting, mashing and copper boiling, refrigeration to cool and store beer, and a scientific understanding of the role of yeast in fermentation. While the first lagered beers in Bavaria were dark and their brewers were tentative innovators until golden Pilsner appeared in neighbouring Bohemia, pale ale brewers stuck their heads above the parapet and boldly announced: 'This is new!' Before the invention of the thermometer, brewers considered that mashing was complete when the steam cleared and they could see their reflections in the wort. Until the arrival of the hydrometer the strength of beer was measured in a rough and ready fashion by weighing the malt used in each brew. The conversion of starch to sugar in the mash tun and the violent transformation of wort into alcohol were spontaneous and uncontrollable forces until Payen and Persoz in France isolated the enzymes in malt, Lavoisier analysed the action of yeast during fermentation, and Louis Pasteur urged all brewers to invest in microscopes. Pasteur visited several British breweries, including Whitbread's in London and Younger's in Edinburgh. He showed them how wild yeasts and other micro-organisms attacked fresh beer and made it sour. As a result of investigations by Pasteur and Hansen of Carlsberg in Copenhagen, brewers isolated yeast strains and stored them in cool places — refrigerators by the end of the century — to avoid contamination.

Cast-iron mash tuns held the heat better than wood, were far larger, holding up to 200,00 gallons of wort, and had longer life spans. Mashing was made more effective and temperature of the grist and liquor maintained by mechanical pre-mashing devices. The mash was stirred by steam-driven rakes, mercifully releasing horses from the toil of plodding endlessly round the tuns to turn the rakes. In the middle of the century Scottish brewers developed the method known as 'sparging',

LEFT: *Pomp and pale ale ... a poster that underscores the links between pale ale and Britain's imperial past.*

INDIA PALE ALE

*Brewed with 100% Fuggles hops,
this IPA has been brewed to reflect the heritage
of the original IPAs of the last century.
Brewed at the Castle Eden Brewery to 5.5% abv.*

*A "Single Varietal" hop bitter
from The Whitbread Beer Company*

from the French *asperger*, to sprinkle. The spent grains were mechanically sprayed with hot liquor to wash out any remaining sugars at the end of the mashing stage. Sparging put paid to the old system of producing three or four beers from the same mash. The mash tun could be utilised more effectively and profitably by pushing a new brew through every couple of hours. Coppers, fired by coal or coke, were turned from open pans into domed vessels that avoided heat loss and retained the essential aromas of the hops.

Cool ships, in which the hopped wort cooled before fermentation, were replaced by heat exchange units where the liquid was pumped through pipes or plates that alternated with pipes holding running cold water. The wort was no longer open to the atmosphere and was free from the risk of infection from wild yeasts. When ice-making machines were invented late in the nineteenth century they were embraced with as much enthusiasm in Britain and Ireland as they were in Bavaria.

New fermenting vessels proved vital to the taste and character of pale ale. The brewers and their customers wanted a clear, sparkling ale. In Burton-on-Trent the 'union set', large oak casks linked together or 'held in union', cleansed the fermenting beer of yeast by placing the casks below troughs. The working beer gushed up pipes from cask to trough, leaving the yeast behind. Brewers throughout the country rushed to emulate their Burton rivals by installing union sets. The determinedly independent Yorkshire brewers developed their own system, the Yorkshire square, made up of two-storeyed slate vessels. The wort was pumped from the bottom storey into the top through a man hole, leaving the yeast behind in the top storey. Beer cleansing not only produced a clear beer but allowed brewers to collect the yeast and store it for the next brew. Consistency of palate from brew to brew was essential as brewers bought chains of pubs and started to market their beers with powerful brand images. Charles Stuart Calverley's lines underscored the importance of brand names and how they impinged on the minds of the drinking public:

O Beer! O Hodgson, Guinness, Allsopp, Bass!
Names that should be on every infant's tongue!

In the pubs, beer was stored in cooled cellars and drawn to the bar by manual pumps known as beer engines. There were only two remaining links with the past: the first pale ales were stored for several months, but that was more a response to a new market, the colonial trade, than any misty-eyed hankering after older practice. The new breed of beer entrepreneurs had no truck with nostalgia, save for the fact that they continued to use top-fermenting yeast strains. Lager brewing was dismissed as a Continental irrelevance by men certain of their place at the heart of the greatest empire the world had known since Roman times: in the late nineteenth century, Bass was the most famous name throughout the lands ruled by the British. The quality of the new pale ales combined with imperial pride made sure that lager beer was to make only a fleeting appearance in Victorian England. The fact that lager was perceived to be a German beer helped limit its popularity. In Charles Chaplin's film 'Limelight' the following exchange takes place between two music-hall musicians: 'Do you know Handel's Largo?'/ 'Yes, but I'd rather have a brown ale!'

The story of English pale ale goes hand-in-hand with the small East

Midlands town of Burton-on-Trent. Long before it was technically possible to brew pale ale, Burton enjoyed a reputation for the quality of its beer, as a piece of nineteenth century doggerel affirms:

> Ne'er tell me of liquors from Spain or from France,
> They may get in your heels and inspire you to dance.
> But Ale of old Burton if mellow and right
> Will get in your head and inspire you to fight.

In 1002 AD, Wulfric Spot, the Earl of Mercia, founded an monastery in Staffordshire and the monks of Burton Abbey settled to their devotions and the brewing of ale. They found that the spring waters from the wells in the area produced a beer with a fine taste and excellent keeping qualities. Many centuries later, when it was possible to analyse Burton's waters, they were found to contain high levels of salts, especially calcium sulphate — gypsum — and magnesium. The salts encouraged a powerful fermentation, drew the best from hops and gave the finished beer a tempting sparkle and refreshing quality in the glass. London water, in contrast, was soft, high in calcium carbonate, and better suited for brewing brown beers.

ABOVE: *Leaving no stave unturned ... coopers at Burton-on-Trent in the late nineteenth century.*

By 1600 Burton had forty-six licensed victuallers who produced ales for a population of just 1,500. Burton ales started to gain a reputation outside the immediate area, which was unusual at a time of rudimentary and slow transport. The beers reached London and became a cult drink in the Peacock in Gray's Inn Lane and the Dagger Inn in Holborn. By the early eighteenth century there were references in London journals to 'Hull ale' but this was almost certainly beer from Burton that had reached the east coast port by way of the Trent and then was taken on to London by sea-going ships. In 1712, 638 barrels of Burton beer passed through Hull en route for London, and Joseph Addison noted in the Spectator, 'We concluded our walk with a glass of Burton ale'. The same paper reported that Burton beer was in great demand in the Vauxhall Pleasure Gardens. The Trent Navigation Act of 1699 had made the river navigable from Burton to Shardlow and by 1712 had been extended to Gainsborough and Hull. The Burton brewers were selling their ales — brown, sweet and well-hopped — all over central and northern England. More importantly they were exporting them to the Baltic ports. Benjamin Wilson led the way. He founded what was to become Samuel Allsopp's brewery, which in turn became Ind Coope & Allsopp. Peter the Great of Russia and the Empress Catherine were said to have been partial to the ales from far-away Burton-on-Trent. But eighteenth-century technology was a bar to developing the export trade. Benjamin Wilson, in a letter dated 1791 to a customer in Elbing (quoted in Colin Owen's 'The Development of Industry in Burton upon Trent') explained: 'From the unusual impatience of the Shipowners and Masters to depart so early in the Spring, I ought to begin to brew before the Winter sets in; but let me tell them and all whom it may concern that it would be very dangerous to the preservation of the ale, which is a material object both for me and my friends to consider. I commonly begin to brew in the beginning of November, and am not willing, notwithstanding the importunity of the shipowners, to open my winter business sooner.' Brewing in Burton as the century drew to its close was still a seasonal affair. Wilson complained that even a mild winter could force him to suspend brewing as he could not control mashing and fermenting temperatures. And brewing methods were still archaic. In a letter to Joseph Brooks in London, Wilson explained: 'Every part of the business is done by hand-pail, from drawing of the mash to filling the casks for exportation. It occurs to me that this quantity of business could be done with the aid of machinery to some great expense, and with equal certainty of purpose.' Country brewing lagged way behind London and other large cities.

Wilson was frustrated by his inability to produce an ale of standardised colour and strength. In a further letter from 1791, in response to customers in the Baltic, he admitted: 'I have committed one fault in the brewing of my ale last winter, and that is, in making it too strong — if I had made it weaker it certainly would have been lighter coloured and would have pleased better at first sight; but it is certainly better for the

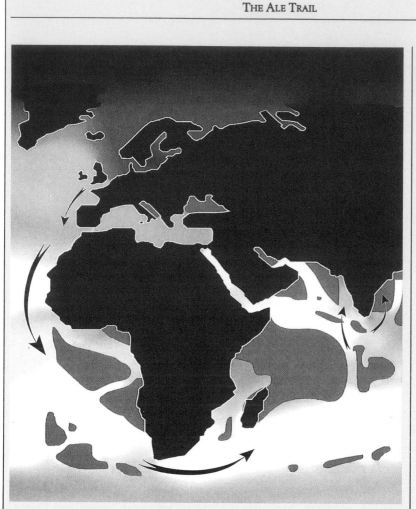

LEFT: *A computer generated map by Thom Tomlinson, brewer of Renegade Red pale ale in the United States, showing the seasonal mean surface temperatures from ship reports from 1855 to 1884. The even gray areas represent missing reports. Most of the journey from Britain to India occurred in moderate to cool temperatures. Maximum temperatures of 25 degrees C occurred in the equatorial areas.*
(Map: courtesy Brewing Techniques)

interest of the adventure to possess strength sufficient for its certain conservation, than to be otherwise and in danger of turning sour.' This is a highly significant letter. Customers were clearly demanding a paler and more refreshing beer. Wilson was anxious to please them but at that stage could not meet the demand for a lighter beer. He also realised, as an experienced brewer, that even a pale beer needed strength to survive the long sea journeys.

It was not just the journey that inhibited trade between Burton and the Baltic, which at its peak accounted for seventy per cent of the brewers' production. Anglo-Russian trade declined as relations between the countries soured. In 1783 tariffs on British goods imported through St Petersburg increased by 300 per cent. Trade ceased altogether in 1800 when Russia placed an embargo on all British ships and merchandise. The Burton brewers turned their attentions to Prussia and

Poland and for a while business was brisk. William Bass, who had sold his transport business in 1777 to concentrate on brewing, by the turn of the century had nine agents in St Petersburg, eleven in Riga, twenty-five in Danzig, one in Elsinore and four each in Hamburg, Bremen and Hanover. But the entire Baltic trade collapsed with the wars with France that lasted intermittently from 1799 to the defeat of Napoleon Bonaparte at the Battle of Waterloo in 1815. As Bonaparte's armies rampaged across Europe they closed port after port to the British. Ships laden with Burton ale could only make the increasingly hazardous sea crossings if they were guarded by the Royal Navy and the British Admiralty had better uses for its men o'war. The effect in Burton was catastrophic. Between 1780 and the mid-1820s the number of breweries in Burton contracted from thirteen to five. The larger brewers, Wilson (now joined by his nephew Samuel Allsopp), William Bass, William Worthington and Thomas Salt, desperately looked for alternative markets. They turned to the colonies for survival.

Britain first colonised India in 1772 and brewers hurried to supply first the soldiers and then the growing number of British civilians with beer to refresh them in that torrid climate. But brown ales and porters were not the best thirst-quenchers and they tended to arrive sour and flat after a sea journey that lasted from three to five months. A brilliant piece of research by Thom Tomlinson, who brews an India Pale Ale called Renegade Red at the High Country Brewery in Boulder, Colorado, working with the Climate Diagnostics Center in Boulder, tracked the temperatures that a shipload of ale would encounter on a voyage from London or Liverpool to India in the mid to late 1800s. (The research appeared in the March/April 1994 issue of *Brewing Techniques*, published in Eugene, Oregon.) The ships left between late November and early February, arriving in India between March and May. The winter departures were timed to make sure the ships reached the Indian Ocean before the monsoon season. Heading south from London, the ships crossed the equator, cruised south along the coast of Africa, rounded the Cape of Good Hope and then crossed the Indian Ocean to Bombay, Calcutta and other ports of call.

'Even though the hogsheads [54 gallon casks] of ale were stored in the lowest level of the ship's hull — the coolest place in the ship — the temperature fluctuations were tremendous,' Tomlinson said. The research showed that for the first few weeks of the voyage, water temperatures were approximately 52° F/11° C. As the ships entered equatorial regions, temperatures climbed to 81°F/25°C. As they rounded the Cape, temperatures dropped to between 65-69°F/17-19°C. In the southern part of the Indian Ocean water temperatures soared to 73°F/21°C. On the final leg of the voyage, nearing the coast of India, temperatures would reach 83-86°F/26-28°C. As Tomlinson drily observed, 'Combine the temperature fluctuations with the normal rocking motions of such a journey and the rough waters off southern Africa and you have one hellish trip for an ale.'

By a strange quirk, the brewer who first seized the opportunity to brew a special beer for India that would withstand the arduous voyage, was based in London not Burton: strange because London in the late eighteenth century, with its soft well water, was not ideally suited to making pale beers. The reason why George Hodgson of Abbot & Hodgson's Bow Brewery, Bromley-by-Bow, East London started to brew an ale specially for the India trade was due to his proximity to the East and West India Docks from where great ships set sail for the sub-continent. Hodgson learned that the ships left half-empty and returned with valuable cargoes of spices and silks that covered the costs of the voyages. Rates for cargo on the outward journeys were low. Hodgson would have heard from ship owners that soldiers and civilians in India were dissatisfied with the ales being sent to them and he reckoned he could make substantial profits by supplying them with a light, refreshing beer.

Little is known about this 'otherwise unremarkable firm', as Gourvish and Wilson describe it in 'The British Brewing Industry 1830-1980'. The brewery, bottling and cask stores, stables, brewer's house, flour mills and wharf alongside the River Lea were sold in 1885 and a block of local authority flats now stands on the site. Most commentators suggest that Hodgson's pale ale was pale only in comparison to the brown ales, porters and stouts of the time. Thom Tomlinson in his research on India Pale Ales in Brewing Techniques says that 'Hodgson's pale ales were some of the first beers in the world that were paler than black or brown'. He describes Hodgson's pale ale as 'copper coloured or reddish bronze'. But no one can be certain what colour the beer was. By the 1790s, Hodgson would have had access to pale malt produced by coke-fired kilns. If he used pale malt only, or pale malt with brewing sugar, there is no reason why the beer could not have been extremely pale in colour. Research carried out by Dr John Harrison, material scientist and brewing historian, for the Durnden Park Beer Circle in Maidenhead, Berkshire, notes that from the early nineteenth century the Burton brewers were using a special East India Malt, also known as white malt, that was closer to present-day lager malts than pale ale varieties. Younger in Scotland used imported malt for its pale ales and that may well have been continental lager malt. Hodgson's pale ale could have been genuinely pale: after all, when the Burton brewers scrambled for a slice of the India market they had to match the colour of Hodgson's beer. It would have been high in alcohol and extremely bitter. George Hodgson had the accumulated knowledge of the India trade from experts in the docks adjacent to his brewery. As an experienced brewer he knew that the best defences against spoilage on the journey to India were alcohol and hops. It is likely that he made his India ale to an original gravity of 1060 degrees (approximately six per cent alcohol by volume) and with twice the normal hopping rate for the time. Additional dry hops may have been added to the casks as a further measure against infection and priming sugar added at the same time to keep the yeast active. Wild

OPPOSITE PAGE: *Brew No. 396 - a parti-gyled brew of India Pale Ale produced in the Allsopp brewhouse in Burton on Trent on Wednesday 15th May 1935. The recipe was reproduced for the British Guild of Beer Writers' seminar on IPAs in London in May 1994.*

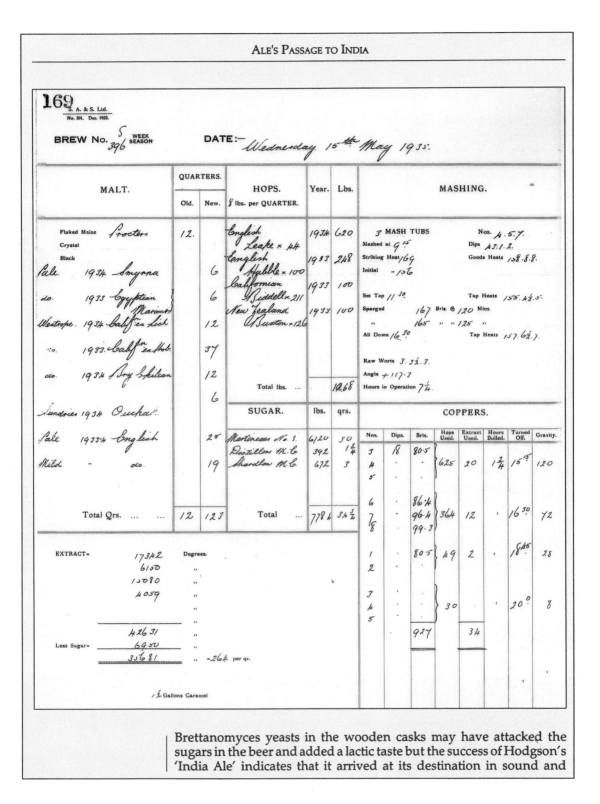

Brettanomyces yeasts in the wooden casks may have attacked the sugars in the beer and added a lactic taste but the success of Hodgson's 'India Ale' indicates that it arrived at its destination in sound and refreshing condition. One matter that is beyond dispute is that because Hodgson was brewing with soft, carbonated London water his ale lacked the sparkle and the quenching edge possible with Burton waters high in natural sulphates. It was not colour but water and the yeast strains developed in Burton that were to lead ultimately to the triumph of Burton pale ales in the India trade.

Mark Hodgson, who succeeded his father, attacked the India market with even greater vigour. In 1750 some 1,480 barrels of beer had left England for India. By 1775 the number had grown to 1,680. In 1800, 9,000 barrels were despatched, an increase that surpasses the entire amount of beer exported to India in the previous one hundred years. Not all the beer came from Hodgson's, but the Bow Brewery was responsible for the bulk of it. (It is not known whether barrels meant thirty-six gallon casks, fifty-four gallon hogsheads or 108 gallon butts). Hodgson had created a virtual monopoly in India but he was ruffling colonial feathers. The Circular on Beer Trade to India complained in 1829 of Hodgson's unethical methods. It said that when Hodgson heard that another brewer was shipping ale to India he would flood the market with large amounts of his own beer, driving down the selling price. The potential rivals made damaging losses as a result. Having seen off his rivals, Hodgson would then exploit scarcity by sending small supplies of ale the following year, driving up prices in order to recoup his diminished profits from the previous year. Prices could fluctuate from twenty rupees a hogshead to two hundred rupees.

Mark Hodgson made the mistake of over-playing his hand. He denied importers credit and then set up his own import business in India. He squeezed out the middle men and made enemies of them. They looked to other British brewers to supply them. Over dinner in 1821 a director of the East India Company named Marjoribanks told Samuel Allsopp of the lucrative pickings to be made from the India trade. The East India Company handled Hodgson's exports but was displeased by his treatment of local importers which could rebound on the company's own reputation and damage Anglo-Indian relations. According to Buchanan's 'Burton and Its Bitter Beer', published in 1858, Marjoribanks told Allsopp that India offered 'a trade that can never be lost: for the climate is too hot for brewing. We are now dependent upon Hodgson who has given offence to most of the merchants of India. But your Burton ale, so strong and sweet, will not suit our market.' Marjoribanks' butler provided the men with a bottle of Hodgson's ale. Allsopp, who had bemoaned the loss of his Baltic trade at the dinner, hurried back to Burton with a sample of Hodgson's beer which he presented to his head brewer and maltster, Job Goodhead. Goodhead said he could kiln his malt to produce an ale of that colour — which suggests Hodgson's ale really was pale — but he spat out the beer when he tasted it, affronted by its extreme hoppy bitterness. Hodgson's beer made a similarly poor impression on George's of Bristol, a major porter brewer which experimented with pale ale. In 1828 a senior partner at

ABOVE: *Now just a museum piece ... Bass's Union Room at Burton.*

George's wrote to Willis & Earle in Calcutta suggesting it would not be difficult to improve on Hodgson's beer. 'We neither like its thick and muddy appearance or rank bitter flavour.' Twenty months later George's shipped twenty hogsheads to India and the same writer noted: 'We made a slight alteration in the Ale by brewing it rather of a paler colour and more hop'd to make it as similar as possible to some samples of Allsopp's ale'. For despite his first revulsion and under pressure from Allsopp, Job Goodhead had made a trial brew of a pale ale, using a tea pot as his mash tun. Allsopp soon had a supply of ale ready for the India trade. In a small town such as Burton, news of the development spread round the other breweries like a bush fire and Bass and Salt were quickly experimenting with their own ales for the India market. They were taking a considerable risk. They had to invest in large casks — hogsheads and butts — and, unlike Hodgson, had to pay transport costs to get the beer to London or Liverpool by canal before meeting the additional costs of the passage to India. And when the ales reached their destination they had to pass muster with tasters who could accept or reject a whole consignment. Allsopp heard to his horror that his first consignment, while accepted by the tasters, earned only twenty rupees a hogshead while Hodgson's rated twenty-five. The second and third consignments from Allsopp brought forty rupees per hogshead each and the Burton brewer never looked back. A letter from a J C Bailton had given Allsopp great heart: 'With reference to the loss you have sustained in your first shipments, you must have been prepared for that, had you known the market as well as I do: Here almost everything is name, and Hodgson's has so long stood without a rival that it was a matter of astonishment how your ale could have stood the competition; but that it did is a fact, and I myself was present when a butt of yours fetched 136 rupees, and a butt of Hodgson's only eighty rupees at a public sale'.

Within ten years Allsopp and Bass accounted for more than half the beer shipped to Calcutta, almost twice as much as Hodgson. Throughout the 1830s, the two brewers sent some 6,000 barrels a year of pale ale to India. The key to the success of Burton-brewed ales, which quickly eclipsed Hodgson's, sending the brewery into decline and closure, lay in the yeast developed for the Burton union system of fermentation and the spring waters. Paul Bayley, the current head brewer at Marston, Thompson & Evershed, the last Burton brewery to use the union set method of fermentation, has described the yeast strain developed by the system as 'greedy'. It attacks the sugars in the wort ferociously, producing dry, fully-attenuated beers with little residual sugar. The use of substantial amounts of brewing sugar in the copper which, unlike malt sugars, is almost totally fermentable, adds to the dryness and high alcohol of the finished beer. The beer is extremely stable but in cask it needs far longer to condition and mature than non-union-brewed beers. It would survive the journey to India better than most beers and, according to Bayley, the active yeast left in the casks would fight bacteria. Burton water, 'brewing liquor', played an equally important role in the flavour and keeping qualities of pale ale. According to Bayley: 'Calcium reduces sugar and helps produce more alcohol. It keeps the yeast active, reduces haze, decreases beer colour and improves hop utilisation. The result is a more bitter beer. Magnesium acts in a similar fashion and sulphate gives a drier flavour and enhances bitterness.'

In Boulder, Colorado, brewer Thom Tomlinson agrees with this assessment of Burton water. 'The secret to the Burton brewers' success came from the water, an ingredient often downplayed in beer recipe formulation. The sulphates of the Trent basin helped the Burton beers achieve their clarity and bitterness and allowed the Burton brewers to far exceed Hodgson's India Pale Ale in clarity, hopping rate, and marketability. The high sulphate content allowed brewers to use hopping rates well beyond that compatible with the carbonate water of London. Sulphates actually change the mouthfeel and perception of bitterness. High sulphate content results in a sharp, clean bitterness, unlike the harsh, clinging bitterness of highly hopped beers brewed with water high in carbonates.'

Few records survive from the last century but Bass archivists claim that export ales brewed until the 1970s were based on recipes dating back to the 1850s. If true, this means that a Bass pale ale for India would have had an original gravity of around 1060 degrees (approximately six

per cent alcohol). This is not exceptionally strong for the time but assuming the casks were primed with sugar and a vigorous second fermentation took place, the final alcohol could have been higher. The ales were heavily hopped in the copper, between three and four pounds per barrel. Dry hops were added in the casks at around six ounces per barrel. The units of bitterness, had they been capable of measurement in the 1850s, would have reached seventy or eighty, almost twice as high as a modern bitter, but the bitterness would have softened during the sea voyage. Bass used Fuggles and Goldings from Worcestershire and Kent. Many British brewers were using both Californian and German hops, as much as fifty per cent of the hop content of their beers, as well as imported barley. The relative cheapness of sea-borne imports allowed brewers to blend a wide variety of malt and hops, balancing out imperfections in any one particular batch.

With the growth and astonishing success of India Pale Ales, brewers moved away from vatting their beers. Two American writers, Wahl and Henius, said in a book published in Chicago in 1908 that the vatting of pale ales went out of vogue with the success of the Burton brewers. Vatting had been the hallmark of strong stock ales made by country brewers and porters blended with vatted stale beers. But IPAs were brewed with long sea journeys lasting up to five months in mind. Vatting before racking into casks was unnecessary. The high final alcohol rating of IPAs meant that, unlike vatted beers which were not fully attenuated in order to leave some residual sweetness, there was little sugar for either Lactobacillus or Brettanomyces to get to work on. India Pale Ales — a term, incidentally, Bass never used, preferring just 'Bass Ale' — did not have the lactic character of porter. Some beer went to India, Australasia, the Caribbean and even Latin America in bottle as well as cask, though the risk of breakage was high. Most India ale was bottled on arrival and stayed in good drinkable condition for three months. The beers threw a sediment, indicating that conditioning in the bottle took place. It is not known how the bottles were stored in India and other hot climates but every effort would have been made to keep them away from the heat either in underground cellars or steeped in cool water.

For all its importance in changing the face of British brewing, the heyday of India Pale Ale was brief, not more than thirty years. By the 1880s exports were falling fast. The Brewers' Journal in August 1882 castigated the big brewers, Bass, Allsopp, Barclay Perkins and Guinness, for not seizing the chance to dominate the world export market in beer. 'Bottled Bass,' proclaimed the journal, 'has been found in every country where Englishmen had yet put foot' but now Bass and the others had become complacent and were failing to match the zeal of the Germans. The lager revolution was in full swing and the cold, light beers were being snapped up in hot climates. Lager breweries were being established in colonial countries as well: two Germans founded the Gambrinus brewery in Melbourne in 1885 and were followed soon after by the Foster brothers from New York. In 1900 a Swiss brewer named Conrad Breutsch was invited to New Zealand specifically to brew lager. Ironically, he brewed at the Captain Cook Brewery in Auckland, named in honour of the Yorkshire sea captain who had brewed a rough ale there to cure his crew of scurvy. A colonial critic of the British brewers complained that their beers had 'too much alcohol, too much sediment, too much hops and too little gas'. A modern ale connoisseur would consider that a curious critique. The brewers had no intention of changing tack. They had invested massively in new plant and equipment to make pale ale and were not prepared to switch to even more capital-intensive lager plant. Anti-German feeling at home meant there was no demand for lager beer and the brewers now had a new mass market to satisfy that was cheaper to supply than the colonies.

In 1827 a ship carrying some three hundred hogsheads of India Pale Ale was wrecked in the Irish Sea. Both Allsopp and Bass have claimed the beer was theirs. A Bass guide book published in 1902 said: 'A quantity saved was sold in Liverpool on behalf of the Underwriters. The quality was so much appreciated that the fame of the new "India Beer" spread in a remarkably rapid manner throughout Great Britain.' That is an exaggeration. Pale ale sales did not start to boom until 1839. Up until that date the Burton brewers had had to rely on slow transport by canal. But in 1839 the 'iron horse' gave yet another technological boost to British brewing. The opening of the Birmingham to Derby railway gave the Burton brewers rapid access to Birmingham, England's second city, the smoke-stacked powerhouse of the industrial revolution, and from there into the national rail network. The rapid development of the railways transformed both the brewing industry and Burton-on-Trent. The brewers could move their beer around Britain swiftly and in prime condition. They built their own internal railway systems to transport beer and raw ingredients within their plants. At its peak, the Bass internal railway had sixteen miles of track, eleven engines and 450 wagons and vans. Michael Thomas Bass had taken to the railways with great enthusiasm. He was the Liberal Member of Parliament for Derby and was a typical Victorian benefactor. His own fortune was assured and he could afford to be generous to the less fortunate. It was not just altruism that encouraged him to donate to the funds of the first railway trade union, the Amalgamated Society of Railway Servants. A contented workforce would transport his beer better than a disgruntled one. Bass would start a railway journey by walking up to the engine cab to shake hands with the driver. On one occasion, after a journey lasting more than ten hours, Bass went back to the cab and was horrified to find the same man in charge. Bass threatened to withdraw his beer from the railway company unless they agreed — and they did — that no driver should work a train for more than eight hours.

During the 1840s the output of Burton's breweries increased from seventy thousand to 300,000 barrels a year. By 1851 the number of breweries had increased to fifteen. Bass and Allsopp were responsible

RIGHT: *The great Victorian breweries had their own railway systems. Those shown here are the Bass Burton sidings.*

for seventy per cent of the output. Between 1850 and 1880 Burton brewing trebled in size every ten years. Bass forged ahead of Allsopp. Allsopp was plagued by financial problems as a result of rashly buying hundreds of pubs in London and venturing unsuccessfully into lager brewing. By 1874 Bass, with an annual output of 900,000 barrels, had become the largest brewing company in the world. In went full bore into the twentieth century with a yearly production of one and half million barrels and a work force of 2,760.

The major London brewers were in a quandary. They could not 'do a Hodgson' and brew an inferior pale ale from their home base as Burton beers were now widely available in the capital: when St Pancras railway station was built in London the cellars were designed specifically to accommodate hogsheads of Bass beer. With the abolition of the tax on glass in 1845 pewter tankards gave way to glass pots. Drinkers could see what they were getting and many preferred the pale and sparkling pale ales to darker brown ales and porter. Lacking the ability to treat the soft London waters, brewers hurried to set up bases in Burton to brew from the hard spring water available in abundance there. Middleton, Nunneley and the large Romford brewer Ind Coope opened breweries in Burton in the 1840s and 1850s. Others were slower to follow but the increasing success and prosperity of their Burton competitors finally forced Charrington, Mann Crossman & Paulin, and Truman to move to Burton. Provincial brewers followed them. Boddingtons of Manchester, A B Walker and Peter Walker from Warrington, and Everards of Leicester set up shop in what was now the undisputed capital of British brewing.

With the exception of Ind Coope, which was to merge eventually with Allsopp in 1934, the incomers were not greatly successful. Manns, for example, enjoyed a fine reputation in London for its mild ale but failed to produce a pale ale that was as highly regarded as those from the indigenous Burton brewers. The brewery was sold in 1896 and a director, John Crossman, said of the Burton venture: 'It came like a shooting star and quickly disappeared, paying the cost and leaving behind it a street named Crossman and a little church (endowed)'. Truman was widely thought to brew an especially fine pale ale in Burton but found it hard to compete with the likes of Allsopp and Bass because the Burton brewers enjoyed a superior reputation. Truman blended its Staffordshire beer with London pale ale, with results that were satisfactory neither to the brewery nor its customers. By the end of the century brewers had the ability to treat their waters with salts to replicate the Burton waters — a system known world-wide as 'Burtonisation' — and they cut their losses and retreated back to their heartlands.

But every brewer now had to have an India Pale Ale in his portfolio. As early as 1855 the Stafford Brewery's price list included X Ale, XX Ale, XXX Ale, XXXX Ale, Stafford Imperial, AK Ale, IPA, Porter, Single Stout and Double Stout. Many also had a Burton Ale, a strong amber ale: a Victorian price list in the visitor's reception area, known as the Sample Room, at Young's Brewery in London includes a Burton Ale, indicating the hold on drinkers' imagination exercised by the small East Midlands town. When Sir Edward Greene, a Suffolk brewer and Member of Parliament, died in 1891 after fifty-five years in the business, the London Star newspaper said in its obituary: 'He was one of the first country brewers to discover that beer need not be a vile, black turgid stuff, but brewed a bright amber-coloured liquid of Burton type which he sold at a shilling per gallon and made a fortune'.

Pale ale was not cheap and its price was pitched above those for mild and porter. Pale ale cost around seven to eight pence a quart against four or five pence for mild or porter. Richard Wilson, in The British Brewing Industry 1830-1980, argues effectively that 'Quality and cost ... made it [Burton pale ale] a status drink for the expanding lower middle class of clerks and shopkeepers, the armies of rail travellers, and those "aristocrats of labour" [highly-skilled workers] whose standards of living rose appreciably after 1850. The other factor in its impact on beer tastes was the ease with which a generation of country brewers succeeded in imitating, usually more cheaply, its light, sparkling, bitter qualities. Making a good Burton-type ale was the *sine qua non* for that generation of brewers who reaped the rewards of the great increase in consumption in 1860s and 1870s.' When duty on glass was lifted, pale ale looked good in the glass, Wilson says. 'It became the high-fashion beer of the railway age'. The pale ale brewers exploited the switch to glass in a second way: their beers were available in bottle for home consumption. This gave them a snob value. The new and growing lower middle classes, conscious of their status, could now drink beer in the comfort of

RIGHT: *Mashing a special IPA for the 1994 seminar at the Ind Coope brewery, Burton-on-Trent*

their homes, freed from the necessity to visit those dens of iniquity, public houses.

The giant brewers — and the likes of Allsopp and Bass by the late nineteenth century were vast — were anxious to maximise profits by brewing beer in the most efficient way possible. Pasteur's work *Etudes sur la Bière* had a profound effect on them. It was now possible to isolate pure yeast strains and prevent infection and spoiled beer. In 1895 the Journal of the Institute of Brewing noted caustically that the time had gone when a brewery could be regarded as 'the last resource for a young man when, having failed for the Army, the Church, or one of the learned professions, his premium is paid and he is shipped off to some pupil-taking brewery with the idea that "at least we can make a brewer of him".' The journal stressed that the modern brewer should be 'essentially a chemist, as brewing is practically the conversion of certain substances into certain chemically different substances by what is more or less a chemical process'. Even before Pasteur had published his findings in 1876, Allsopp had taken on a brilliant young German chemist, Dr Henry Böttinger of Wurtenburg, as the company's scientific adviser. Bass appointed John Matthews as its 'chemist and principal brewer' and he was joined by the legendary Cornelius O'Sullivan in 1865. O'Sullivan's outstanding work won him many awards and in 1885 he was appointed a Fellow of the Royal Society. It was his pioneering research that enabled brewers to move from seasonal brewing to all-year-round production. Dr Horace Tabberer Brown at Worthington carried out far-reaching research into barley germination, yeast nutrition and microbiology. He, too, became a member of the Royal Society. His half-brother, Dr Adrian Brown, worked for Thomas Salt until 1900 when he left to establish the British School of Malting and Brewing at the University of Birmingham. The brewing scientists in Burton formed a scientific circle with the tongue-in-cheek name of the Bacterium Club. They were aided in their work by the generous support of their employers, who paid them handsomely and made sure they had suitable premises and the most up-to-date equipment: Cornelius O'Sullivan was paid £3,500 a year by Bass, an enormous salary for the time.

An anonymous article in the Daily News in 1880, reprinted as a pamphlet, gives a graphic picture of Bass as a vast Victorian enterprise and also serves as a remarkable description of the brewing process of the day. William Bass had started his company little more than a century before on an acre of land. In 1880 the Bass empire occupied 140 acres. It used 267,000 quarters of malt a year, 36,000 hundredweight of hops, and paid £300,000 to the government in excise duty. Weekly wages amounted to £2,500. 'Bass has in use 47,000 butts, 160,000 hogsheads, 140,000 barrels and 200,000 kilderkins [eighteen gallon casks]; a stock of casks in all, in store and scattered over the country, exceeding half a million.' The writer's description of the brewing process stresses how all the new technologies had been assimilated. When the wort has been run off through the slotted base of the mash tun 'the malt left is "sparged" by a shower bath of hot water to extract from it the last remains of saccharine-matter'. The wort is pumped by steam power to the coppers where hops are added and the wort is boiled. It then has to be cooled before fermentation. The writer notes that before the arrival of refrigeration the temperature was often too high to allow brewing to take place. But now the hopped wort is pumped to heat exchangers: 'It is difficult to make these out to be anything else than huge boxes; but by climbing up and peeping over the edge, we see a shallow lake, laced by successive long straight coils of copper piping ... the boiled wort is flowing slowly from the coolers through this mighty submerged snake, while the cold water that covers it has given to it a slow, steady motion at right angles to the flow of the wort, so as to intensify the refrigerating power.'

Once fermentation has started, the fermenting wort is transferred from vessels called squares to the great union room, where it continues to work inside large wooden casks linked together by one long pipe. 'What a ball-room would this Union-room make if its floor were clear ... but instead of dancers it hold 2,500 casks, each one containing 160 gallons'.

The nature of the beer brewed by Bass and its competitors was changing. India Pale Ale had been a means to an end, to carve out a

ABOVE: *Fit for a king ... Cornelius O'Sullivan, Head Brewer at Bass, Burton examining the King's Ale brewed in 1902. O'Sullivan was appointed a Fellow of the Royal Society for his work on brewing.*

lucrative export market to replace the trade lost to the Baltic states. Those ales, by necessity, had not only to be high in alcohol but also massively hopped. By the 1880s drinkers in Britain, the middle class consumers of pale ale in particular, were demanding weaker and less bitter beers. Critics of both IPA and well-hopped porters and milds complained of the beers' 'narcotic' effects, causing sleepiness and well as drunkenness. As the hop is a member of the same family as cannabis, its narcotic effect when used in abundance should not be dismissed as a Temperance conspiracy theory. The brewers were driven as much by the need to improve cash flow as consumer preference. They had had a difficult time in the late nineteenth century. Changes to the 1830 Beer Act, which had allowed anyone to open a beer house on payment of one guinea — the rudimentary pubs were known as 'Tom and Jerry houses' — had ruined many of the pub owners. Commercial brewers had 'loan tied' many of these pubs: publicans agreed to take the products of one brewery in return for generous loans and discounts. When the pubs crashed, the brewers lost their investments. In 1896 Barclay Perkins was owed two million pounds by bankrupt publicans and Allsopp was so badly affected that it went into receivership and had to be financially restructured. The brewers rushed to buy the countless thousands of failed pubs now on the market but the property scramble sent prices soaring. The brewers paid extravagant prices in order to create new 'tied estates'. As many of them were now public companies and faced angry shareholders, they had to take urgent action to restore their fortunes. They were no longer prepared to lock up capital in vats and casks, waiting months and even years for the cash to come in. They moved away from vatted porters, stock ales and IPAs stored in cask for months to what were dubbed 'running ales'. E R Moritz, consulting chemist to the Country Brewers' Society, wrote in the Brewers' Almanack of 1895: 'It is ... essentially within the last ten years that these lighter ales, both of pale and mild character, have come especially to the front. The public in this period has come to insist more and more strongly upon extreme freshness of palate with a degree of brilliancy and sparkle that our fathers never dreamt of'. A visitor to the Northampton Brewery in 1875 wrote admiringly that 'Improved systems of brewing cause beers to mature in a period that would have astonished our grandfathers, and old ales are now drunk that have been brewed in less time than was of old required to make the sweetest and mildest ales even moderately drinkable, and men of the time of the Whitbreads, the Meux's and the Calverts who wasted fortunes in building vats each larger than the other would almost turn in their graves could they learn that their successors have their beers fit for consumption in less time than it took to fill their gigantic tuns'. In 1905, Julian Baker, in The Brewing Industry, noted that 'the light beers, of which increasing quantities are being brewed every year, are more or less the outcome of the demand of the middle classes for a palatable and easily consumable beverage. A good example of this type of beer is the so-called "family-ale", and the cheap kinds of bottled bitter beers and porters'.

The new pale ales were the product of scientific research and practice. All brewers could Burtonise their liquor. Treated with sulphates, brewing liquor contributed to better extraction of malt sugars, improved hop utilisation and cleaner fermentations. Malting had been greatly improved and the move to pale malt meant that more extract could be produced from smaller amounts of grain. J M Hanbury told his fellow directors of Truman Hanbury & Buxton in 1902: 'Better barley means more weight, better extract, better quality of extract, better beer, increase in trade, decrease in returns, and better reputation'. The scientific understanding of yeast was also a powerful impetus to producing running ales. Pure strains meant that fermentation could be better controlled. Yeast packed down and cleared in casks within a few days, enabling beer to 'drop bright' and be served within a day or two of arriving in the pub cellar. Running beers came to dominate the draught beer market, especially as the brewers built their substantial 'tied pub' accounts through which they could control the supply of beer. With a quick turnover of beer, brewers' bills were being paid within a month. The move to running beers accelerated with the government restrictions on strength in World War One. The average gravity of beer in 1913 was 1052 degrees. In 1918 it stood at just 1030: one degree less and it would have qualified as 'near beer' under American Prohibition. By 1920 the average had climbed back to 1042 but beer was never again to enjoy the powerful gravities and hop rates of Victorian times. And the averages included those for mild ales as well as pale ales and porters. Brewers also faced a growing demand for bottled beers. Whitbread, seeing the writing on the porter vat, had moved first into pale ale production and then invested in bottled beer in the early part of the twentieth century. Its advertising was aimed heavily at the middle class, showing smartly-dressed men and women enjoying Whitbread Pale Ale at home. At first the bottled versions of running bitters conditioned in the bottle but brewers soon had the machinery to hand to filter, pasteurise and artificially carbonate bottled beers. But many brewers, notably Bass, Guinness and Worthington, remained faithful to beers that matured naturally in the bottle. Bulk beer for pub sale — which accounted for more than eighty per cent of total beer consumption — was supplied in unfinished form and underwent a secondary fermentation in the cask in the pub cellar. While almost every brewery in the world, under the impact of lager, transferred to brewery-conditioned beers, British brewers remained faithful to cask-conditioning. This was the strength of the tied-house system: publicans were trained by their breweries in the arcane rituals of tapping and venting casks, allowing them to undergo a secondary fermentation and then 'drop bright' before they could be served. It was not until the 1950s that brewers experimented with brewery-conditioned 'keg' beers, the result of which was to spawn the most dogged and influential consumer revolt in Britain that restored cask ale to its rightful place in the pantheon of beer.

RIGHT: *A poster showing the Hook Norton brewery in Oxfordshire, a fine redbrick Victorian building built on the 'tower' system, with the brewing process flowing from floor to floor by gravity.*

BELOW: *American brewmaster Garrett Oliver who brewed a superb IPA at the Manhattan Brewing Company, seen at the London pale ale seminar in 1994.*

There is considerable confusion today over the terms India Pale Ale, pale ale and bitter. Some beer writers and historians think the terms are interchangeable. They are not. Historically, IPA meant a 'keeping beer', brewed to withstand long journeys and with a bitterness that would have made them undrinkable save for the fact that the beers softened and lost some of the bitterness during the sea journeys to the colonies and the Americas. Although the term 'bitter' was used as early as 1858, as in Buchanan's book Burton and its Bitter Beer, the term did not come into vogue until the twentieth century and the development of 'running ales or bitters'. Pale Ale was a modified version of IPA, brewed for consumption in the British Isles with sometimes a lower alcohol level and a great reduction in hop bitterness. After World War One, the term bitter tended to dominate. It marked a clear distinction with mild ale, which still commanded more than half of beer sales — bitter only overtook mild after World War Two. It was also easier to pronounce than pale ale: those of us saddled with Cockney accents and its glottal stops can only manage a strangulated 'pow-lal'. Brewers today mark the difference between bitter and pale ale in their bottled versions of draught beer. Light Ale is the bottled version of a bitter of up to four per cent alcohol while Pale Ale represents a Best Bitter of more than four per cent in bottled form.

The 1994 edition of the Campaign for Real Ale's *Good Beer Guide* lists fewer than a dozen draught beers called IPA. Of those, only two are more than four per cent alcohol. Standard bitters of 3.5 per cent alcohol may be good beers but it is an abuse of history to call them India Pale Ales. The American brewer Garrett Oliver, who brewed a superb IPA at the Manhattan Brewing Company — now sadly closed — says no beer should be called an India Pale Ale unless it could withstand a long sea journey. His own beer was stored for two to three months in cask before being served. The modern brewing industry, dominated by the 'pile 'em high and move 'em out' philosophy, is unlikely to respond to Oliver's suggestion. A few British brewers experimented with IPAs in 1993 and 1994 but the only beer regularly available in Britain today than can be called a true descendant of India Pale Ale is Worthington White Shield, brewed by Bass, a bottle-conditioned beer that rates 5.6 per cent alcohol, 20.5 units of colour and forty units of bitterness. It is brewed from Halcyon and Pipkin pale malts, has a tiny amount of black malt for colour and is hopped with Challenger and Northdown varieties. After primary fermentation the beer is sterile filtered then primed with sugar and re-seeded with yeast. It is the last fragile hold on a once great style that reflected Britain's imperial grandeur and declined with it.

THROUGH A GLASS BRIGHTLY

The improved knowledge and appreciation of pale ale in Britain is due largely to the enthusiasm of one man. Mark Dorber works in a City of London law firm by day but his fascination with pale ale has led him to devote most of his spare time to working in the cellar of an imposing pub in south London, the White Horse at Parson's Green. Working closely with Bass, which owns the pub and has allowed him to experiment with its own and other brewers' beers, Dorber perfected his cellar techniques until the White Horse won a just reputation for serving the finest pint of Draught Bass in the capital. Dorber learnt from his experience of both the Bass beer and Marston's Pedigree Bitter than Burton-brewed pale ales undergo such a volcanic second fermentation in the cask that they need as much time as a harassed publican can manage before being drawn to the bar. He allows his beers to stand for a good two weeks before they are sold. Burton beers served too young tend to have what brewers call a 'green' character, unbalanced by rough yeasty aromas and palate. As his experience deepened, Dorber determined to share his love of the style with others. In 1990, working with Dr Keith Thomas of Brewlab, he organised a seminar on Burton Pale Ales at the White Horse. Brewers from Bass, Burton Bridge and Marston's were joined by experts in malt, hops and good cellar practice as well as leading beer writers. Dorber published the papers presented to the seminar and was determined to improve his understanding of the subject. In 1993 he approached Bass and suggested the company should brew an IPA for a festival of pale ales at the White Horse. Bass executives were enthusiastic and called in a retired brewer, Tom Dawson, for his advice. Dawson recalled brewing a beer called Bass Continental for the Belgian market from the 1950s to the 1970s. The beer was based on recipes for Bass pale ales brewed in the 1850s and represented an unbroken line with the original IPAs, which were all fermented from original gravities in the region of 1063 degrees. He consulted old brewing ledgers going back to the 1880s and then drew up a recipe for

ABOVE: *Mark Dorber at the White Horse, Parson's Green, south-west London, ensuring the quality of the Draught Bass in his cellar.*

the White Horse India Pale Ale project.

On Saturday 19 June a team of young brewers under Tom Dawson's guidance assembled at Burton-on-Trent to brew the beer. They were assisted by Mark Dorber and cellar staff from the White Horse. The atmosphere, according to Dorber, was electric as they attempted to brew a taste of history. They used the tiny five-barrel pilot brewery in the Bass Museum, first used as an experimental brew house at Mitchell's and Butler's brewery in Birmingham in the 1920s. Two brews were necessary to meet the White Horse order of the equivalent of six hogsheads or 324 gallons. Brewing lasted for almost thirty hours before the exhausted but exhilarated participants announced themselves satisfied.

Tom Dawson's recipe was made up of ninety per cent Halcyon pale malt and ten per cent brewing sugar. East Kent Goldings and Progress whole hops were used at the rate of twenty-two ounces per barrel and were added in two stages during the copper boil. The hopped wort circulated over a bed of Progress in the collecting vessel after the boil to give additional hop aroma. When the fermented beer was racked into casks it was dry hopped with East Kent Goldings for aroma at the rate of six ounces per barrel. The yeast used was a two-strain Bass one that dates back to the time the company used union yeast cleansing casks.

The major surprise in the recipe was the fact that no coloured malts were used. Most modern pale ales and bitters use crystal malt to give them a copper or tawny colour. But it seems that crystal malt was not widely used until the end of the last century. The beer reached 7.2 per cent alcohol with a stunning eighty-three units of bitterness. The bitterness was far more than Tom Dawson had planned but modern varieties of hops such as Progress are some forty per cent higher in alpha acids than nineteenth century varieties. The beer was aged in casks for five weeks before it was served at the White Horse on 31 July 1993.

I hurried to the pub and reported my findings in What's Brewing, newspaper of the Campaign for Real Ale. 'The beer is burnished gold in colour. The colour rating is eighteen units. Placed next to a glass of modern Draught Bass and classic Pilsner Urquell lager beer, the White Horse IPA was mid-way between the two. The aroma was pungent and resiny. Hops dominated the palate and the long, intense bitter finish. "It's like putting your head inside a hop pocket [sack] from the Kent fields," Mark Dorber said. Malt and yeast also had their say in the aroma and palate of the beer. Ripe bananas, pear drop and apple esters began to make themselves felt as the beer warmed up. The fruitiness was most apparent when the beer was tasted in the pub cellar, straight from the cask. Dorber said a slightly higher fermenting temperature in the brewery than planned had helped create the fruity esters. Mark Dorber said the beer would remain in drinkable condition for some three months. Tom Dawson, with his long experience of Bass yeast, thinks it will survive for even longer. Both think the beer will become softer over time but will not lose the enormous hop character.'

The interest in IPAs led to Dorber and the author, with the support of the British Guild of Beer Writers, organising a further seminar on the subject in the summer of 1994. We invited brewers in both Britain and the United States to participate, and to contribute beers for sampling. In preparation for the event, I asked Carlsberg-Tetley, the company that now owns the Ind Coope brewery in Burton-on-Trent, if they would consider recreating an IPA, as Samuel Allsopp had brewed the first Burton pale ale on the site. They responded favourably and I went to the brewery to watch the beer being brewed. Ind Coope has a pilot plant known as the Samuel Allsopp Brewery. It is a miniature version of the group's brew houses in Alloa in Scotland and Wrexham in Wales, built in the Netherlands and designed to produce lager. There was a certain historic irony in watching an IPA being mashed in both a mash kettle and a lauter tun, for the system is the classic lager brewing one in which the wort is clarified not in the mash tun but in the lauter vessel. Lager brewers traditionally use malts that are less 'modified' — the starches in the grain cannot be attacked so easily by enzymes — than ale malts and need a more thoroughgoing mashing regime.

As a result of takeovers and a turbulent financial history, the longest surviving recipes in the brewery date back only as far as 1935, one year after the merger of Ind Coope and Samuel Allsopp. Production director Peter Sunderland chose the recipe for an IPA that was brewed on 15 May 1935. It was a 'parti-gyle' brew that produced a 1040 degrees bitter, a 1041 IPA and 1046 best bitter, the brew being treated with liquor after fermentation to produce beers of different gravities. The fact that the IPA was a lower gravity than the best bitter indicates how far the style had been Bowdlerised by the 1930s. The grist composition was fascinating. The brewery used Smyrna, Egyptian Marrioutt and Ouchak imported six-row barleys along with English pale and mild malts, probably Spratt Archer. The hops came from California (Biddell variety) and New Zealand (Buxton) as well as England. The English varieties were Hubble and Leake, both now extinct. Peter Sunderland said it was common in those days to use imported barleys from warmer climates while Californian hops were free from European diseases and high in alpha acids. As well as malt, three types of brewing sugar were used: Martineau's, Distiller's and Shardlow. With none of the ingredients available today, Peter Sunderland and his team — Nick Bathie, Andy Lea and Ben Elson — recreated the beer with modern varieties. Their task was made easier with the knowledge that the IPA was identical to a beer called Diamond that was brewed until 1960. The 1046 gravity best bitter became better known as Double Diamond which lives on today in cask-conditioned form as Ind Coope Burton Ale.

Sixty barrels of 1994 India Pale Ale were brewed from Halcyon pale malt, with fifty kilos of crystal malt and five kilos of chocolate malt, with twenty-five per cent brewing sugar. The hops were equal amounts of Fuggles and Goldings and the finished beer was dry hopped in the cask at the rate of four ounces per barrel. The beer was 4.2 per cent alcohol by volume, had nineteen units of colour and twenty-two units of bitterness. The beer was similar in colour to the special Bass brew but, as the bitterness rating indicates, had a more gentle hoppiness. The Goldings nevertheless gave a fine peppery and citric fruit aroma, there was more tart fruit in the mouth and the finish was quenching and finely balanced between malt and hops.

When the seminar assembled in the imposing surroundings of Whitbread's Porter Tun Room in the old Chiswell Street brewery in London it had attracted not only brewers, historians and beer writers but leading wine writers Oz Clarke, Andrew Barr and Andrew Jefford. Dr John Harrison, the brewing historian, outlined the history of the style. The average gravity of export ales in 1846 was 1068 degrees, he said. Hodgson and his competitors had learnt that the best way to send pale ales to India and other countries was to bottle or cask them 'flat'. Before the beers went into the holds of ships they were unsealed and purged of natural carbon dioxide. Once the bottles or casks were capped or bunged again, a slow secondary fermentation would take place during the voyage. The system avoided containers bursting as a result of too much gas and also ensured the beers would arrive at their destination in fine, sparkling form. To prove that IPAs could survive the journey to India and further afield, Dr Harrison had brewed a pale ale to a nineteenth-century recipe and kept it in his garage at a temperature of 80°F/25°C during the famous British hot summer of 1976. It was in good drinking condition the following Christmas.

For the seminar he had brewed a beer that was as close as possible to what his research suggested Hodgson's India Ale would have been like. He used Thames Valley well water and one hundred per cent pale malt, with no brewing sugars. The hops were East Kent Goldings with 5.5 per cent alpha acid, used at the rate of 2½ ounces per gallon and dry hopped at the rate of half an ounce per gallon. It was fermented from an original gravity of 1072 degrees using a yeast strain from Truman's. The beer was six weeks old at the seminar and had been fined three weeks earlier. It had a powerful resiny aroma of Goldings hops, it was packed with tart fruit in the mouth and the finish was exceptionally dry and bitter with a touch of astringency.

BELOW: *Power house of reform ... Whitbread's Castle Eden Brewery where several revivalist beers have been brewed.*

Paul Bayley, head brewer at Marston's of Burton, brought samples of an IPA that was 5.2 per cent alcohol and brewed from one hundred per cent Pipkin pale malt. Bayley used three hop varieties, Challenger, Fuggles and Goldings, and the beer was dry hopped at the rate of four ounces per barrel. The beer was well matured at eight weeks. It had a pungent sulphury nose — the famous 'Burton snatch' — with undertones of grain and peppery hops, there was tart gooseberry fruit in the mouth and the finish was subtly fruity and hoppy.

Whitbread's Castle Eden Brewery, the former Nimmo's company in North-east England, brewed an IPA with 5.5 per cent alcohol from pale malt and ten per cent torrefied wheat. The recipe was devised by head brewer Tony Rowsell. Only Fuggles hops were used and the wort was

late hopped in the copper for aroma. The colour, an appealing burnished gold, was fourteen units with forty-two units of bitterness. The aroma had a ripe orange/citric character with resiny hops, there was tart fruit and hops in the mouth, and the finish was a fine and complex balance of quenching fruit and hops.

There was great interest in the Bass White Horse ale, by then eleven months old. Mark Dorber said that to counter the pronounced banana ester on the beer he had dry hopped the casks a second time in the pub. The beer had become much softer over time. The fruitiness was almost Madeira-like, with a pungent apricot fruit on the nose, fruit, hops and nuts in the mouth and a big bitter-sweet finish.

From the United States Thom Tomlinson brought a sample of Renegade Red from Boulder, Colorado, which had won the gold medal at the 1993 Great American Beer Festival. Tomlinson said he Burtonises his brewing liquor to enhance the fruitiness and bitterness of the beer. He uses pale and ten per cent crystal malt and the beer is hopped with two US varieties, Cascade (seventy-five per cent) and Chinook at the rate of two pounds per barrel. The beer is brewed from a gravity of 1064 degrees and has an astonishing ninety units of bitterness. Bitter hops and tart fruit dominated aroma and palate and the finish was stunningly dry.

Teri Fahrendorf of the Steelhead Brewery in Eugene, Oregon, brews her Bombay Bomber from two-row pale malt and six-row Munich and Vienna coloured malts. It is 5.3 per cent alcohol by volume with forty-five units of bitterness. Fahrendorf adds gypsum to mountain water and hops with Chinook and Mount Hood. The beer is dry hopped with Chinook which give a pungent gooseberry note to aroma and palate. With a lower bitterness level than Renegade Red's, the beer was a fine balance between malt and hops, was refreshing in the mouth and dry in the finish.

Garrett Oliver's IPA from the Manhattan Brewery has an original gravity of 1066 degrees and is brewed from imported two-row East Anglian pale malt produced by Munton & Fison, with twenty-five per cent brewing sugar. It is dry hopped, primed with cane sugar and stored for three to four months. It reaches fifty-five units of bitterness. The aroma is redolent of apricots and oranges with great hop character in the mouth and a big hoppy/bitter finish.

The seminar concluded with a call to British brewers to make commercial versions of India Pale Ales available to the public. Those present felt that any beer labelled 'IPA', if it is true to the style, should not be less than 5.5 per cent alcohol and forty units of bitterness.

In recreating India Pale Ales, brewers should pay careful attention to history but should not be hide-bound by it. Modern ingredients, hops in particular, are different to Victorian and Edwardian ones and that must be taken into account when devising recipes. Drinkability is as important as history and there are few sun-drenched colonialists slavering on the Calcutta quayside for beers brewed to survive a storm-tossed voyage round the Cape and through the Indian Ocean.

Part Two
The mystery

Chapter One
Sugar and spice and all things nice

There is mystery involved in any fermented drink. As yeast turns sugars into alcohol, mere mortals can only stand back in redundant wonder, for this is a complex, spontaneous and natural process that requires no outside intervention or stimulation. But brewing is the most mysterious of all the methods used to make alcohol. Even in today's high-tech culture, few people know how beer is made or even the ingredients that go into it. Wine or cider are easy: crush the fruit, allow the natural yeasts on the skins to go to work on the sugars in the fruit and alcohol is the end result. But crush an ear of barley and nothing happens.

How many are aware that barley is the staple raw ingredient of beer? I grew up in the East End of London where one of the local brewers advertised its products with posters that carried the slogan 'There are more hops in Ben Truman', illustrated by a bibulous pirate hopping on

BELOW: *In the beginning ... the brewing process starts with the harvesting of barley.* (Photo: Robin Appel Associates)

his peg leg. Even in the post-war world of the 1950s, many East End families still went to pick hops in Kent every September. The small green plants were ever-present in our lives and it was not surprising that we assumed beer was made from them. When I first started to drink beer I discovered a strong ale called barley wine but I still thought weaker brews were made from hops. In the late 1970s, when I wrote my first book on beer, the publisher phoned me to say he had enjoyed the manuscript but added: 'I never knew, until I read your book, that beer was made from barley'. Where beer is concerned, ignorance can still be bliss.

But in order to enjoy beer to the full and to understand and appreciate the brewer's skill, knowledge of the ingredients and the brewing process can only deepen our pleasure. Hops are important to beer but, as history shows, are not essential to its production. Without grain, though, there can be no beer. Over many centuries, barley has become the preferred grain to such an extent that brewers call it 'the soul of beer'. Wheat is still used, but in small proportions: it accounts for just one per cent of the grain used in brewing throughout the world. Some brewers may add a dash of oats or even rye, while light lager beers often have a sizeable dose of rice or corn. But barley is the heart as well as the soul of beer, the belt as well as the braces.

All cereals are developments of tall grass. Barley is the best grain because it produces a sweet, clean beer and has the most 'extract' of fermentable sugars. It differs from most other modern grains because it has a husk. The husk acts as a natural filter during the mashing stage of brewing while other huskless grains tend to clog up pipes and valves. Belgian and German 'wheat' beers usually have around fifty per cent of barley malt in their composition. Wheat has a robust and distinctive tart fruitiness but is difficult to brew with. Oats give a smooth, creamy character to beer while rye has a dark, aromatic quality, but both grains produce far smaller amounts of extract than barley. Other cereals -- rice, maize and sorghum -- have to be cooked first to make them soluble. Rice and maize are used extensively in the United States to make rather bland and uninteresting lagers while sorghum is the basis of many lagers and ales — even dark stout — in Africa.

MALT

Before there can be beer, barley must become malt. A barley kernel looks scarcely different to a grain of malt yet the natural chemical changes that take place during malting turn a starchy cereal into a sugar-rich source available for fermentation. For centuries breweries did their own malting but today most prefer to buy in their malt requirements from specialist firms. This allows them to blend malts from different companies to balance any slight imperfections in any one batch.

Brewers will select a variety of barley with enormous care and will attempt to remain with that variety to ensure consistency of flavour in their beer. Yeast can react with disdain if it is suddenly confronted by a

BELOW: *Germinating barley, where starches begin the transformation into fermentable sugars.*

new type of barley malt and will refuse, like a sulky child, to produce a satisfactory beer. The preferred type of barley for ale brewing is 'two-row', so called because there are two rows of grains within each ear. The finest type of two-row is known as maritime barley as it is grown close to the sea. In England, the pick of the crop comes from East Anglia, the eastern-most region made up of the counties of Cambridgeshire, Norfolk and Suffolk. Much of the land has been reclaimed from the sea or from the low-lying watery fens and the soil is rich and dark, ideal for cereal growing. In Scotland, the best malting barley comes from the Lowlands, the narrow neck of the country with water on both sides, while the barleys of Flanders are also grown within sniffing distance of the North Sea. In warmer climates, six-row barley is the norm. It produces a malt that imparts a more biscuity, grainy texture to beer. Many perfectionist ale brewers in the United States import carefully selected two-row malt from England as they feel it gives their beers more authenticity of aroma and flavour. Ale brewers also tend to prefer hardy winter barleys grown in the autumn for their muscular taste while lager brewers choose spring barleys for their softer, maltier notes.

Only a small proportion of barley is suitable for malting. Most goes for cattle feed or to be turned into breakfast cereals, bedtime drinks or as a

BELOW: *The brewing process at Arkell's brewery om Swindon showing the traditional ale system of mash tuns, coppers and fermenters.* (Courtesy Khadija Buckland/Red House, from the official history of Arkells)

ABOVE: *McMullen's brewing team examine amber malt for their Traditional IPA, specially made for the brewery by French and Jupps. Head Brewer Tony Skipper (centre) was named Brewer of the Year in 1995 by the British Guild of Beer Writers.*

constituent of children's chocolate bars. Barley for malting must be low in protein and nitrogen: if they are too high the finished beer may be hazy. In an age when farmers are often heavy-handed and insensitive in their use of fertilisers and pesticides, high nitrogen barley can be a problem. Farmers are also threatening some of the most respected malting barleys as a result of pressure from bigger brewers to grow high-yield crops that produce more per acre. Low-yield barley varieties, such as Maris Otter in England and Golden Promise in Scotland, are fighting for survival. The difference between a high-yield and a low-yield variety makes only a fraction of a penny difference in the price of a glass of beer. But the giant British brewers buy malt in such vast quantities that fractions can add up to large amounts of money. Not one of Britain's big five brewers, which account for around three-quarters of beer production, now uses Maris Otter, which has been de-listed as an official malting barley. It has to be contract grown to order. In spite of these petty restrictions, many regional and micro-breweries have remained true to Maris Otter. Ken Don, the head brewer at Young's of Wandsworth, a family-owned company in south London renowned for its characterful and uncompromising ales, told me he would stick to the variety because he was prepared to pay the premium price to ensure the quality of his beers. Ironically, Young's beers are several pennies a pint cheaper than national brewers' beers, so the savings in using high-yielding modern varieties such as Halcyon or Pipkin are not being passed on to the drinker. George Gale, another fine family brewery in Hampshire, southern England, is a dedicated Maris Otter user. The brewing staff made some trial brews using high-yielding barley malt and found that their yeast reacted badly and was unhappy with the new variety. Gales said that while big brewers would solve such problems by throwing industrial enzymes into their fermenters it was not prepared to compromise the flavour of its ales. When Whitbread, one of Britain's giant brewers, launched a series of high-profile quality ales in 1994 with such names as Glorious Goldings and Imperial Fuggles it switched back to using Maris Otter. There are no short cuts to quality.

When the brewer has chosen his barley he turns to the skill of the maltster to make the finest brewing material for him. I have visited two types of maltings, traditional floor maltings where the grain is turned by hand, and more modern plants where manual labour is replaced by mechanically rotated drums. Traditionalists believe that floor malted barley gives a cleaner flavour to beer. While I am a great believer in traditional values, after a day spent in Crisp's maltings in East Dereham in Norfolk I am glad I do not have to spend my life bent under a low roof, endlessly raking and turning grain in a warm, moist atmosphere.

When the barley reaches the maltings it is steeped — soaked — in water in a deep cistern or trough called the steep or in large tanks in more modern plants. Steeping lasts for some three days. The water is changed frequently. Steeping is surprisingly like fermentation, with the water appearing to boil as the grain heaves to the surface. The reason is

ABOVE: *David Jupp of French and Jupps shows samples of malt, from pale to chocolate.*

that bacteria attacks wild yeasts on the husks of the grain: a primitive form of fermentation takes places but it must be stopped by regular washing to clean away the bacteria. Unless it is removed, bacteria would interfere with the subsequent development of the embryo in the grain. During steeping the grain will absorb large amounts of moisture — the moisture content will increase from around fourteen per cent to forty. This is vital to encourage germination.

When the right level of moisture has been achieved the steep is drained and the barley is left to stand for six to ten hours. It is then transferred to the floor of the maltings where it is spread out to form what maltsters call a couch. The grain starts to germinate and the biochemical changes that take place produce surprising heat. The temperature of the malting floor is kept at 12° C/55° F but the heat of the grain, known collectively as a piece, will rise to 17° to 18° C/65° to 70° F. The piece has to be turned regularly by hand by workers with rakes to allow the grain to breathe and to stop the build-up of heat. In a modern maltings the grain is placed in large drums that are turned three times a day. Germination will last from between six and ten days in a floor maltings, four days in a drum maltings.

During germination, the embryo of the plant, the acrospire, starts to grow while tiny roots break from the husk: the root is called the chit and maltsters say "chitting" has started. The process now underway is known as modification. The grain is made up of two parts, the inner

endosperm made up almost entirely of starch, and a tough outer layer, the aleurone layer, that protects the endosperm and contains vital proteins. As the acrospire grows it triggers complex chemical changes that turn proteins into enzymes, which are organic catalysts. At the same time the starches are made soluble as part of the transition to brewing sugar — maltose.

A day later and the rootlets have grown with great speed to stand proud of the husk. When the acrospire has fully grown, modification is judged to be complete and the endosperm, previously hard and steely, is now soft and friable. The maltster tests the grain by chewing it: if it is soft and chewy in the mouth he knows that modification is satisfactory. The skill of the maltster is to stop partial germination at just the right moment: if modification goes too far then the grain will start to consume its own sugars.

As much of the protein as possible has been broken down. Ale brewers want a fully modified malt so that enzymes will work quickly during the infusion mashing stage in the brewery. In traditional lager brewing, malt is poorly modified, with substantial amounts of undegraded protein remaining. This is caused by the poorer quality of lager malts with a higher nitrogen level that require a more thorough decoction mashing in the brewery.

The grain is now called green malt and is loaded into a kiln. A traditional kiln looks like an indoor chimney, with the malt spread on a mesh floor and heated from beneath by a coke or wood fire. But with few exceptions, brewers do not want a malt that has come into contact with smoke, which gives the grain a burnt, acrid and bitter character. Most malt today is heated in drums or roasting machines that are heated externally.

The heat from the kiln is low to start with — around 60° C/150° F — to gently dry the malt, stop germination and preserve the enzymes. Then the heat is turned up to kiln or cure the malt. The temperature of the kiln will determine the type of malt produced. Pale malt will usually make up eighty to ninety per cent of an ale's recipe as it will produce the highest amount of sugar extract. The temperature of the kiln will be raised to 80° C/190° F and held for twenty-four hours. Pale malt looks almost identical to barley but if you chew it you get a pleasant biscuity flavour in the mouth.

Higher temperatures will produce darker malts. Malts that are heavily kilned will have no live enzymes and can provide no sugars in the brewing process. They are used for colour and flavour.

ABOVE: *Cleaning the malt in the steep.*

Most dark malts are produced today in roasting machines. In the past, when brown malt was the basic raw ingredient, it was kilned over woodsmoke. French and Jupp's, Britain's specialist dark maltsters based in Stanstead Abbotts in Hertfordshire, close to the East Anglian barley fields, have kept their traditional kiln for visitors. The family-owned company began malting in 1703. At the height of the porter brewing industry in the nineteenth century, French and Jupp's supplied thirty-four quarters — six tonnes — of crystal and black malt to Whitbread every other day. Today the company makes no pale malt. Its products range from carapils, for the lager industry, crystal, amber, brown, chocolate and black malts, as well as roasted barley. Demand for its malts has grown appreciably with the revival of dark beers and the decision by many brewers to abandon caramel and to use proper grain instead. Maris Otter barley is stored at the maltings and on local farms. It is steeped and germinated mechanically and is then transferred to a roasting machine, which works on the same principles as a coffee roaster. I met Reg Collins in charge of the machines and I was bemused at first when he mentioned temperatures of 450 degrees. I discovered that, in common with many older Britons, he has not bothered to make the switch to Celsius and stays faithful to Fahrenheit.

Two and half tonnes of green malt are needed to make two tonnes of roasted malt. The roasting temperatures are 200° C/430° F for chocolate malt, 205° C/440° F for black and 210° C/450° F for roasted barley. Amber malt, rare these days, is heated to a much lower temperature. Reg removes a sample of malt from time to time on a cylindrical shovel to test the roasting. He must be careful not to over-roast or the malt will become carbonised and unusable. Roasted barley, bitter and charred to the taste, has a slight red tinge, while chocolate and black malts have a matt finish.

Crystal malt, widely used by English brewers to give a copper colour to bitters and pale ales, is made by a different method. After germina-

ABOVE: *Testing the colour and quality of roasted malt.*

ABOVE RIGHT: *A roasting machine at French and Jupps for making dark, highly-kilned malts.*

tion, the green malt is not dried but is placed in a sealed kiln so the moisture cannot escape. The temperature is raised to 45° C/150° F, which happens to match the mashing temperature in a brewery. The enzymes inside each kernel of grain convert the endosperm starches into sugar. Each husk now contains a soft, gummy ball of malt sugar. The vents of the kiln are opened and the heat is increased. The sugar crystallises and the colour of the malt deepens. Not all the starch is converted and much of the sugar produced is dextrin rather than maltose. Brewer's yeast cannot ferment dextrin and the unfermented sugar adds not only flavour and colour to beer but also "body", the satisfying roundness and fullness of palate missing from both lagers and home-brewed beers where all the sugar turns to alcohol. Modern brown malt is also a stewed green malt but the temperature is kept low to stop the sugars crystallising.

French and Jupp's, with a long history of making dark malts, says that crystal was not widely used in England until the early part of the twentieth century and coincided with the development of "running bitters" that replaced well-matured pale ales. Running bitters were ready to drink after just a day or two in cask in the pub cellar and crystal helped give body and flavour to the beer.

Malts are given colour ratings. Pale ale malt has a rating of three, crystal twelve, chocolate 110, black 130 and roasted barley 140. The skill of the maltsters in producing this fascinating blend of raw ingredients provides the brewer with the essential staff of life to start the brewing process.

HOPS

An English ale brewer described hops to me as "the grapes of brewing". At first it seemed an odd turn of phrase, for hops contain no starches or sugars to aid fermentation. But while the grape provides both flavour and sugar, beer walks on two legs. Fermentable sugars come from malt, while bitterness and essential elements of the aroma and palate are provided by hops. And a Fuggle or a Golding, a Cascade or a Willamette will give flavour thumbprints to beer as distinctive as Cabernet Sauvignon, Pinot Noir, Gamay or Syrah grape varieties to wine. The hop is not just the grape of brewing, it is the salt and pepper as well.

The Latin name of the small green aromatic plant — the Americans call it a herb — is Humulus Lupulus, the wolf plant. Left to its own devices, it would rampage across the countryside, trailing up fences and intertwining with hedges on its thick stalk or bine. It is a member of the Cannabidaceae family that includes cannabis and the nettle. As well as being a vital prop of the brewing process, the hop can also act as a sedative, can be infused with tea, aid convalescence, combat insomnia (insomniacs sleep on a pillow stuffed with hops) and even make a poultice to cure boils. In the *Complete Book of Herbs*, Geraldene Holt says, rather po-faced, 'Do not take hops internally if you are suffering from depression as it could accentuate your condition'. I suspect Ms Holt has never enjoyed four pints of Adnams' Southwold Bitter on a Saturday night.

BELOW LEFT: *An illustration from A Perfitte Platform for a Hoppe Garden, a seminal work by Reynold Scott.*

RIGHT: *Modern mechanised hop picking.*

BELOW: *Humulus Lupulus, the hop plant, seen in Poperinge in the heart of the Belgian hop-growing region.*

Once the oils, tannins and resins were identified as important elements in the brewing process, the hop was cultivated by encouraging it to grow up wooden poles and then twine round a lattice work of wire. In A Perfite Platforme for a Hoppe Garden, first published in 1774 and the major work on the subject for several centuries, Reynold Scot described in detail how to prepare the soil and then erect poles as soon as hops appear above the ground in order to give them maximum exposure to sun and light, and make picking easier: 'Cut them asunder with a sharpe hooke and with forked staffe take them from the poles'.

Hops are picked in the early autumn. Until mechanisation was introduced in the 1950s, Cockneys from London and Brummies from Birmingham would descend every September on the hop fields of Kent and Worcestershire to earn money picking the plants. In return for a few miserable shillings they would labour all day until their hands were raw from the bines and black from the juices in the plant.

The hop plant is dioecious. This means that the male and female plants grow separately. As the plant can be propagated by cutting, the male is redundant, except in Britain. In the rest of the world, the hapless

male hop is hunted down with all the zeal of the Spanish Inquisition searching for heretics. Only the female of the species is wanted for brewing as its flowers, known as the cone, contain the resins and oils that give bitterness and aroma to beer. Lager brewers want aroma from their hops and avoid, in the main, too much bitterness and astringency. If the female is fertilised and seeded it gives a more pungent aroma, palate and finish to ale, with a pronounced citric character on the nose, a snuff-like pepperiness in the mouth and a tart, dry and intensely bitter finish with a hint of astringency. The hops of the Hallertau region of Bavaria, south of Munich, are classified as 'noble hops' as a result of their fine aroma. British hops, on the other hand, have a more plebeian, down-to-earth pugnacity, characteristics possibly acquired from legions of Cockney pickers.

ABOVE: *Cockneys down on the farm ... the traditional image of hop pickers from the 1930s.*

The cone of the hop contains alpha acids — humulones — and beta acids — lupulones — plus oils essential to brewing. During the copper boil in the brewery, alpha acids give bitterness to the wort while the oils impart flavour. Beta acids and tannins help stabilise the wort.

In classic ale brewing as practised in England, the brewer will use two varieties of hop. The Fuggle gives an intense bitterness to beer while the Golding is used for its piney, resiny aroma. They will be used at different

ABOVE: *A hop pocket at Boddingtons of Manchester.*

stages of the boil to avoid too much distillation of aroma, ending with a late addition of aroma hops just before the boil finishes. Many brewers also add a handful of hops to the finished cask of ale to heighten the aroma. Both the Fuggle and the Golding take their names from their original growers in the eighteenth and nineteenth centuries respectively. Both varieties are susceptible to attack by disease and pests — the Fuggle is especially vulnerable. Hop growers and the industry's research centre, Wye College in Kent, have developed new strains that are resistant to disease and contain both aroma and bitterness within one plant in order to save costs. Modern high alpha hops, such as Challenger, Northdown and Target, have been adopted with enthusiasm by larger brewers but smaller craft brewers prefer to stick to traditional varieties. High alphas may be more economical but they can add a harshness to the finished flavour of beer. Their resistance to attack in the field, however, is an important consideration when a brewer is planning his hop order several years in advance.

The hop is as open to attack from disease and pests as the grape is from phylloxera. Many varieties of hop are especially prone to assault from two types of fungus, verticillium wilt and downy mildew, while aphids and spider mites can also wreak havoc. In Bavaria, the Hallertau variety has been ravaged by disease, as has the English Fuggle in Kent and Worcestershire. The first North American hop gardens were cultivated in New York State and New England by English settlers but a climate not dissimilar to the one they had left behind encouraged them to pick up their bines and transplant them to the opposite side of the country in California. The climate proved too hot there and now the major American hop industry is based in the Yakima Valley region of Washington State, Willamette Valley in Oregon and Snake River Valley in Idaho. The local mountain range, the Cascades, gives its name to one variety grown in Yakima while the Willamette is a close cousin of the Fuggle. The Chinook variety has to be used with caution as a result of the stunning and almost overpowering aroma of grapefruit it gives to beer. Cascades are a pungent and peppery aroma hop while Clusters are used for bitterness. North of the border, Bramling Cross grown in British Columbia are used extensively in Canadian brewing and are exported widely. Australia has a superb bittering hop, Pride of Ringwood, which is used in other countries by brewers attempting to make organic beer in which the ingredients have been grown without fertilisers or pesticides.

Hops must be stored and packaged quickly after they have been picked to avoid oxidation. In Kent, probably the most attractive of the world's hop-growing areas, hops were traditionally dried in oast houses, small round buildings with distinctive white cowls on the roof. The hops were laid out on a perforated drying room floor and heated by a coal fire below. The temperature was maintained at 60° C/150° F for about ten hours. A steady draft of warm air was maintained by rotating the cowl on top of a chimney, which created a suction. Sulphur rock was put on

the fire to help keep the hops stable and pest-free during storage. As a result of a sharp rise in lager consumption in the 1960s and 1970s, hop growing in Kent went into severe decline. Many oast houses were bought as 'second homes' and weekend cottages by Londoners. Some are still used for their original purpose but most hop curing is now carried out in rather more utilitarian buildings.

The hops are packed by compressing them into long sacks known as pockets. The aim of compression, which squeezes a surprising number of plants into a sack, is to prevent oxidation. At a hop store and then a brewery, the sacks are kept in shady rooms as the plant is photosensitive and could continue to ripen and degrade its important constituent parts.

Breweries with traditional coppers and hopbacks (receiving vessels) use the whole flowers of the hop, which act as a natural filter as the wort leaves the copper for the back. More modern breweries clarify the hopped wort in a centrifuge or whirlpool: the wort is pumped to the vessel from a wort kettle that does not have a slotted base. In these cases, brewers need pelletised hops that have been milled to a powder and reduced under great pressure into small green pellets. Hop pellets are easier to store and do not oxidise as easily as whole hops but many craft brewers argue that some essential character is lost by the pelletising

ABOVE: *Traditional oast houses at Crowhurst Farm in East Peckham, Kent, destroyed by fire in 1964.*

process. However, even the most traditionalist of brewers will often use pellet hops to 'dry hop' their casks. Hop oil or hop extract is a far more controversial product. It is produced by boiling hops with hydrocarbons or in an alkaline solution. The extract increases the bitterness of beer but not the aroma and can leave an unpleasant tang and bite at the back of the mouth. Extracts are disliked by craft brewers and distrusted by drinkers who know about the chemicals used in their production.

Just as the colour of beer is measured on an international scale, so is the bitterness. Units of bitterness, known as EBUs, are calculated by working out the ratio of acids in the hops to the quantity used. A high EBU has nothing to do with quality. Brewers will carefully dove-tail the use of hops with the malt in order to conform to the style of beer. A mild ale may have between fifteen and twenty EBUs. Wheat beers, which use aged hops mainly for their antiseptic qualities to ward of infections, have low bitterness units of ten to twelve. Some strong pale ales may have ratings of sixty or more. The American Renegade Red India Pale Ale has ninety units: it is a fascinating beer but I doubt if it can be consumed in quantity as the throat would rebel against such intense bitterness. The beer made by American micro-brewer Bill Owen is called Alimony Ale, has one hundred EBUs and is described by Owen as 'the Bitterest Beer in America'.

WATER

It is a common mistake to consider that water is only a spear-carrier in the drama of making beer. Brewers don't make the mistake. They understand the importance of water and treat it with due reverence. For a start they never call it water. The common or garden stuff that comes from the tap is used for general cleaning purposes in the brewery while the water used for brewing is always known as 'liquor'.

The type of water is crucial to brewing, especially when a brewer is determined to brew to a precise beer style. You cannot make a genuine pale ale with soft water, neither can you make a true Pilsner with hard water. The total salts in the water of Burton-on-Trent, home of the original India Pale Ales, amount to 1,226 parts per million. In Pilsen, where golden lagers originated, the figure is just 30.8.

Before the age of science, when it became possible to treat water in order to suit brewers' — and drinkers' — preferences, breweries would be built in areas where the finest water was available. In Britain, London's soft waters were ideal for making milds, porters and stouts while Burton, Tadcaster and Edinburgh had water better suited for pale ale production. In the rainy climate of Ireland, Arthur Guinness had a plentiful supply when he started brewing in Dublin though it is pure mythology that he used the waters of the Liffey. Guinness used and still uses the soft waters of the Wicklow Mountains.

Water is the result of rain. As rain falls to earth, it picks up gases and pollutants that acidify it. The main acid present in rain water is carbonic acid. As anyone knows who has ever had the misfortune to suffer a burst

ABOVE: *Cool and crisp and resiny ... the hop store in Elgood's brewery in Cambridgeshire.*

pipe, water gets everywhere. When it hits the earth it drains through the top soil, percolates through layers of minerals and porous rock, snakes and winds its way through cracks in non-porous rock until it settles on a table of impervious rock where it waits to be collected. It may force its way back to the surface in the form of a spring or overflow into a river. As it passes through the earth, water absorbs mineral salts. The type and quantity of salts depend upon the rock formation in a given area. Soft water is the result of rain falling on to insoluble rock such as slate or granite. It cannot pick up mineral salts and is almost mineral free.

Calcium Bicarbonate, derived from chalk, is the most common cause of hardness in water. It is a nuisance to brewers. Its ions — dissolved salts — impede fermentation, reduce the effect of far more important sulphate ions and interfere with the fining or clearing of the finished beer. Brewers ensure that only minimal amounts of calcium bicarbonate are present in their liquor.

Calcium Sulphate, popularly known as gypsum, is as welcome in the brewery as bicarbonate is unwelcome. It is highly beneficial to the brewing of ale, pale ale in particular. It helps create the right level of acidity in the mash, known as the pH, short for 'power of hydrogen', and encourages enzymic activity as starches are turned into maltose. It ensures the best extraction of the aromas and flavours of hops, clarifies the wort, encourages a powerful fermentation but discourages too much astringency in the finished beer. Calcium sulphate also counters harshness in beer. It was the high levels of gypsum in the spring waters of Burton-on-Trent that enabled the early brewers of pale ale to use generous amounts of hops to help the beer withstand the long sea journeys to the colonies. In contrast, the IPA brewed by Hodgson in London, using soft water, may well have been harsh to the taste.

Magnesium Sulphate — Epsom Salts — is also found in unusually high levels in Burton water. Yeast thrives on magnesium and helps account for the 'greedy' nature of traditional Burton ale yeasts developed in the union room method of fermentation. The salt also helps stabilise the wort when it is boiled with hops in the copper.

Sodium Chloride — common salt — is present in high proportions in soft London water. It is not true that salt is imperative to the production of mild, porter and stout. Salt enhances flavour and improves the 'mouthfeel' of ale. It was widely used by brewers centuries ago during fermentation but the effect would have been negligible.

Brewers world-wide now 'Burtonise' their water for pale ale brewing by adding gypsum and Epsom salts. They will also remove bicarbonate and then carefully filter and clean water several times to remove impurities, a vital procedure in an age when water is heavily polluted with agricultural chemicals. It is a sad fact of life that brewers in Burton-on-Trent and other parts of the East Midlands, the internationally renowned home of pale ale, can no longer use many of the local wells as a result of excessive pollution and now use the public supply instead.

Whether water comes from a well, a pond, river or even in the form

ABOVE: *Two essential components of the brewing process, water and the Maltings (Munton and Fison).*

of desalinated sea water matters little today as all the supplies will be treated to ensure absolute purity and the correct balance of salts. The end result is a vital part of the brewing process as water will account for some ninety per cent of a glass of even the strongest beer.

YEAST

Ale and beer have been made as long as civilisation has existed. Yet it was not until the Dutch scientist Anton van Leeuwenhoek in the eighteenth century and the Frenchman Louis Pasteur in the last century analysed yeast that its role in brewing was understood. Until then fermentation was considered to be some kind of witchcraft and the foam produced by this strange alchemy was looked on in wonderment and awe. There was even some opposition to Pasteur when, with the aid of the microscope, he demonstrated that the production of alcohol was the result of a natural chemical reaction in which yeast cells multiplied as they turned sugars into alcohol and carbon dioxide. The act of producing alcohol was a vital function of the living cell, Pasteur argued, analogous to the respiration of higher organisms. He called the process 'la vie sans air' — life without air.

Yeast is a fungus, a single celled plant that can convert a sugary liquid into equal proportions of alcohol and carbon dioxide. There are two basic types of brewer's yeast: ale yeast and lager yeast. Ale yeast is classified as Saccharomyces cerevisiae, cerevisiae being the Latin word for ale. Lager yeast is classified as Saccharomyces carlsbergensis, as the first pure lager yeast strain was isolated in the Carlsberg brewery in Copenhagen, Denmark. It is now also known as Saccharomyces uvarum. The two different types are often referred to as 'top fermenting' and 'bottom fermenting' strains. This is because ale yeast rises to the surface of the wort during fermentation while lager yeast falls to the bottom. The terms are misleading for many people think, wrongly, that ale yeast works only on top of the wort while lager yeast works at the foot. Any type of yeast must work at all levels of the liquid in order to turn as much sugar as possible into alcohol. Better terms would be 'warm fermentation' and 'cold fermentation' for ale yeast will only work at 12° C/55° F and above while lager yeast is tolerant to cold and will happily work at temperatures down to 5° C/40° F.

Modern ale brewing reflects its history. It still often takes place in open vessels and the warm temperature at which it works and the brevity of primary fermentation — about a week — produces compounds known as esters that add distinctive aromas and flavours reminiscent of fruit to ale. The slower, cooler fermentation used in lager brewing and the carefully cultured single strain yeast produces a cleaner beer almost totally devoid of fruitiness.

When ale yeasts were analysed in the last century it was found that any one brewer's yeast included several different strains. They would fight one another and impede a thoroughgoing and successful fermentation. Prompted by Pasteur, breweries set up laboratories and began to isolate pure yeast strains. But many brewers prefer to work with two-strain and even multi-strain yeasts that will ferment different sugars at different speeds and are essential when secondary fermentation is needed in bottle or cask. Britain's leading premium cask-conditioned ale, Draught Bass, is produced by a two-strain yeast that originated in the brewery's union room in Burton, while the classic bottle-conditioned Trappist ale from Belgium, Chimay, is fermented with a multi-strain yeast. The monks have carefully cultivated the yeast for decades and believe its composition is vital to the fruity and spicy character of their beer.

Yeast is not a neutral substance. It does more than make alcohol. As the same strain reproduces itself many times over during the course of each fermentation it does not die out. There is always a fresh supply of refrigerated yeast on hand. It picks up, retains and imparts vital flavour characteristics from one brew to the next. It becomes used to its brewery and the careful blend of malt and other cereals. Take it away from its friendly environment and it will change character. Paul Bayley, the head brewer of Marston's in Burton-on-Trent, told me that if his voracious yeast strain was transferred to another brewery using not

RIGHT: *Yorkshire square fermenters still in use at the Tetley brewery in Leeds.*

only different ingredients but a different method of fermentation it would change its character after just a few brews. Change the yeast and not just the aroma and flavour change. Drinkers may change too, preferring to drink the beer of another brewery. That is why brewers not only jealously guard and protect their yeasts but also deposit samples in special yeast banks. Nearly every British brewery deposits samples of yeast with the National Collection of Yeast Cultures in Norwich. If they get an infection in the brewery they can start again with a batch of the same yeast from the national collection. And infections can happen even in the best organised brewery. In the 1980s, the Suffolk brewery of Adnams, famous for its fruity and seaside-salty cask-conditioned ales, got a yeast infection when it was extending its brewhouse. Fortunately, Norwich is just a short drive from Adnams' base in Southwold.

Brewer's yeast has two methods of respiration: aerobic, with oxygen, and anaerobic, without oxygen. It works with oxygen at the start of fermentation as there is plenty of dissolved oxygen in the wort. The brewer aerates the wort before pitching his yeast to encourage yeast development. It grows rapidly, with bubbles of gas rising to the surface of the wort while a brown slick begins to cover the surface. When all the oxygen is used up the yeast reverts to anaerobic respiration. Activity slows down but it is only during the anaerobic stage that alcohol is produced. A day later a dense, yellow-white, rocky head is formed, streaked with brown and black from the proteins in the wort. The head forms peaks all over the top of the fermenter, which brewers call 'cauliflowers'.

In the strict scientific sense, it is not yeast but enzymes released by it that produce alcohol and CO_2. There are three types of sugar present in the wort: maltose and dextrins from the malt, and sucrose from cane sugar if brewing sugar is added during the copper boil. (Lactose, milk sugar, is sometimes added for certain types of beer such as 'milk' stout). Brewer's yeast can only ferment maltose and sucrose. It cannot ferment dextrins, which remain to give residual sweetness and body to beer, or lactose. The yeast enzymes are maltase, which attacks maltose to produce glucose, and invertase which breaks down sucrose into glucose and fructose. The converted sugars are assimilated by the yeast, which is also busily reproducing itself by cells dividing, fusing and creating fresh spores.

All the frantic activity surrounding fermentation causes considerable heat. Ale yeast is pitched at around 15° C/60° F but fermentation will increase the temperature as high as 25° C/80° F. The wort becomes rough or 'green' beer after about seven days: brewers say they like to give their ales 'two sabbaths' in the fermenters. As the yeast tires it clumps together and rises to the surface. This is known as flocculation. The yeast head is skimmed off to encourage younger yeasts in suspension in the wort to continue to produce alcohol. When there is virtually no yeast left in suspension the brewer will judge that fermentation is complete. Throughout the process he has been taking constant readings with his hydrometer to measure the density of the wort. When the hydrometer indicates that most of the sugars have been converted, primary fermentation is at an end. Finished, drinkable, ale is almost to hand.

ADJUNCTS

In Germany, with its famous 'Pure Beer Pledge', the Reinheitsgebot, there is no problem about adjuncts in beer: they are illegal. Brewers can use only malted barley or wheat and they frown upon beers from other countries where adjuncts — unmalted cereals and sugars — are allowed. But are a German Alt or Kölsch, both members of the ale family, necessarily better than a Belgian Trappist or an English bitter because they abjure adjuncts? It is a controversial subject and I freely admit that I tend to agree with the last brewer I spoke to. Miles Jenner, head brewer of Harvey's in Lewes, Sussex in southern England, told me he uses small amounts of adjuncts, such as flaked maize, because it allows him to 'play tunes' with his beers. He makes some splendid cask ales, including one of the best of the revivalist porters. But the danger with adjuncts is that one brewer's sublime concerto is another's silly symphony.

Adjuncts got a bad name in the 1970s and 1980s when consumer watchdogs in the United States discovered that giant brewers were using massive amounts of cheap materials and industrial enzymes to make 'lite' lagers. The beers were virtually devoid of taste and character but they were immensely profitable because of the cheap way they were made. Ale brewers should not be tarred with the same brush as lite-fingered American lager brewers. They use adjuncts primarily for colour, for flavour, to counter nitrogen haze in the finished beer and to encourage head retention. These problems arise as a result of the comparatively brief fermentation and maturation of a warm-fermented ale. In Germany, where ales as well as lagers are produced by decoction mashing followed by several weeks lagering and then filtration, the problems do not arise.

Adjuncts can contribute to the sugar extract in the mash tun but they do not possess enzymes. It is left to the enzymes in the pale malt to convert the starches in the adjuncts as well as in the malt.

Torrefied grain, either barley or wheat, is a widely-used adjunct in ale brewing. Torrefied means scorched. The grain is similar to popcorn. The high temperature used explodes the endosperm and gelatinises the starch which can then be attacked by the malt enzymes in the mash tun. Flaked grains and grits are made by steaming or milling the grain to gelatinise them. Wheat flour, probably the most extensively used adjunct in British ale brewing, gives a delightful flavour to beer and counteracts any hardness of palate. As with malted wheat, it can only be used in small amounts for fear that it clogs up every inlet and outlet.

Sugar is not strictly an adjunct because it does not need to be converted by malt enzymes. Brewer's sugar is called invert sugar. It has been inverted into its component parts of glucose and fructose and is attacked by invertase enzymes in the yeast. The problem with sugar is that because it is almost totally fermentable — unlike malt sugars which include unfermentable dextrins — it adds alcohol to beer but also makes a thin drink if used in large quantities. I would be anti-sugar but for the fact that some superb ales use substantial amounts. Belgian Trappist ales, for example, make extensive use of candy sugar. Marston's Pedigree Bitter, one of the finest of England's cask-conditioned ales, is made from 83 per cent pale malt and 17 per cent sugar. Head brewer Paul Bayley says the sugar allows him to make a 'subtle' ale for its strength of 4.5 per cent alcohol by volume. If he reduced the sugar content, he says, the beer would be too robust for most drinkers' tastes.

On the other hand, the revered Samuel Smith's brewery in Tadcaster, Yorkshire, has stopped using any brewing sugars in its Old Brewery Bitter, Museum Ale and its extensive range of magnificent bottled ales, including a brilliant porter and imperial stout. There has been no noticeable effect on the uncompromising flavours of the beers.

Health-conscious drinkers will demand fewer sugars and purer beers. I don't want to stop Miles Jenner playing his mash tun melodies but I think it would be sensible for the industry to agree to a malt content of 90 per cent in all ales. And while they are about it they could also stop using caramel — burnt sugar -- altogether. As brewers constantly tell me that sugars and adjuncts are no cheaper than malt, I see no reason to use burnt sugar for colour when dark malt could be used in its place. If nothing else, it would stop brewers producing 'milds' or 'stouts' that are just their basic bitters with colour added.

Chapter Two
A life in the day of a brewery

Brewing is not for the faint-hearted. It begins as early as 4.30 or 5pm in the morning when most sensible people are still a-bed. I suspect this ungodly hour is actually very godly and stems from the time when brewing was done by monks who would stir the mash and light the copper at dawn before hurrying off to their devotions.

I have visited hundreds of breweries. But by the time I have arrived at them most of the work has been done. The invitation from Eldridge Pope was different. I was to be nominally in charge of production, head brewer for the day. It was too good an invitation to miss, for Eldridge Pope is a revered brewer of both cask and bottle-conditioned ales. Its beers include the legendary Thomas Hardy's Ale, the 12 per cent alcohol bottled beer that improves with age and was inspired by the great West Country novelist's description of the ale of 'Casterbridge', his name for Dorchester. Eldridge Pope's handsome red-brick Victorian brewery is in Dorchester, hard-by the railway station and I stayed overnight in the Station Hotel to avoid the ignominy of being late for work the following morning.

It was a low-risk strategy on the part of the brewery. The ale I was to brew was a one-off winter product called Old Spiced Ale. If I made a complete hash of making fifty barrels, there was time to brew another using more skilful hands. And I was surrounded by so many helpers and minders that as I moved around the brewhouse I felt like the QE2 coming into harbour with a full panoply of tugs and pilots' cutters fore and aft. Head brewer Dan Thomasson even pandered to my soft, sedentary life-style by making a late start to the day, though seven-thirty still seemed a trifle brusque to me on an icy winter's morning. I was joined in the brewhouse by Alex Bardswell. She chairs the local branch of the Campaign for Real Ale and the winter brew was due to be on sale at the branch's beer festival a few weeks later. Alex had a proprietorial interest in the brew and it was good to have a brewster on the team.

The beer we had to make was a stronger version of Eldridge Pope's premium cask ale, Royal Oak. This rich and fruity ale is five per cent alcohol. Old Spiced Ale would be six per cent, with a starting gravity of 1058 degrees. It would be lightly hopped at less than half a pound per barrel compared to one pound per barrel for Royal Oak. The aim was for fifteen units of bitterness — Royal Oak has thirty — so that the hops did

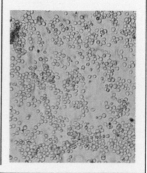

BELOW: *Alive and kicking ... yeast spores under the microscope.*

RIGHT: *The brewing team beside the copper at Eldridge Pope: Dan Thomasson, Alex Bardswell, Arthur and David Caddy, Arthur Dyke and the author.*

not overwhelm the spices that would be added. Nutmeg, cinnamon and cloves were carefully balanced to make sure the cloves, the most aromatic of the three, did not overpower the other two. They would be added in small bags as a sort of bouquet garni to each cask of finished ale.

The brewing day began by checking the liquor, the brewing water. Eldridge Pope's liquor comes from a bore hole on the site and originates in the soft chalky hills of Dorset. Dan Thomasson prefers the bore hole water to the public supply, which is too chlorinated for his liking. He adds calcium sulphate (gypsum) and magnesium (Epsom salts) to harden it and get the right level of acidity, the pH. The water was shockingly cold, sharp on the tongue, slightly effervescent with a hint of saltiness. It wasn't my usual brew to kick-start the day but it certainly cleared the palate and perked me up.

The liquor was ready. Now we had to check the malt. When malt arrives in the brewery it is ground or 'cracked' in a mill. There are two mills at Eldridge Pope and they have different settings to produce different weights of cracked malt. Most of the malt is ground to a flour but it is blended with coarser grits and the rough husks of the grain. The husks are vital as they act as a natural filter in the mash tun. The blend of cracked malt is known as grist and, with the liquor, it goes into a large vessel known as a mash tun.

In charge of the tun were two Arthurs, Dyke and Caddy. They run the brewhouse and their job is to look after the mash and the copper boil. 'We've warmed the tea pot,' they said in unison as we arrived in our regulation white coats. Mashing in a traditional ale brewery is an infusion of malt and liquor, similar to the infusion of tea with boiling water in a tea pot. Many people talk of 'mashing' the tea, probably not realising that the term predates the arrival of the tea leaf in Britain by several centuries. There was a pleasing symmetry in having a man called Caddy in charge of the brewery 'tea pot'.

Alex and I used one of two mash tuns that have been in place since

1922. The Arthurs had pumped hot liquor into it to raise the temperature. It is made of cast iron and is insulated with slats of deal. The lid is made of two semi-circles of wood raised by pulleys. Poised above the lid is a large tube called a Steel's Masher. This is a Victorian invention that mixes grist and liquor at the right temperature and consistency inside the tube by an Archimedes screw. Temperature is crucial to all aspects of brewing, none more so than at the start of the proceedings when a degree out can physically as well as literally gum up the works. The liquor has been heated to 75° C/180° F — the 'strike heat'. The mashing temperature is lower (65° C/150° F) but the malt will quickly reduce the heat of the liquor. If the temperature of the mash falls below 65° C the Arthurs pump more hot liquor into the tun through its slotted base. If the temperature is too high it will destroy the enzymes in the malt. If it is too low the enzymes will work sluggishly and will not convert all the starches into sugar. The Arthurs also have to avoid 'cold spots' in the tun where the malt would clog into a paste and glue up the works.

Liquor flooded into the mash tun and covered its base. Then the flood thickened as the Steel's Masher added the malt, a blend of Pipkin pale and crystal. Liquor and malt are mixed in the ratio of one kilo of malt to two barrels of liquor: the mixture is called 'the goods'. It looked like porridge and smelt like it too, reminding me forcefully that I had yet to breakfast. The mash would stand for one and a quarter hours while saccharification takes place: the conversion of starch to sugar. The biological catalysts, enzymes, present in the malt grist are known collectively as diastase. The two most important enzymes are alpha-amylase, which convert starches into maltose and dextrins, and beta-amylase which produces only maltose. Maltose is a highly fermentable malt sugar while dextrin cannot be fermented by brewer's yeast.

We left the Arthurs in charge of the mash tun while we went on the brewer's rounds. It is similar to a doctor's rounds because we had to check the health of the various beers in the brewhouse. In the brewer's sample room we tasted some recently racked brews of Dorchester Bitter, Best Bitter and Thomas Hardy Country Bitter, three cask-conditioned ales. Country Bitter is also sold in bottle-conditioned form. The beers were 'green' or immature: cloudy, yeasty, sweet and with no acidity. But Dan's practised eye and tongue told him the ales were developing well, with no off-flavours from wild yeasts or bacteria. He also tested the 'copper break' from a previous brew. During the copper boil a sediment of hops and protein is separated from the liquid. Dan could tell from the sample that the boil had been clean and effective, leaving behind a rich silt of protein.

It was time to return to the mash tun for the 'first runnings'. Brass taps are fitted to the side of the tun. The Arthurs turned the taps and the hot, cloudy, tawny liquid poured into tall glasses. They could tell, from long years of experience, that the smell and the taste confirm that saccharification is taking place. The sweet liquid is known as 'wort', pronounced 'wurt'. It comes from the Old English wyrt, meaning root.

That morning it had a delicious malt loaf smell and was sweet and biscuity in the mouth. If there is any doubt about the state of starch conversion a chemical test can be made. It is called the 'starch end point'. A small sample of wort is mixed with a few drops of iodine. If the iodine turns blue-black then starch is still present in the wort. If it stays clear, then full starch conversion has taken place. A simpler test for experienced brewing staff is to note when the wort runs clear rather than cloudy from the taps.

The mash was progressing well and it was time for breakfast. Brewers get and deserve a gargantuan feast, a full English breakfast with all the toast-and-marmalade trimmings plus — and I was told this was part of the tradition — a glass of Guinness stout. Food and alcohol made a new man of me. Fully awake now and fighting fit, I hurried back to the brewhouse to continue my labours. The mash was over. The Arthurs were satisfied that starch conversion was at an end. It is dangerous for mashing to continue once most of the starches have been transformed into malt sugars. Tannins are extracted from the malt as well as sugar and if the mash stands for too long it will acquire a harsh and unpleasant flavour, like stewed tea. Mashing is halted by simply raising the temperature of the mash with more hot liquor, which kills the enzymes.

BELOW: *Adding hops, with much spillage, in the copper.*

The slotted bottom of the mash tun was opened and the wort began

105

to drain through the thick cake of spent grains. They act as a filter and the wort extracts stubborn sugars during its exodus. To ensure that no sugars are left behind, perforated tubes in the roof of the mash tun revolved, sprinkling or 'sparging' the grains with more hot liquor. When the run-off is finished the spent grains are sold to farmers as cattle feed.

Run-off takes two hours. We used the time to tend to other brewer's duties in the brewhouse. Dan took us to the hop store where supplies are kept in large hessian 'pockets' or sacks. He removed handfuls from different pockets to check the aroma and feel of the plants, which are used in their natural whole flower state, not compressed into pellets. For years Eldridge Pope stayed faithful to Fuggles and Goldings but their increasing price encouraged a move to high-alpha Challenger and Northdown varieties. Northdown is especially rich in alpha acids, tannins and resins and with them Dan can use fewer hops to get the same balance of aromas and flavours he wants. But he still uses Kent Goldings for 'dry hopping', adding a handful of hops to each cask of ale as it leaves the brewery for the pub cellar.

With our nostrils filled with the fine peppery, piny aromas of the hops, we clambered down from the store room to the laboratory to run checks on the yeast. All the effort that goes into making beer can be destroyed if the yeast is not up to scratch. Yeast cells are invisible to the naked eye but spring to life on a slide under a brewery microscope. They dart and glide in a frisky fashion, ready, willing and anxious to get to work on a sugary liquid. Dan was satisfied with their condition. Yeast cells have to be white. Too many blue ones means some are dead and there will be insufficient for a successful fermentation. Black rods among the cells means there is an infection and the yeast batch has to be scrapped. From the laboratory we returned to the sample room where Dan ran checks on the colour, acidity, carbonation, original gravity, alcohol content and bitterness of all the brews on site. Nothing can be left to chance. If a bad brew hits a pub, the brewery's reputation will suffer.

Eleven thirty. We returned to the brewhouse, this time to the copper room. The wort had been pumped to the copper room from the underback or wort receiver. Many modern 'coppers' should fail the Trades Description Act as they are made of stainless steel. Eldridge Pope's coppers are the real McCoy, great gleaming, domed vessels with large air-tight portholes, for all the world like deep-sea diving bells. They work on a similar principle to a coffee percolator. There is a central column inside the copper topped by a peaked cowl called a 'Chinese hat'. Boiling wort gushes up the column, the calandria, and into the main body of the vessel where it agitates the rest of the liquid. The entire liquid foams and rises as the boil progresses.

Hops are added at the start of the boil. The task for the apprentice brewers is a simple one: open the porthole and pour in hops from a pocket. To the distress of Dan and the Arthurs, Alex and I manage to spill

ABOVE: *Preparing for the final confrontation between yeast and sugary wort in the fermenter.*

almost as many precious green plants on the floor as we get through the opening. In spite of our efforts to the contrary, the boil is at last under way. It will last for an hour and a half. It is the simplest process in the brewery but its importance should not be minimised. The boiling wort extracts the alpha and beta acids, tannins and oils from the hops, kills any bacteria, destroys the enzymes and stops any further saccharification, causes proteins to coagulate which improves the stability of the finished beer, and caramelises some of the sugar to give colour and flavour to the beer. Brewing sugars are also added during the boil. In the case of Old Spiced Ale, fifteen per cent of the recipe is accounted for by sugar. It dissolves immediately and will provide a rich additional source of 'fermentable material' for the yeast. Not all the hops are added at once. Much of the vital aroma is boiled away, so hops are added in stages, including a final burst ten or fifteen minutes before the end of the boil to give the wort as much aroma as possible. Copper finings are added to clarify the wort. They are made from Irish moss, also called carragheen, which is not a moss at all but dried and powdered seaweed.

Proteins are removed during the boil, ensuring that the finished beer will be bright and free from nitrogen haze. After the boil has been underway for some time the proteins come out of solution and coagulate into a dark, sticky substance that settles to the bottom of the copper. This is known as the 'hot break' and the protein matter is called trub. At the end of the boil, when the hopped wort begins to cool, further protein will collect in what is called the 'cold break'. The trub and the spent hops act as a filter as the wort is pumped out of the copper into a receiving vessel called the hop back.

It was mid-day. We said farewell yet again to the Arthurs and went back to the sample room, the brewer's home-from-home. With the sun officially over the yard-arm, we could taste some beer. It seemed a long time since Guinness at breakfast. The aim of the exercise was to judge the maturity and flavour of beers at different stages of their development. Royal Oak two days after 'rack' — filling into casks — was yeasty, with little discernible hop in the mouth and a harsh, bitter flavour. At nine days the ale had developed with startling speed. It had a pungent aroma of Golding hops, ripe pears in the mouth and a complex finish with a powerful hop note. We ran our taste buds over the range of Dorchester Bitter, Best Bitter and Hardy Country Bitter before receiving the summons to return to the coppers.

BELOW: *Checking the conditioning in the sample room.*

The boil was over and the hopped wort had been pumped to the hop back, a vessel similar to a mash tun with a slotted base. The term 'back' comes from an old Dutch word and is similar in derivation to bucket. Buckets or tubs were used in earlier times as receiving vessels. The spent hops cover the base of the back like giant tea leaves and filter out the trub. The temperature of the wort was now 95° C/220° F and it had to be brought down to 18° C/66° F in preparation for fermentation. This is achieved by running the wort through a heat exchange unit. This looks like a series of car radiators, with every other radiator filled with cold water and the intervening ones containing the wort. I have been to a few breweries, mainly in Belgium and one in England (Elgoods of Wisbech in the Cambridgeshire fens) were the hopped wort is cooled in flat open trays called 'cool ships'. As the wort is open to the atmosphere it is also open to attack from wild yeasts or bacteria, but Elgood's head brewer assured me he never had this problem.

Time for lunch. As breakfast is the brewer's main meal of the day, lunch is a quick stop for a snack and a beer. But at last we could drink some beer in quantity, let it pass over our tongues and down our throats instead of spitting into a bucket (or should it be a 'spit back'?) Once more in the Station Hotel, I reacquainted myself with Blackdown Porter, one of the best of the new breed, full of chocolate, liquorice and fruit character.

Then it was time for the moment of truth. Ernest Hemingway should have written about fermentation rather than bull-fighting. In the brewery, only yeast cells die, but they do not die in vain. The fermentation room at the brewery is packed with splendid old vessels made of heavy, dark wood and lined with copper to stop bugs hiding in crevices and attacking the wort. The sides of the fermenter are high and boards can be added to the tops in case the fermenting wort gets too excited and attempts to overflow the vessels. Before the change in the way in which duty on beer was levied, the density of the wort would be measured to see how much sugar was present. Water has a density of 1,000 degrees. If a beer has a starting or original gravity of 1036 degrees that means there are thirty-six parts of fermentable sugars present. Duty was paid on that 'original gravity' but the system is now based on the finished alcohol. But brewers still carefully measure the starting gravity with a hydrometer to make sure the density is correct.

David Caddy, Arthur' son, was in charge of fermentation for the day. In my East End youth it was the norm for jobs in the docks or the printing industry to pass from generation to generation and it was good to see the paternal system surviving in brewing, ensuring continuity of skills and dedication. The wort was running in a thin stream from a pipe above the fermenter. It was foamy and agitated, for air had been pumped into it to encourage the yeast. The yeast is mixed in or pitched at the ratio of one pound of pressed yeast for every gallon of wort. It would take two days for the yeast head to form but we could measure the violence and the passion of the process by walking round the rest of the room. In some of the fermenters there was just a thin brown slick on top of the wort. In others a dense, white-brown rocky head had formed. In still more, the head was enormous, threatening to over-run the container like some terrible extra-terrestrial beast from a John Wyndham novel. During fermentation, the temperature of the wort rises from 18° C/56° F to 22° C/74° F. If the temperature rises higher, the yeast will work sluggishly and sugars will not be converted. Modern fermenters are fitted with coils through which cold water is pumped to keep the temperature at the required level.

RIGHT: *Yeast press where liquid is removed and the yeast is then recycled for the next brew.*
(All Eldridge Pope photographs in this chapter by Doug Pratt)

The air above the fermenters was rich with heady carbon dioxide and ripe fruity aromas. As the enzymes in the yeast, maltase and invertase, attack the sugars, compounds called esters are created. The esters produce powerful fruity aromas. Depending on the amount and type of malt used, esters may be reminiscent of apples, pear drops, bananas, molasses, liquorice and even a tannic, polished leather. When fermentation is complete after a week, 'green' or rough beer is held in conditioning tanks for a few days to allow rough and unwanted alcohols and esters to be purged.

For Alex Bardswell and me, the brewing day was over. We could do no more. The brew was left to its own imperious devices, mutating and changing with every passing day until declared fit for consumption.

So I didn't get to put the little spice bags in the casks. My ham-fisted addition of hops in the copper had been noted and more delicate work was clearly deemed beyond my capabilities. But when I phoned Dan Thomasson a few weeks later he assured me the finished brew had been fine — 'Like liquid Christmas pudding' — and had been a great hit at the Dorchester beer festival. It was called simply Old Spiced Ale. I had half hoped for 'Protz's Old Spiced Ale' but for some unaccountable reason Eldridge Pope seem to hold me in less regard than Thomas Hardy.

Chapter Three
Tap and spile

Britain is the only major brewing country where substantial amounts of beer leave breweries in a rough, unfinished form to reach maturity in pub cellars. Many other countries, Belgium in particular, produce beers that condition naturally in the bottle. But it is only in Britain that around twenty per cent of draught beer production is naturally conditioned. Draught beer, whether it is ale or lager, reaches the bar in most parts of the world having been filtered, often pasteurised and then propelled to the drinker's glass by some form of pressurised dispense. Britain's unique contribution to the world of beer comes in cask-conditioned form, popularly known as 'real ale'. It has survived and revived against the odds, in spite of mass marketing techniques that demand both long shelf life and high profits from beer, because of the dominance of the British pub. Close to three-quarters of the beer drunk in Britain is in draught form in pubs. In most other countries beer in the main comes from bottles and cans, and is consumed at home. Sales of draught beer in bars and cafés tend to be slow. It is the rapid turnover of draught beer in British pubs that has enabled cask-conditioned ale to prosper.

ABOVE: *The enduring image of the English pub ... a pint and a game of dominoes.*

Louis Pasteur's impact on brewing practice was a double-edged one. He revealed the workings of yeast and impressed upon brewers the need for absolute cleanliness to avoid infection in their beer. But his belief in heating liquids to deter bacterial attack did little for the flavour or character of beer. Pasteurisation may have a place in the farmyard and the cow shed but it should be unnecessary in breweries kept scrupulously clean. However carefully it is done, heating beer upsets the balance of delicate aromas and flavours. It has an especially deleterious effect on hop character and, at worst, imparts aromas reminiscent of cardboard, stale toffee or cat's pee. At the point of dispense, over-enthusiastic use of carbon dioxide can also damage the balance of beer by making it unacceptably fizzy and giving it a carbonic bite.

Cask-conditioned ale avoids filtration and pasteurisation. At the end of fermentation it is held in conditioning tanks for a few days. The yeast will begin to sediment out, carbon dioxide will build up and the maturing beer will purge itself of unwanted rough alcohol and ester flavours. Clarity of the beer is aided by the addition of finings in the form of isinglass made from the swim bladder of the sturgeon fish. The sturgeon has a wretched life, hunted by the rich for its eggs to turn into caviar and then deprived of its bladder to provide clear beer for the hoi-polloi. Beer will clear naturally of its own accord but it is a slow process that takes several weeks. The London and Country Brewer, published in the 1730s, mentioned several methods for clearing beer including brandy with bean flour, treacle and oyster shells, eggshells, chalk and sugar, lime and isinglass. Obadiah Poundage, in his famous discourse on London porter published in 1760, noted that the improved 'transparency' of porter had been achieved by the use of isinglass. Isinglass was seized upon by brewers at the turn of the twentieth century with the development of 'running bitters' or cask-conditioned ales. With a home market to satisfy rather than a colonial one, the pale ale brewers wanted beers to be up and running within a day or two of arriving at the pub and isinglass proved an important help in this respect.

Sturgeons' bladders look like giant and translucent potato chips. They have exotic names depending on which part of the world they are caught in. Saigon is considered the finest isinglass and other varieties include Brazil, Karachi, Indian and Penang. The bladders are reduced to a thick, white viscous liquid by being placed in a bath of acid. When a small amount is added to beer, isinglass gives off a positive charge while yeast cells are negatively charged. As every school child knows, unlike poles attract and, in the green beer in both the conditioning tank and then in the cask in the pub cellar, the finings attract the yeast cells and slowly drag them to the belly of the cask.

At the end of primary conditioning the beer is racked or run into casks. A cask is a container wider in the middle than at the ends. It has two openings: a large bung hole on top which is used to fill the cask with beer and is then sealed with a wooden or plastic bung, and a tap hole at one end, also sealed, which will be connected to a tap and lines in the

RIGHT: *Swim bladders of fish are turned to isinglass or finings, used to clarify beer.*

cellar to draw the beer to the bar. Casks come in various shapes and sizes, ranging from a nine-gallon firkin, through eighteen-gallon kilderkins, thirty-six gallon barrels to fifty-four gallon hogsheads. Metric sized casks are also used. Some ale lovers have a romantic fascination with wooden casks and feel the most flavoursome beer comes from them. But wooden casks are expensive to repair and most cask ale is stored in metal containers today. Both metal and wooden casks have a plastic lining to avoid possible contamination of the beer. Before a cask is sealed in the brewery liquid sugar may be added to encourage a strong second fermentation and a handful of hops put in for aroma.

BELOW: *Racking ale into casks at the Vaux Brewery in Sunderland.*

When a cask arrives at the pub it is rolled down to the cellar and placed, belly down, on a wooden cradle known as the stillage. If the pub landlord has rotated his stock with care he will let the beer settle for a few days. The longer a beer can rest before it is vented the better the aromas and flavours will be. In order to avoid the cask being moved and disturbing the sediment, it is normal to hammer in the serving tap with a mallet on arrival. As soon as the beer is next in line for serving, the cellarman will take a small porous peg of wood, the size of a piece of schoolroom blackboard chalk, and hammer it into the bung. Within the circle of the bung there is a seal called the shive. It has a tiny central core known as the tut. This is knocked through into the cask as the venting peg, the spile, is hammered into place. It must only be finger tight as it will have to be removed from time to time.

The beer will start to 'work' as secondary fermentation takes place.

RIGHT: *Serving a pint of Charles Wells Eagle straight from the cask.*

RIGHT: *Serving a pint of Charles Wells Eagle straight from the cask.*

After a short time, froth and bubbles will appear at the top of the spile as carbon dioxide is produced. The yeast is slowly producing alcohol from the remaining sugars in the beer as the finings drag it inexorably to the belly of the cask. The amount of extra alcohol produced by secondary fermentation is small but the maturity and flavour of the beer is enhanced immeasurably by the process. The cellarman will gently wipe the venting peg from time to time. When froth stops appearing, fermentation is at an end and he will remove the soft spile and replace it with a hard, non-porous one. This will stop carbon dioxide escaping to the atmosphere. It is vital to retain CO_2 within the cask to give the beer 'condition' or sparkle. Beer is ready to be served within one or two days of being vented. The cellarman will run off small amounts through the tap to judge how the beer is conditioning. At first it will be cloudy and yeasty but gradually it will clear in the glass, will form a good head of natural foam and will have fine aromas of malt and hops. The beer will be deemed to have 'dropped bright' and is ready to serve. A line or plastic tube is attached to the tap so the beer can be drawn to the bar above. It is essential that the cask is not moved or shaken or the lees, the layer of detritus in the cask—yeast cells, proteins and spent hops—will be stirred and make the beer cloudy.

Once a cask is vented it is open to the atmosphere. While ale is being served, the hard spile has to be removed to stop a vacuum occurring. As the beer is under attack from the air it will stay in drinkable condition for only a few days.

Most British draught beer is drawn to the bar by a handpump and beer engine. The engine was invented in the eighteenth century and is a simple suction pump. When the handpump on the bar is pulled back,

BELOW: *All hands to the pumps ... a sample of handpulls available to British publicans.*

a cylinder within the engine is pushed down and displaces the beer. Pubs without cellars may keep casks stillaged behind the bar and will draw the beer by gravity dispense straight from the tap. In some parts of the North of England and the Midlands, electric pumps replace handpumps while in Scotland a system of air pressure, in which the beer is driven to the bar, is the favoured method of dispense.

There are a number of myths about cask ale. 'Warm beer' has international reverberations. Even those under the sway of the Mullahs probably know that the British prefer tepid beer. The myth-makers would not like to live in rooms heated to just 12° C/55° F for that is the recommended cellar temperature for storing ale. At that temperature it should be cool and refreshing. Served to cool, ale will be hazy and the subtle aromas and flavours will be masked. Served too warm and ale will take on unpleasant off flavours. Many devices are used to keep beer cool, ranging from wet sacks placed over casks, to cooling jackets inside which cold water circulates.

The second myth is that the British like 'flat' beer, without a collar of foam. The head on cask beer is formed by a combination of the effort that goes into serving it — whether it is drawn through a pump or straight from a cask — the level of carbon dioxide in the beer, and the protein structure of the liquid. Beer devoid of any head will be either too young to drink or stale and out of condition. There is a cultural divide, though, between those in the south of England who prefer their beer with a thin collar of foam and those in the north who like a thick head. The northern head is achieved by forcing the beer through an agitator attached to the spout of the beer engine. The agitator, or swan neck, has small holes drilled in it that force the CO_2 out of solution. The result is a glass of beer that eddies and surges until the head separates from the liquid. The beer has a smooth and creamy appearance and taste while the hop character is forced into the head, giving an attractive aroma that persists as the foam clings to the sides of the glass while the beer is drunk. Southern beer is not meant to be served in this way but the popularity of certain heavily-promoted Yorkshire bitters in the 1980s and 1990s has encouraged brewers in other areas to use swan neck dispense. The character of southern beers has been badly affected by this practice, making them unbalanced and lacking in hop character. But this is a neighbourly dispute, one that can be settled over a few pints. Many southern brewers, the two big London independents Fullers and Youngs in particular, ensure their beers are served in the manner that best suits their character.

Whether it is served with a large or small head of foam, from a beer engine or straight from the cask, this is the highest form of ale brewing. After all the agitation in the brewery, the mashing, boiling and fermenting, followed by maturing and conditioning the pub cellar, real ale — cask beer — is now ready in all its rich diversity to please and refresh legions of drinkers and to prove that it is one of the wonders of the world of brewing.

ABOVE: *A quiet lunch-time pint at the Highland in Leeds.*

PartThree

Chapter One
The catalysts

CAMRA

If the Campaign for Real Ale had not been formed in the early 1970s ale would by now be just a footnote to the history of brewing. A few small regional brewers in England and Wales would have remained true to cask beer. But its impact would be minimal today, confined to a handful of pubs and sought after as a cultural oddity, occasionally filmed for television and put on a par with conker fights and recreations of battles between Cavaliers and Roundheads in the English Civil War. Save for a few disgruntled mega-brewers, few would dispute that CAMRA turned the British brewing industry on its head, saved regional brewers from closure and spawned the micro-brewery revolution. But its impact has not been confined to the British Isles. When CAMRA stirred the British brewing pool, ripples washed up on many shores. In the summer of 1994 I made an extensive tour of revivalist ale brewers in California and the Pacific North-west of the United States. The name of CAMRA was an Open Sesame. Americans are naturally warm and hospitable but I was beered, dined and made welcome beyond the bounds of duty by the simple mention of the curious rubric. Belgium's magnificent array of ales now has a wider appreciation and has come out from the shadow of a mass Pils market as a direct result of CAMRA's activities across the North Sea. In Australia, the Netherlands, Scandinavia and even in France ale is reappearing and gaining a new understanding.

The international influence of CAMRA has come as a pleasing shock to its founders. In 1971, when four young men decided to launch an organisation that would attempt to halt the emasculation of Britain's cask ales, they did so more in hope than expectation. Michael Hardman, Graham Lees, Jim Makin and Bill Mellor, from the Manchester and Liverpool areas, went on a pub crawl one evening before they were due to fly to Dublin for a boozing holiday. They were distressed by the quality of much of the ale they supped that night. By the time they reached Dublin and marvelled at the quality of the Guinness there they decided that a drinker's organisation to protect and revive British ale was needed. The Campaign for the Revitalisation of Ale, as the body was first called, remained just a bibulous gleam in the eye for a year until a meeting was called and the group was formally constituted. CAMRA

ABOVE: *Founding fathers ...the men who created CAMRA celebrate the first ten years; left to right, Jim Makin, Bill Mellor, Michael Hardman and Graham Lees.*

was a mass movement waiting to happen. A number of people with great knowledge of brewing, the British pub and a thirst for good beer hurried to join it. By 1973 it had one thousand members. The simple suggestion to drop 'revitalisation' from the title in order to coin the phrase 'real ale' was the turning point. Although brewers have never liked this popular term for cask-conditioned ale it struck an immediate chord with the drinking public. Hardman, Lees and Mellor were journalists. Aided by writers such as Christopher Hutt, author of *The Death of the English Pub*, and Frank Baillie with his *Beer Drinker's Companion*, they were able to garner a great deal of media attention at a time when the brewing industry and pub trade were undergoing changes of seismic proportions.

The changes were rooted in World War Two. Many experienced publicans were killed during the war, either doing military service or as a result of bombs falling on their pubs. They were replaced by younger people who lacked the training and skill to look after cask beer. The brewers, freed from war-time restrictions on ingredients and strength, were keen to get people back into pubs and paid scant attention to training publicans. As a result many murky and vinegary pints were served. Searching for consistency, drinkers switched in droves to bottled beer. Aided by clever advertising campaigns, sales of bottled Bass, Double Diamond and Guinness soared. The swing to bottled beer boosted the profits of larger brewers who had the capital to invest in new, sophisticated bottling machines. The fortunes of smaller brewers were in the doldrums as the larger ones grabbed an ever bigger market share through poster advertising and the arrival of commercial television in 1956. Brewing became dominated first by large regional brewing groups and then, following a frenzy of takeovers and mergers in the 1960s and 1970s, six national giants. The spur for merger mania was a new type of bulk beer known as keg. With the success of bottled beer, most of its filtered, pasteurised and artificially carbonated, the bigger brewers hit on the idea of putting bottled beer in bigger containers for their pubs. Kegs, shaped like giant cans and known as 'beer dustbins' to their detractors, had a shelf life of several months. Keg beer had been tried on a limited basis for social clubs by Watneys before the war and Flower's brewery in Stratford-on-Avon enjoyed great success with it in the 1950s. Sales soared in the 1960s when the big regional brewers rushed to follow Bass, which had become a national giant as a result of swallowing such famous names as Charrington in London, and Mitchells and Butlers in Birmingham. Within a few years Bass's hegemony was under attack by other new giants: Allied Breweries, formed by a merger of Ansells, Ind Coope and Tetley; Watney Mann and Truman, later the brewing division of Grand Metropolitan which also acquired Websters, Wilsons and Ushers; Scottish and Newcastle, a merger of Scottish Brewers — better known as Youngers and McEwans — and Newcastle Breweries; Courage, which had merged with Barclay Perkins in the 1950s and spread west and north from its London base by buying Simonds of Reading and John Smiths of Tadcaster; and Whitbread which had feasted on a glut of takeovers and closures to turn itself into a national group, closing fifteen breweries between 1960 and 1971.

The brewing industry had been transformed almost as if by a magician's wand. A cosy industry in which hundreds of brewers provided their beers on a level playing field had been changed virtually overnight. Six giants now dominated to such an extent that they accounted for around three-quarters of beer production and owned more than half the country's pubs. The 'Big Six' set out change the entire pattern of beer drinking. Before the giants were created, Britain was to beer drinking what France was to wine — highly regionalised. There were wide variations in regional styles and fierce loyalties to those styles. The new giants had no truck with such sentimental nonsense. They were national brewers with a new mass market at their feet. The brief to their brewers and marketing departments was to develop keg beers that could be promoted throughout the country with great flare and élan. Hoardings, the press, and commercial radio and television were suddenly awash with slick advertising and, in the case of the broadcasting media, catchy jingles for Bass's Worthington E, Allied's Double Diamond, Watney's Red Barrel, Courage's Tavern, Whitbread's Tankard,

ABOVE: *A panoply of ale ... beer stands at the Great British Beer Festival in London.*

and Scottish and Newcastle's Tartan. Keg beer's share of the market grew from one per cent in 1959 to sixty-three per cent by 1976. The keg market was built not from consumer demand but by advertising and promotion. Between 1976 and 1977 the total advertising spend on beer for the year was £20.34 million, a staggering sum for the time and almost all of it accounted for by the Big Six. The reverse side of the coin was the savage reduction in choice for drinkers: between 1966 and 1976 the number of beer brands brewed in Britain fell by more than half, from three thousand to fewer than 1,500. Within a decade cask-conditioned ale declined from being the dominant form of draught beer in Britain to a sideline, leaving drinkers in many areas with no choice but to drink cold, over-carbonated and largely tasteless keg beers.

The challenge that faced the fledgling Campaign for Real Ale in the 1970s was a daunting one. It required tackling the might of rich and powerful conglomerates that had successfully changed the face of British beer. They dismissed CAMRA as an irrelevance that harked back to the past. They saw themselves as an important element of the new fast food and drink culture, harbingers of the 'leisure industry', anxious to get consumers to part with their 'leisure pounds'. But they found that CAMRA could not be laughed into oblivion. The campaign had found rapport with the drinking public. When CAMRA members dressed as undertakers protested against brewery closures, the media took notice.

When CAMRA produced well-documented evidence to show that keg beer was both more expensive and weaker than cask ales, drinkers took notice. When the campaign started to organise beer festivals to spotlight the brewers still producing fine-tasting ales, drinkers flocked to them. By the late 1970s the campaign had grown to 28,000 members. The annual Good Beer Guide, which listed pubs serving real ale, was in the top ten best-selling books. CAMRA produced national and local newsletters and pub guides. Carefully researched reports sent to the government showed how the national brewers abused their market share through price fixing and controlling a monopoly of outlets in some parts of the country. Analyses by brewing experts and scientists detailed the cost-cutting and inferior ingredients used by the big brewers to maximise their profits.

From the outset CAMRA was a brilliantly professional organisation. Founder member Michael Hardman edited both the Good Beer Guide and the campaign's national newspaper What's Brewing and had an unerring eye for every media opportunity. The campaign was organised like part-political party and part- underground guerrilla movement. With an elected national executive at its head, it was divided into regional groups and local branches. Each branch with a brewery in its area appointed a liaison officer to report on how the company was performing and lobbying it to produce more cask ale.

ABOVE: *Mistress of all she surveys ... GBBF organiser Christine Cryne.*

CAMRA chimed with the times. The 'Swinging Sixties' had given way to the nostalgic seventies. People preferred the traditional to the flashy and modern, and didn't like what brewers were doing to beer. But such inchoate feelings of discontent could never have become a mass movement for change but for the British pub. Campaigns for 'real cheese' and 'real bread' have had only limited success because consumers of these products do not hang around in cheese shops or bakers to discuss the issues. But drinkers do stay in pubs, sometimes for an hour, sometimes for a whole evening. Much of CAMRA's campaigning was done in pubs because that was where cask ale was sold—or should have been sold. When they complained that modern keg beer was inferior to cask they were cutting with the grain, for since time immemorial drinkers have always felt that 'beer isn't what it used to be'. Now, at last, here was a body that not only agreed with the sentiment but was prepared to do something about it.

Many drinkers had fond memories of cask beer and didn't like the fizzy keg replacements. When Watneys replaced Red Barrel with an abysmal keg beer called just Red, CAMRA laughed it to oblivion. The campaign cruelly dubbed Watneys 'Grotneys'. The name stuck and the group was told by its financial advisers to stop painting its pubs an easily identifiable red in the hope that some drinkers might be encouraged to go to them. The fall out from the Watneys Red fiasco affected all keg beers. The national giants hit back in two ways. They started to brew and market lager and also to gingerly feel their way back into the cask ale market. Lager was a more difficult target for CAMRA to hit. Unlike keg,

ABOVE: *John Cryne, national chairman of CAMRA, at GBBF.*

lager was not replacing something drinkers preferred. It was new to Britain and was aimed specifically at young people. Research showed that many women didn't go to pubs because they didn't like the taste of bitter beer. Lager was brewed to be bland and inoffensive. As an executive of the Harp Lager Company said about his product: 'There's not much you can say for it, but on the other hand there's not much you can say against it'. The first British-brewed lagers — often using such absurd Germanic names as Hofmeister and Sazenbräu to give them a fig leaf of respectability — had little in common with the genuine article. Some were even top-fermented ales made from pale malt. Those brewed using lager yeasts were stored for days rather than months. Excessive carbonation and low serving temperatures masked the fact that the beers were largely devoid of taste. They were also expensive, up to ten pence a pint more than milds and bitters of similar or greater strength. But lager was an enormous success thanks to clever marketing aimed at the young. Many were from working-class backgrounds and were enjoying the first cheap packaged holidays to European resorts where they acquired a taste for lager. As sales of lager roared ahead, increasing from seven per cent of the beer market in 1971 to a quarter by 1977, the national brewers, who accounted for nearly all lager production, confidently said it would grow to eighty per cent by the 1990s. It didn't happen. While CAMRA found it harder successfully to attack lager than keg — as a real ale campaign it was sniping from the sidelines on this issue — it saw lager grow to fifty per cent of total beer consumption, then dip back. By the 1990s, sales of 'standard' — ie weak — lager were declining fast. Better-produced premium lagers were developed and imported lagers of real quality from Germany and the Czech Republic were finding favour. The market share for lager has always been distorted by its dominance of the supermarket and beer shop sector. In pubs, lager has had a much smaller share and has been outsold by all types of ale, cask, keg and stout.

Of greater importance to the campaign was the rekindling of interest in cask among the nationals. In 1976 Allied Breweries' Ind Coope division launched a strong pale ale called Draught Burton Ale. It was a sensation. Ind Coope had expected to put it into a few, carefully chosen outlets. As demand soared, the company supplying Ind Coope with beer engines to serve the beer put its employees on permanent overtime. The success of Burton Ale opened the floodgates. Other national brewers rushed to supply what they now dubbed a 'niche market'. It had been a mass market until they effectively closed it in the 1960s. Bass discovered it had a rather fine ale called Draught Bass. Courage began to sell Directors Bitter outside of a few chosen pubs. Scottish and Newcastle found there was more to life than Tartan Special and launched Youngers and McEwans cask ales in southern England. Whitbread stopped calling all its ales Trophy and began to bring back revered names such as Fremlins and Wethereds. Even Watneys, which had stopped all cask beer production, experimented with real ale, albeit served from converted kegs as the group had no genuine casks to put the beer in.

The return to cask ale production by the nationals encouraged regional brewers to stay true to the cause. Many had tinkered with keg. Some had considered, like Watneys, that there was no future in cask at all. A few, such as Youngs in London and Holts in Manchester, had thumbed their noses at keg and found renewed success in the small but now firmly ensconced real ale market. The regionals, boosted by their pride of place in CAMRA publications, reduced or stopped keg production. Many regionals decided not to brew lager. They became reborn cask brewers.

Suddenly pubs everywhere had banners and posters announcing they sold real ale. The success of the regionals prompted a new wave of small or 'micro' brewers in the early 1980s. They came from several strands: disillusioned brewers from national groups, keen home-brewers wishing to use their skills commercially, small business people who thought they could make money from real ale. Many crashed in the deep recession of the early eighties but some survived and added to the growing pleasures of good beer. The second wave of micros in the late eighties and early nineties had learned the lessons of the first wave. They were better capitalised, had researched their local markets better and even bought a few pubs in which to sell their products.

CAMRA was a victim of its own success. Membership slumped in the early 1980s. With so many pubs now selling cask beer, drinkers saw no reason to continue in membership. At one stage membership dipped below 15,000. The organisation regrouped. It had to change from a single issue guerrilla movement into a more broad-based consumer organisation. The beer drinkers in green berets came down from the hills and changed into suits. But they left a cache of guns behind in case they were called to arms again. The move away from being a single-issue campaign led to some heart-searching and disgruntlement. But it created renewed media interest and slowly membership began to recover. CAMRA became the friend of pub users as well as cask ale drinkers. It lobbied hard to save pubs threatened by closure. Both nationally and locally it organised Pub of the Year competitions which rewarded good pub design and argued that architects should honour traditional values and avoid flashy 'refurbs', to use a vulgar piece of brewerspeak. The campaign tackled the problem of the monopolistic grip of the national brewers in papers prepared for the government and its many departments and watchdogs. It called for a relaxation of the absurdly restricted pub licensing laws in England and Wales with the result that flexibility was introduced in 1988, allowing pubs to open from eleven in the morning until eleven at night every day except Sunday. The campaign took a keen interest in the way in which beer was brewed and the ingredients used. CAMRA's Technical Committee, aided by the indefatigable Dr Keith Thomas of Brewlab, established credentials as firm critics of shoddy brewing practice and cheap adjuncts. The com-

ABOVE: *CAMRA's impact is international ... The Czech paper Pivni Kuryr (Beer Courier) gave the campaign a special award for its efforts to save the Czech brewing industry from foreign take-overs.*

ABOVE: *Olympian heights - top-level view of the Great British Beer Festival.*

BELOW: *And now for something completely different ... Terry Jones serves beer in a Monty Pythonesque manner at the opening of the Great British Beer Festival in 1977.*

mittee also helped boost the image of cask ale through the annual Champion Beer of Britain competition, with panels of judges required to use precise parameters to mark the appearance, aroma, palate and finish of beers. The spin-off from this work was a major change in the approach of the Good Beer Guide. As well as listing the best pubs, its brewery section included tasting notes for all cask beers.

Beer festivals were central to CAMRA's new-found success. As many as fifteen a month are now held throughout the country. Some offer just the beers from a particular locality. Others draw beer from further afield, some include beers from other countries, a few are devoted to particular styles, with winter ale festivals especially popular. The pinnacle of the beer festival year is the Great British Beer Festival. It has been staged in different towns and cities in Britain but has settled on London as its home base. In the ornate setting of the grand hall at Olympia, the festival offers some three hundred cask-conditioned ales, along with bottle-conditioned ones, selected ales from other countries, cider and perry, good food and entertainment. The 1994 festival broke all records, came dangerously close to running out of beer on the last day, created enormous media attention and recruited more than one thousand new members.

The need for a strong and vigorous campaign was demonstrated many times during the 1980s. The acquisitive nature of big brewers took on an international perspective when Elders IXL, the Australian owners of Foster's lager, bought the Courage group. When Elders then attempted to buy Scottish and Newcastle, CAMRA mounted a major opposition to the move, culminating in a demonstration through the sedate streets of Edinburgh. Elders dropped the bid. A second recession, declining beer consumption and over-capacity in the industry prompted Elders' decision but there is no doubt that CAMRA's voluble opposition also had a part to play. The campaign also fought against a bid by Scottish and Newcastle for the Lancashire brewery of Matthew Brown, which in turn owned the famous Yorkshire brewery of Theakstons. S&N's intention was an asset-stripping one. Short of strong cask brands itself, it badly needed Theakston's name on its bars and in its massive free trade accounts. So ham-fisted was S&N's first attempt to buy Browns and so powerful was CAMRA's opposition that the national giant had to admit defeat and won control only after a second, protracted and costly bid. More regional breweries were to close. The most outrageous example of greed and skulduggery came when Greenall Whitley, a regional giant based in North-west England, bought and closed the much-loved Simpkiss Brewery in the 'Black Country' region of the Midlands centred on Wolverhampton. Greenalls wanted the Simpkiss site merely as a convenient depot and it showed its contempt for brewing tradition, quality and heritage by pouring the final batch of Simpkiss beer down the drain.

With the national and larger regional brewers threatening to run riot once more, CAMRA lobbied the government's Office of Fair Trading for an investigation. The OFT asked the Monopolies and Mergers Commission to look at the supply of beer and at an industrial structure that acted against consumer interest. The MMC report in 1989 was a bombshell. It said the grip of the Big Six brewers did constitute a monopoly that not only affected the consumer through lack of choice and high prices but also prevented smaller brewers extending their operations and new brewers entering the industry. The commission's recommendations included the right of every tenant who ran a pub owned by a national brewer to buy a 'guest beer' of his own choice, a ban on cheap loans and discounts which allowed the nationals to dominate the 'free trade' of pubs not owned by breweries, and the demand that the nationals turn a substantial minority of their pubs into free houses offering greater choice. The Big Six went into over-drive to oppose the report, which they condemned as a CAMRA-inspired document. The government watered down most of the MMC's proposals but it did implement the 'guest beer' proposal. Intensive lobbying by CAMRA officials blocked a major loophole in the proposal. The term 'guest beer', they argued, was so open to misinterpretation that the big brewers would twist the recommendation to their own advantage by offering their tenants heavily-branded national lagers. Far from increasing drinkers' choice, it would decrease it. The government saw the sense of the argument and rephrased its proposal. Now pub tenants would be free to buy a guest *cask-conditioned ale* of their choice. It was a master-stroke by CAMRA that for the first time opened the doors of big brewers' pubs to regional and micro breweries.

The guest beer policy has been a considerable success. It has undoubtedly boosted drinkers' choice. But in general the government's heavily doctored version of the MMC proposal has not halted the onward march of the mega brewers who had a bigger market share after the commission's report was published than before it. Asked to turn some of their pubs into free houses, the giants preferred to sell pubs. They helped set up pub chains owned by seemingly independent businessmen. But many of them came from executive positions with the national brewers. They were given financial help by their former employers and in return signed deals to take their beers exclusively from those companies. In order to increase market share, the national brewers launched a discount war to drive regional brewers out of free trade pubs and supermarkets. And in a move of blatant cynicism, Grand Metropolitan left brewing by swapping all its breweries for Courage's pubs. In one fell swoop, both groups were freed from the government's 'beer orders', which only covered breweries with tied estates, and they signed a deal whereby Courage would be the sole supplier of beer to Grand Met's vast pub estate for seven years. Elsewhere, the famous Manchester independent Boddingtons sold its brewery to Whitbread while Allied Breweries merged its brewing division with Carlsberg. In 1995 Scottish and Newcastle bid £425 million for Courage.

CAMRA worked ceaselessly against all these changes. The media

ABOVE: *It concentrates the mind ... taster at work in the Champion Beer of Britain competition. He is Barrie Pepper, chairman of the British Guild of Beer Writers.*

ABOVE: *So quiet you can hear a pin drop ... tasters in action during the final rounds of the Champion Beer of Britain Competition.*

publicity given to the MMC report and its aftermath brought the brewing industry to the attention of millions of people. People were aware there was something wrong in the way beer was sold by the nationals. The result was a sudden rise in the campaign's membership, increasing first to thirty thousand, then to thirty-five, on to forty and, by the autumn of 1994, to forty-six thousand, forcing the organisation to move to new premises in St Albans in Hertfordshire, where it had been based since the mid-1970s. With increased muscle, CAMRA took up its many fights with renewed vigour, spotlighting in particular the grotesque imbalance of beer duties between Britain and its European partners. When the European Union announced an open market in 1993, cheap beer flooded into Britain from mainland Europe, hitting brewers and retailers and depriving the government of millions of pounds in lost revenue.

On the credit side, sales of real ale continued to increase. A report on the cask ale market by Carlsberg-Tetley in the autumn of 1994 showed that it was growing by nine per cent a year and was the only growth sector in an otherwise declining beer market. If the big brewers' predictions in the 1970s had been correct, cask ale would not have existed in the 1990s. Lager would have confined it to the history books. CAMRA had saved it and brought it to a new, wider and more appreciative audience. It had helped create a climate in which regional and micro brewers could flourish and it had focused attention not only on British beer but on fine ales in other lands.

Those are CAMRA's great and enduring achievements. But there will always be fresh challenges to face. The European Commission will decide by 1997 whether brewers can both produce beer and sell it in their own pubs. If the commission says no, it would be a body blow to the British 'tied house' system without which the regional brewers could not survive. Meanwhile the national brewers, interested more in volumes than quality, have developed new types of canned and keg beers with a mix of nitrogen and carbon dioxide dispense to give a smoother and creamier palate. They are aimed at the cask ale market, attempting to replace cask with beers with greater shelf life and profitability. Once again CAMRA will take up the cudgels, refighting the battles of the 1970s in order to save real ale for the twenty-first century. As its national newspaper What's Brewing observed in an editorial in the October 1994 issue, 'The price of beer drinkers' liberty is eternal vigilance'.

EBCU

In 1990 three beer organisations met in Bruges in Belgium to set up the European Beer Consumers' Union. The founding members were CAMRA from Britain, PINT from the Netherlands and OBP from Belgium. PINT (pronounced with a short 'i' as in 'hint') stands for Promotie Informatie Traditioneel Bier — Promotion and Information about Traditional Beer. It was founded in 1980 to campaign for tradi-

BROUWERY = DE RIDDER =

tional beer and pubs in the Netherlands. It produces a bi-monthly magazine and runs beer festivals, including the annual Bokbier (strong beer) Festival in Amsterdam in October. OBP was set up in Belgium in 1984. The full name of the organisation is Objectieve Bierproevers, Objective Beer Tasters in English. It is first and foremost concerned with designating beer styles in a punctilious fashion. OBP's best-known member, Peter Crombecq, publishes the Bierjaarboek with detailed information and tasting notes about every beer brewed in the country. It campaigns against the monopolistic tendencies of large brewing groups such as Interbrew and Riva and has lobbied the Belgian government to defend the status of lambic and gueuze beers brewed by spontaneous fermentation.

The EBCU has become an effective lobbying force in Europe with important contacts in the European Commission and within the European Parliament. As well as exchanging information among member groups, it campaigns for a European-wide agreement on ingredients listings for beers — at present British brewers do not have to give any indication of the ingredients they use — and has a won Appellation Contrôlée status for the lambic and gueuze ales of Belgium.

The organisation has widened its influence with new members: Sö in Sweden and Finnlibs in Finland. Les Amis de la Bière in France is an associate member as the group covers only a small area of France in the

ABOVE: United in defence of good beer ... members of the European Beer Consumers' Union at the De Ridder Brewery in Maastricht.

ABOVE: *Drew Ferguson of CAMRA Canada.*

Nord-Pas de Calais region. Groups from Denmark, Norway and Switzerland are expected to join.

CAMRA CANADA

With a large number of British expatriates living in Canada it is not surprising that beer lovers there sought inspiration from CAMRA when they set up an organisation in the early 1980s. They were too late to save Canada's brewing tradition, which had been lost in a series of mergers and takeovers that created three giants, Canadian Breweries, Molson and Labatt. Canadian Breweries became Carling O'Keefe and is now part of Molson. The vast country is effectively controlled by just two beer companies. The problem of Canada's size is compounded for any small producer by the curious restriction that will not allow a brewery in one province to export to another. Molson and Labatt get round the restriction by having breweries in every province but such luxuries are beyond small entrepreneurs. The giants destroyed Canada's great ale brewing tradition and now concentrate on mass marketed lagers and such new, high-tech products as 'ice beer' that prove that if you try hard enough it is possible to produce a beer quite devoid of taste and flavour. They supply much of their draught beer in unpasteurised form but the government insists that imported beers must be pasteurised. This gives the two local giants an enormous advantage as they can stress the freshness of their products. CAMRA Canada started when both ex-pats and native Canadians got together to pool resources and brew good tasting ale at home. That was not as easy as it seems as home brewing was illegal. Brew pubs were also banned in several provinces.

CAMRA Canada has waged war on several fronts. It has had home brewing legalised and has lifted the ban on brew pubs. 'It was like dealing with ten different countries,' according to CAMRA Canada president Drew Ferguson. 'We took politicians to bakeries and said "What's the difference? They use flour, water and yeast".' The organisation has also arranged with the governments of Quebec and Ontario for micro breweries to have tax advantages over the national brewers.

Brew pubs are now appearing in many towns and cities. On the west coast of Vancouver and British Columbia the driving force has been British ex-pats inspired by the spread of micros in the Pacific North-west of the United States. In Ontario, ex-pats have combined with local entrepreneurs. French-speaking Quebec has always has a strong ale tradition and the province is a huge outlets for Belgian ales. It is harder going on the west coast where people of Scottish and Irish descent stick with Guinness and even Watneys Red Barrel, which no longer exists in Britain and is brewed solely for the North American market. 'There must be a nuclear reactor full of that stuff somewhere!' Drew Ferguson said.

According to Ferguson, most micros produce keg beers. Only a handful produce cask-conditioned ale as bar owners are not prepared to look after it. Ferguson is concerned that too many micros concentrate on five per cent ales. 'They're too strong for comfort, but Canadians

127

want "the best bounce for the ounce".' CAMRA Canada responds by arguing for taste and quality in ale rather than strength. Ferguson says the future of the campaign must be political: lobbying provincial and central governments for a sliding scale of tax on beer to favour the micros, more freedom in the market, easier access for imported beer, and lifting restrictions on micros and home brewers.

AMERICAN HOME BREWERS' ASSOCIATION

There is no consumer movement comparable to CAMRA in the United States and the US does not have a large body of British ex-patriates, as does Canada, to spread the ale message. The revival of interest in quality beer — lager as well as ale — has come from the American Home Brewers' Association, though some of the new wave micro brewers, Anchor of San Francisco in particular, predate the association by many years. The AHA has provided a forum for home brewers to pool ideas and resources. It has become a publishing power-house, starting with a highly professional magazine, Zymurgy (from the Greek word for the art and science of brewing) and spreading to a superb series of books on beer styles that includes pale ale and porter. The AHA has encouraged British producers of beer kits, raw ingredients and brewing equipment to export to the US. The AHA has been a genuine catalyst, inspiring many home brewers to move up several gears to commercial brewing. The association has turned the definition of beer styles into an art form. I have sat in on judging panels in the US organised by the AHA and have been struck by the awesome attention to detail of the association's trained tasters who will throw out, say, a porter if it does not meet the laid-down criteria of the style for ingredi-ents, colour, aroma and palate. The high-spot of the year is the Great American Beer Festival. The inspiration clearly comes from CAMRA's Great British festival though the American one is not confined merely to ale. Its awards to commercial and home brewers in a vast number of categories are much sought after. The influence of the AHA can be seen in the fact that both the two US brewing giants, Anheuser-Busch and Miller, are now producing ales and stouts that fly in the face of their belief in a mass market dominated by bland lagers.

ABOVE: *1993 Great American Beer Festival at Denver.*

Part Four
The Tapestry

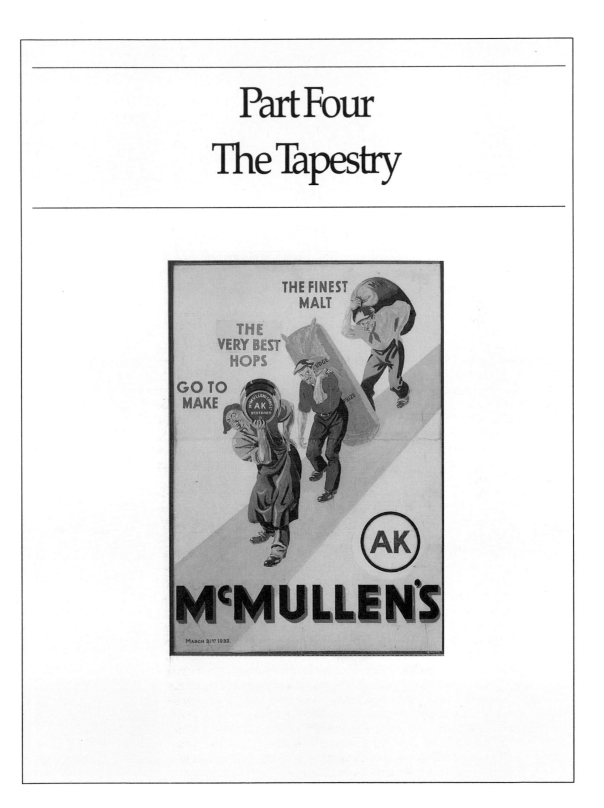

Chapter One
England

Cask-conditioned ale is alive and well in England. There are close to one thousand brands available and the number will grow as new micro-breweries are launched with almost every passing week and established brewers extend their range. A beer style that seemed doomed to oblivion twenty years ago has clawed its way back from the abyss.

England today is to beer what France is to wine, a land flowing with an abundance of choice and regional diversity. Malts ranging from pale to black and hops with superb aromas of peppery tannins and resins combine to provide ales rich and fruity in character, matching anything the grape can offer. A clockwise trip round the country finds strong, tawny ales in the North-east; Yorkshire's complex creamy beers, rich and malty, underpinned by tart hoppiness; the malty milds and bitters of the West Midlands balanced by the sulphury and delicately fruity ones from neighbouring East Midlands; the ripe beers from the East Anglian grain basket with their citric fruitiness; uncompromisingly hoppy beers from London, the Thames Valley and the South-east; the nutty, bitter, slightly astringent ales of the West Country; and the full-flavoured beers of the North-west with an astonishing abundance of choice in the mecca of Manchester.

Bitter is king of the beer styles, the twentieth century's adaptation of the previous century's pale ales. But mild ale retains great affection and support in a few pockets, especially where factories and mines still struggle to survive in the post-industrial society. Seasonal beers have appeared again in recent years, with winter warmers, old ales and barley wines followed by spring, summer and harvest ales. Porters and stouts are back to remind drinkers of their brewing history and heritage.

That heritage is underscored by the determination of master brewers to remain faithful to style and tradition. Nowhere is that determination more fierce than in the red-brick Victorian brewery of Marston, Thompson and Evershed at the heart of the capital of pale ale brewing, Burton-on-Trent. There are only six breweries operating in Burton today. Three are micros and one of them brews only occasionally. Of the three large commercial companies, only Marston's — which started brewing in 1834 and moved to its present site, the Albion Brewery in 1898 — stays true to the traditional system of brewing in the town, a system rooted in the union room. The union method went hand in hand

BELOW: *Strength in the Unions ... Marston's Union fermentation room at Burton-on-Trent.*

ABOVE: *The cathedral of brewing ... overhead view of Marston's union room.*

with the growth of pale ale brewing in the nineteenth century. The new style of beer was marketed on its clarity and natural sparkle. As glass replaced pewter as drinking vessels in pubs, drinkers became more aware of the murkiness of dark beers and the pleasing translucent quality of pale ale. But producing clear beer was not easy. Yeast was in suspension in the fermenting wort. It could be skimmed from the top of the vessel but it was impossible to remove it entirely, with the result that finished beer could be cloudy at a time when pub-goers, to use modern marketing language, were 'drinking with their eyes'. The problem was solved with the unions. Although the method is indissolubly linked with Burton-on-Trent, it was invented by the Liverpool brewer Peter Walker, who briefly had a brewery in Burton at the height of the pale ale revolution. Walker simply took a medieval method of fermentation and stood it on its head. In the middle ages fermentation took place in large wooden casks. The spontaneous violence of the action of the yeast drove fermenting wort out of the open bung. Brewers collected liquid and yeast in buckets or troughs beneath the casks. They returned the liquid by hand to the casks and retained the yeast for later brews. The simple genius of Walker's method was to place troughs above the casks. The troughs retained more yeast and, because they were slightly inclined, allowed the fermenting wort to run back into the casks. The system was effective, virtually ran itself, and brewers throughout the country hurried to instal union sets. They went out of favour in the twentieth century because they were capital intensive, needing constant repairs and attention to the casks. They were replaced by more effective skimming methods, in particular the 'parachute', a large metal funnel placed apex-down in the fermenter so that the yeast can collect in it. But while modern methods and carefully cultured, single-strain and well-behaved yeasts make the production of bitter an easier process today, Marston's believes that only the unions can produce the true flavour of a genuine pale ale. The company is so committed to the system that in the early 1990s it commissioned an additional union room with thirty casks at a cost of more than one million pounds. This involved importing the right type of oak from Germany so that the specialist cask makers, Buckley's of Greater Manchester, could build the new union sets.

Marston's devotion to the unions is based on its belief that the yeast strain developed in the system is not only crucial to the flavour and character of its ales but would change dramatically if it were asked to work in conventional fermenters. This belief has been underscored by the experience of Bass, also based in Burton, which scrapped its unions in the 1980s. While its best-selling cask ale, Draught Bass, is still a good beer it has unquestionably lost some of the delicate fruity-hoppy complexity of its hey-day.

The union rooms at Marston's are the cathedrals of brewing. Due reverence is shown by workers and visitors, who tend to speak in hushed tones as they walk the floors and gangways of the vast rooms, where the only other sounds are the hiss of carbon dioxide and the drip, drip of foaming wort gushing from the union casks and up into the 'barm troughs' above them — barm comes from an old Norse word for yeast and is a dialect expression in Staffordshire and the North.

Fermentation at Marston's begins in open square fermenters, based in rooms above the union sets. The open vessels are unusually shallow. Head brewer Paul Bayley says that one of the many curious character-istics of yeast developed in the union system is that it will refuse point-blank to work in a conventional deep vessel. Thirty-six hours after fermentation has started, the wort is 'dropped' (run by gravity) from the shallow vessels into the union casks below.

The term union stems from the fact that the great oak casks, each one holding 144 gallons, are linked in rows by pipes and troughs — 'held in union'. A union 'set' is made up of two rows of casks, eight casks to a row, with a barm trough set above them. Each cask is cooled by water pumped through internal pipes or attemperators. As fermentation continues, carbon dioxide drives wort and yeast up swan-neck pipes built into the bung holes of each cask and which overhang the barm trough. The wort runs back into the casks via union pipes while some

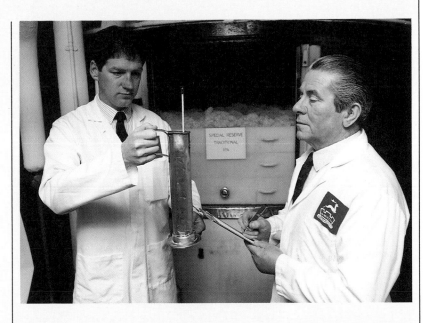

of the yeast sediments in the trough. By the time fermentation has finished, nearly all the yeast has been collected in the troughs, leaving a clear beer in the casks. A tap at the bottom of each cask is opened and the green beer pours into a trough below, where it runs into a collecting tank or 'back'. It stands in the tank for a day before being racked into casks and transported to pubs.

Marston's Pedigree Bitter (4.5 per cent alcohol), the result of all this activity, is a beer of marvellous subtlety and complexity. The aroma, known locally as 'the Burton snatch', is a powerful 'burning match' sulphury one from the gypsum in the brewing liquor. This slowly thins to reveal malt, hops and delicate fruit. The fruit is a clearly definable hint of apple, which also used to be evident on the aroma and palate of Draught Bass when it was brewed in the unions. The fruitiness lingers in the mouth and the finish, balanced by a robust bitterness from Fuggles and Goldings. Only Pedigree is brewed in the union rooms as it is Marston's biggest volume ale. But all the other beers in the company's portfolio are fermented with the same union-derived yeast strain. In the autumn of 1994 I tasted a new Nut Brown Ale from Marston's and it had the unmistakable sulphury, fruity character of a union room beer. Marston's has done a great service to beer appreciation by persisting with a system of fermentation that flies in the face of the 'wisdom' of marketing departments and accountants concerned more with quick profits than quality.

In Yorkshire, the 'square' system of fermentation tackles not only the problem of cleansing beer of yeast but also the nature of the yeast strains used in that vast region of northern England. Unlike a Burton yeast, greedily attacking malt sugars, Yorkshire yeasts are highly flocculant. This means that yeast cells clump together and separate from the fermenting beer. Unless the yeast is roused on a regular basis it will not attenuate far, leaving a high level of unfermented sugar in the finished beer. The problem was overcome with the square vessel, made first from stone, later from slate and more usually today from stainless steel. The square is a two-storey vessel. The two chambers are connected by a manhole with a raised rim or flange, and also by 'organ' pipes. The top chamber, known as the barm deck, is open. The bottom chamber is filled with wort and yeast. As fermentation gets under way, yeast and wort rise through the manhole. The yeast is trapped by the rim of the opening while the wort drains back into the bottom chamber via the organ pipes. Every two hours or so wort and yeast are pumped from the lower chamber to the top one via a fish-tail spray. This aerates the wort and mixes in more yeast. When fermentation is finished the manhole is closed and the green beer is left in the bottom chamber for two days before being racked into casks. Yeast is recovered from the top chamber. Beers brewed by the system are notably full bodied as a result of the presence of unfermented sugars.

Unlike the Burton union, Yorkshire squares are widely used in the North. I have come across them in the Mansfield Brewery in Nottingham and surprisingly, given the famous antipathy between Yorkshiremen and people on the other side of the Pennines, in the Tetley-Walker Brewery in Warrington. The regular aeration of the wort creates high levels of carbonation that help produce the thick collar of foam on a glass of beer, the 'creamy head' popular in the North. Paul Theakston, who opened the Black Sheep Brewery in Masham, North Yorkshire, in the early 1990s, was determined to buy second-hand 'Yorkshire' squares — actually from Nottinghamshire — in order to produce the right flavour in his ales. When squares were made of stone or slate the natural coolness of the materials helped check the rise in temperature of the wort during fermentation. Modern stainless steel vessels have cooling systems built in. The first brewery in Yorkshire to develop stone squares was Bentley and Shaw of Huddersfield. It is thought the company may have been encouraged by the work of the famous chemist Dr Joseph Priestley who unravelled the mysteries of 'fixed air' — carbon dioxide — as a result of living next to a brewery in Leeds that later became the famous Joshua Tetley company. Priestley's research led to the production of carbonated water and later the soft drinks industry. More importantly he presented a paper to the Royal Society, an association founded to promote scientific research, on the absorption of gases in liquids. Although there is no written evidence to prove the case, Priestley's work may have led Bentley and Shaw to develop a method of fermentation that created a high level of carbon dioxide.

The small town of Tadcaster near York is known as the 'Burton of the North'. It has three breweries, a small offshoot of Bass, and two plants

ABOVE: *Still rolling out wooden barrels at arch-traditionalists Samuel Smiths of Tadcaster, Yorkshire.*

named Smith. Samuel Smith's Old Brewery was built in 1758 and is one of the oldest surviving breweries in England and certainly the oldest in Yorkshire. It is vigorously and rigorously independent. Behind a gritty, no-nonsense, bluff Yorkshire façade of horse-drawn drays and beer served from wooden barrels there is a sharp business sense that has built success from a dedication to tradition. With the aid of the Bavarian Ayinger brewery, Sam Smith's brews some of the only drinkable English lagers. It produces magnificent ales using the only remaining stone squares in the country. Old Brewery Bitter (3.8 per cent) and Museum Ale (5.2 per cent) have generous amounts of crystal malt in their grist — nine and ten per cent respectively. As a result, the ales have a rich nutty and, in the case of Museum, winey character. They are both well hopped with Fuggles and Goldings and have a complex creamy maltiness and flinty dryness. In the early 1990s, Sam Smith's took the decision to phase out all brewing sugars from its beers as it felt that adjuncts were detrimental to quality and unnecessary where cost-saving was concerned. It produces a superb range of bottled beers of which its Taddy Porter, Oatmeal Stout and Imperial Stout are classics. As with Marston's, Sam Smith's dedication to tradition has paid a rich dividend.

At the turn of the century, a row in the Smith family led to John Smith walking up the road and opening his own brewery. The Magnet Brewery, named after his most famous ale, was one of the most beautiful

135

in the world, with a great fermenting room full of Yorkshire squares. But John Smith became part of the Courage group and now the squares have given way to modern conical fermenters.

The simplest way to cleanse yeast from beer is the dropping system. In the days before vacuum scavengers were designed to literally suck the excess yeast from the top of the fermenters, it was difficult and costly to remove yeast manually. Some yeast always remained in suspension and, if the temperature dropped, fell to the bottom of the vessel. As brewing historian Graham Wheeler has noted in 'Home Brewing — the CAMRA Guide', 'It was not long before some bright spark realised that, rather than try to remove the yeast from the beer, it would be far easier to remove the beer from the yeast; and thus the dropping system was born'.

The dropping system is still used by Brakspear of Henley-on-Thames. Primary fermentation begins in conventional open squares on the first floor of the brewery. When fermentation is well under way, with a good rocky head on top of the wort and about half the sugars consumed, the wort is 'dropped' by gravity into a second bank of fermenters immediately below. It is a brilliantly simple yet effective method, the Yorkshire square upside down. Dropping the wort leaves behind all the 'trub' or spent matter such as spent hops and dead yeast cells that have collected on the bottom of the fermenters as well as both the yeast head and yeast in suspension. The wort is thoroughly roused and aerated, and a new and much cleaner yeast head soon forms as fermentation continues.

LEFT: *One good turn ... traditional cooper at work at Theakstons.*

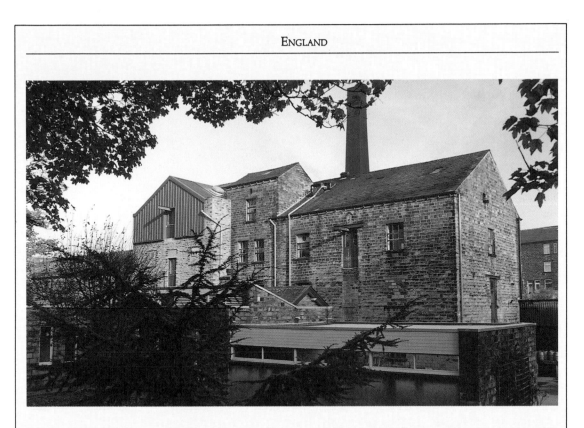

ABOVE: *True Yorkshire grit ... Timothy Taylor's brewery in Keighley.*

Brakspear is an old Thames Valley family that may have been distantly related to the only English Pope, Nicholas Breakspear: the brewers stress the possible link by pronouncing their name in the same way. Their beers are noticeably fruity, with a pronounced orange note on the aroma of the 3.6 per cent Bitter and more exotic fruits on the four per cent Special. As well as Maris Otter pale and crystal malts, Brakspear also adds a touch of black malt for colour and flavour.

England has an abundance of classic ales, many of them brewed by long-established family-owned companies. Samuel Smith's rugged traditionalism is matched by another Yorkshire brewery, Timothy Taylor of Keighley. In superb old stone buildings, the evocatively named Knowle Spring Brewery—which provides the liquor for brewing—has a cupboardful of prizes for its ales, including three times winner of CAMRA's Champion Beer of Britain accolade for Landlord, its premium bitter. As was the case with many Victorian brewers, Timothy Taylor was a maltster who decided to expand into brewing. His first brews appeared in 1858 and he moved to Knowle Spring five years later because of the abundance of fine water there. Timothy's grandson, John Taylor, has been ennobled and as Lord Ingrow takes home supplies of the spring liquor to mix with his whisky as he knows of no finer water. The aroma and palate of Taylor's ales comes from the unusual blend of ingredients. The brewery uses Scottish malt, Golden Promise, with a small amount of crystal in the Best Bitter. But both Golden Best, a light-

LEFT: *Hops are added to the boiling wort at McMullen's brewery.*

coloured mild, and Landlord are made from 100 per cent Golden Promise, with no darker malts or brewing sugars. Whole hop flowers are Fuggles and Goldings in the copper with Styrian Goldings (actually an off-shoot of the Fuggle) used for aroma. The brewery does not dry hop in the cask but allows the hopped wort to circulate over a deep bed of Styrians after the copper boil. Landlord, 4.3 per cent alcohol, is one of the most complex bitters in England, with a pungent orange-and-lemon aroma from the Styrians, fruit and hops in the mouth and a long, rich, hoppy and citric fruit finish.

Brewers in Eastern England can draw on the finest malting barley in the country and their ales have a deep fruitiness as a result. Adnams, based in the picturesque Suffolk seaside town of Southwold dominated by its stubby, whitewashed, in-shore lighthouse, has expanded from its isolated rural base into one of the most successful of small regional brewers. Just thirteen per cent of its production goes to its own pubs as it supplies other outlets throughout the country. Its success has been built on its remarkable 3.8 per cent Bitter brewed from Maris Otter pale malt and some invert sugar. The tart, quenching and aromatic quality of the beer, as with the other ales in the portfolio, is based on Adnams love affair with the Fuggle. Challenger, Fuggles and Goldings are used in the boil and the ale is dry-hopped in the cask with Fuggles. With thirty-three units of bitterness, Adnams Bitter has a stunning aroma of peppery Fuggles and orange fruit, a complex fruit, malt and hops palate and a deep finish packed with citric fruit and hop resins. The Fuggle character is even more evident in the 4.5 per cent Extra, named Champion Beer of Britain in 1993. Brewed with pale and crystal malts, the ale drains through a deep bed of Fuggles in the hop back after the copper

RIGHT: *The Old Ale of old England .. an Adnams' poster for a beer style that played a central role in the development of the early Porters and Stouts.*

boil. With thirty-six units of bitterness, Extra has a pungent, spicy hop nose that also dominates the palate and finish.

McMullen in the county town of Hertford shares an Irish connection with Adnams. The McMullen's ancestors were Irish while Adnams' directors include members of the Irish Loftus family. McMullen has one of the finest Victorian brewhouses in England from which come some of the most distinctive cask ales. The company is one of a select band that brews more mild ale than bitter. The biggest selling McMullen ale is AK, sold for most of the twentieth century as a light mild but repositioned in

LEFT: *Giddey up! Horse-drawn dray at Adnams in Suffolk, still used to deliver ale to local pubs.*

the 1990s as a bitter. The company felt that mild had the wrong, old-fashioned, working-class image. But milds brewed with little dark malt are such a rare breed that it is a pity to deny AK's humble origins. It is, nevertheless, a brilliant ale and is unusual in several respects. It has an original gravity of 1033 degrees but is fully attenuated to achieve 3.8 per cent alcohol. Brewed from 80 per cent Halycon pale malt, flaked maize, maltose syrup and just a touch of chocolate malt (one per cent) AK has a lilting hop aroma thanks to Goldings and Whitbread Goldings Variety, which despite the name is a Fuggle derivative. AK has twenty-two units of bitterness and a complex palate and finish, with an almost winey fruitiness that comes from the distinctive Whitbread B yeast strain used at Hertford. AK's big brother, Country Bitter, is another well-attenuated ale, 1041 degrees gravity making 4.6 per cent alcohol, with a big hop character, a delicious nuttiness from crystal malt and dark fruit and vanilla in the finish.

The most unusual aspect of AK is its name which has taken on all the trappings of a mystery novel. No one is certain what the letters stand for. Many fanciful cases have been put forward, such as 'Asquith's Knock-out', commemorating the occasion when the Chancellor of the Exchequer raised beer duty savagely in his budget. But that was in the early twentieth century and AK's origins are nineteenth. Other suggestions are based on the assumption that less than literate brewery workers marked casks with the letters AK to indicate that the beer was 'All Klear' or 'All Korrect', which is taking us into the realms of fantasy that surround the origins of porter. Brewing historian Martyn Cornell,

who has written a two-thousand word essay on the subject for the Brewery History Society, believes A stands for ale and K comes from a Flemish word kyte, meaning small beer. It is an interesting theory but almost too intellectual for comfort. The famous insularity of the English and their inability to grasp foreign languages would have given the cheeky imposition of Flemish words short shrift. I think the origins of AK are much simpler and stem from the practice of branding casks to indicate strength. Two famous Burton ales, Double Diamond and Worthington E, take their names from cask markings: Ind Coope branded its casks with diamonds to indicate strength (single, double and triple D) while Worthington's pale ales ranged from the letters A to E. The letter X, from medieval times, was used to indicate beer strength. If you cut an X vertically you get a K. I suspect this was used by McMullen and other brewers — Fremlins in Kent had an AK mild — to indicate an ale of lower strength. As nineteenth-century brewers produced more than one mild but almost certainly from just one mash, with liquor added to achieve different strengths, A would have been the first mild ale produced from a gyle. But the debate will doubtless continue.

London, once one of the world's great brewing cities, is now reduced to just two independent companies. But Fuller, Smith and Turner of Chiswick, and Young's of Wandsworth brew such distinctive ales that they have kept London proudly on the map. Fuller's ales, with deft touches of crystal malt alongside the pale, have a rich, fruity complexity underscored by a generous hoppiness. Young's ales are paler, eschewing darker malts, and are uncompromisingly bitter as if they sprang, ready brewed, from the hop fields of Kent. Fuller's best known products are the deeply complex London Pride (4.1 per cent), with its dark fruit and bitter hop character, and the astonishing Extra Special Bitter (5.5 per cent), which has been likened to alcoholic Cooper's marmalade as a result of a deep fruitiness reminiscent of oranges, lemons and gooseberries.

Young's has pride of place in CAMRA's pantheon of cask ale brewers. In the dog days of the 1960s and 1970s, John Young, the redoubtable chairman of the company, set his face against keg beer. He has a passionate love of his brewery's beers and he was unwilling to compromise them at a time when marketing wisdom said you either brewed keg or died. He was for years a lone southern voice in the keg wilderness. He tells with relish the story of a meeting of the Brewers' Society in London at the height of the keg boom. During a break in the proceedings the assembled brewers were standing by a window overlooking the street as a funeral procession passed by. 'There goes another of your customers, John!' one brewer guffawed, to general merriment. John Young had the last laugh. As the real ale revival took hold, Young's ales became much sought after and the brewery remains one of the best-known independents in the country. John Young and his family have been unflinching standard-bearers for quality and tradition, attitudes that spill over from their brewhouse into their splendidly run estate of pubs. The remarkable Victorian brewhouse, with restored coppers and beam engines, is set amid the terrible traffic snarl of south London and yet has an almost sylvan charm and quiet. Great dray horses deliver to surrounding pubs while the brewery yard has a flock of geese and a lively ram, the company mascot. The two main ales are Bitter (3.7 per cent) and Special Bitter (4.8). The Bitter is always known as 'Ordinary', a curious name for the antithesis of the humdrum. Extremely pale (fourteen units of colour), brewed from Maris Otter malt and a little torrefied barley and brewing sugar, it has a nostril-expanding hop aroma due to the generous use of Fuggles and Goldings (32-34 units of bitterness). It is tart and bitter in the mouth with a splendidly quenching and bitter finish and a strong underpinning of citric fruit. Special Bitter has been transformed from a rich but overly malty ale into a beautifully balanced one by the simple expedient of dry hopping it since the early 1990s. Fuggles and Goldings are joined by Target to achieve thirty-two units of bitterness. A peppery hop aroma balanced by ripe citric fruit is followed by a mellow maltiness in the mouth and a big finish packed with hops and citric fruit. Young's also brews one of the best-known English seasonal ales, Winter Warmer, a port-winey, ruby-coloured ale in such demand that in goes on sale every autumn and stays in Young's pubs until the following spring.

Fittingly, the Cotswolds, the captivating area of Gloucestershire full of small towns and villages of mellow stone buildings, has the most idyllic brewery in the country. The Donnington Brewery near Stow-on-the-Wold is fronted by a mill pond where geese, swans and weeping willow trees provide an exquisite backdrop. The water turns the wheel

ABOVE: *John Young, the chairman of Young's Brewery in South London.*

RIGHT: *The loveliest setting in England ... water wheel at the Donnington Brewery near Stow-on-the-Wold in the Cotswolds.*

RIGHT: *The loveliest setting in England ... water wheel at the Donnington Brewery near Stow-on-the-Wold in the Cotswolds.*

of a mill that still provides all the power for the small brewhouse. The mill was once part of a feudal estate that dates back to 1291. In the sixteenth century it was used as a cloth mill and was converted to grind corn around 1580. It became a bakehouse until the Arkell family from Swindon, Wiltshire, bought the mill and its associated buildings in 1827 and Richard Arkell started to brew in 1865. His grandson, Claude, who is a distant relation of another Arkell family still brewing in Swindon, carries on the slow, bucolic tradition of making fine-tasting country beers. His brewing liquor comes from a spring beside the mill pond while his Fuggle hops are from neighbouring Worcestershire. Local

barley was used until the 1960s but today Claude Arkell buys the finest Maris Otter from Norfolk. Leafing back through the old leather-bound brewing books, he showed me recipes from 1874 for a Christmas Ale of 1078 degrees gravity along with porter, table beer and best ale. The brewery in those days was using Californian and Bavarian hops as well as Kentish varieties.

Today Claude Arkell brews a BB bitter, 3.5 per cent, and an SBA of four per cent. He is sad that demand for mild is so small that his XXX mild is BB with caramel added for colour. His bitters are rich and rounded, dominated by splendid, earthy Fuggle hop bitterness and complemented by biscuity malt. Donnington's owns fifteen pubs within striking distance of the brewery, several offering accommodation as well as fine ale and simple country food. Brewery and pubs combine to offer havens of peace and tranquillity in the harsh modern world.

Palmer's Brewery in Bridport, Dorset, runs Donnington a close second in the 'beautiful brewery' stakes. It is close to a stretch of coastline dominated by high, chalky cliffs and the charming harbour town of Lyme Regis, the setting for John Fowles' novel 'The French Lieutenant's Woman'. The brewery is partially thatched and, like Donnington, has a large water wheel, though this one no longer provides power. In a county with two bigger commercial breweries, Eldridge Pope and Hall and Woodhouse, Palmer's lovingly-crafted ales tend to be overlooked and under-rated. When I included Palmer's IPA in a collection of lesser known regional ales in a tasting for the British Guild of Beer Writers they were overwhelmed by the quality of the ale and voted it the best in show. At 4.2 per cent alcohol and twenty-eight units of bitterness, the beer does not quite match the strict criteria of the style. But with a fine balance of malt and Goldings hops on the nose, a delectable nutty character from crystal malt and an intensely dry and well-attenuated finish (the original gravity is 1039 degrees) it is a fine drinking and characterful ale. Palmer's also brews Bridport Bitter, which, at 3.2 per cent alcohol, is one of the last surviving examples of what is known in the English West Country as 'boy's bitter', a dismissive term for a low strength beer. I mourn the loss of the breed, for in their day they offered wonderfully tasty and refreshing ales. Generous hopping in Bridport Bitter (Goldings and Styrians producing twenty-six units of bitterness) gives the beer a delightful floral hop aroma and palate, a clean balance of malt and hops in the mouth, and quenching finish with hops, light fruit and nut from crystal malt.

The North-west of England is a vast region that ranges from the serene beauty of the Lake District to the great cities of Liverpool and Manchester. Like the people, the beers tend to be passionate and uncompromising. The classics are Joseph Holt's mild and bitter from Manchester. It is a family-owned, dynastic brewery with little truck with the modern world. It serves a tight-knit community of austere pubs decorated with mahogany wood. It has virtually no free-trade business and refuses to supply beer for CAMRA's Great British Beer Festival on the grounds that it is held outside its traditional trading area. It doesn't bother with marketing departments or public relations agencies and makes no effort to build links with the media. In 1992 I was the first journalist ever to be allowed into the brewery. When I asked about Holt's advertising policy I was met with the puzzled response: 'Do you mean our beer mats?' In spite of this take-it-or-leave-it attitude, Holt's enjoys enormous success. The demand for its beers is insatiable and is

RIGHT: *Shiver me Timbers! Famous children's author Arthur Ransome lived close to the Mason's Arms in the Lake District. The pub brews its own beers, including a fruit beer that uses local damsons.*

145

delivered to pubs that have large enough cellars to take fifty-four gallon wooden hogsheads. With no advertising and low delivery costs, the beer is astonishingly good value at around £1 for a pint of mild and a few coppers more for bitter.

The mild is a revelation. It is a modest 3.2 per cent alcohol yet has thirty units of bitterness, high for a modern mild. It is brewed from a blend of three pale malts, Halcyon, Pipkin and Triumph, with crystal and black malts, flaked maize for head retention and dark invert sugar. Whole hops flowers are Goldings and Northdown. There are fine resiny hops on the nose with a hint of chocolate, it is bitter-sweet in the mouth with hops and dark chocolate on the finish. The four per cent bitter is not for the faint-hearted. The recipe is identical to the mild's save for light invert sugar in place of the dark. The hops achieve forty units of bitterness and give a magnificent resiny aroma to the beer balanced by tart citric fruit. Malt and hops balance the palate followed by a deep bitter finish with delicate citric fruit notes.

ABOVE: *The calandria that keeps hopped wort boiling and bubbling inside the copper.*

The splendour of well-established English ales has been underscored by the booming micros. Although many of them own a pub or two, they are so reliant on other brewers' outlets and the free trade that they tend to kick over the traces, and are bold, imaginative and dare-devil in their choice of brews and the names they give them. In County Durham, Butterknowle's High Force (6.2 per cent) is named after a local waterfall. Black Sheep is a tongue-in-cheek name chosen by Paul Theakston of the famous brewing family when he opened his own plant cheek-by-jowl with the long-established Theakston's in Masham, the latter now part of the giant Scottish and Newcastle group. Cropton, near Pickering in Yorkshire, calls its standard bitter Two Pints. When you ask why, you are told that surely you will not be satisfied with just one glass. Still in Yorkshire, Franklin's of Harrogate pulls no punches: its strong (six per cent) ale is named, simply, Blotto. Nearby, Marston Moor near York calls its five per cent ale Brewers Droop: male drinkers have to weave a dangerous course between drinking and sexual satisfaction. In East Anglia, Crouch Vale Brewery near Chelmsford is also concerned with the nether regions of male drinkers: its winter ale (6.5 per cent) is Willie Warmer. There is contrapuntal brewing in the region. Mauldon's in Suffolk named its Black Adder porter (5.3 per cent) after a popular television programme and Woodforde's near Norwich responded with Baldric (5.5 per cent) after a character in the same series. Both breweries have won CAMRA's Champion Beer of Britain competition. Bunce's Brewery near Salisbury is dismissive of its bitter called Pigswill (four per cent) while Uley in Gloucestershire goes the whole hog, so to speak, by giving all its beers a porcine character with Old Spot Prize Ale (five per cent) named after a breed, Pig's Ear IPA (also five per cent and brewed from lager malt) and Pigor Mortis at 5.5 per cent. In Warrington in the North-west, Coach House has won a fistful of awards in just a few years of operation with the likes of Gunpowder Strong Mild (3.8 per cent), Post Horn (five per cent), and Blunderbus porter (5.5). To Robinwood of

RIGHT: *Mash tun fed by a Steel's Masher that blends `liquor' and grist at the Hook Norton brewery.*

BELOW: *Belinda the Brewster ... Belinda Elgood of Elgood's Brewery in Cambridgeshire who may take control when her father retires.*

Todmorden in Yorkshire — a region famed for the bluntness of the people — goes the dubious prize for the most down-to-earth-closet name for its 5.4 per cent premium ale: Old Fart.

MILD: BACK FROM THE DEAD

Mild Ale, once the biggest selling beer in Britain, is hanging on for dear life. The dedication of a handful of brewers and a vigorous promotion by CAMRA have helped the style survive. Mild has such a pivotal role in the history and development of ale brewing in England that it would be tragic if it were to succumb now, especially at a time when other dark brews such as porter and stout have become revivalist beers. It is a powerful link with the past. It has existed for some three hundred years and both porter and stout developed from it. At a time when beers were conditioned and matured for long periods of up to a year in oak vats, mild was the term given to a young, 'green' and immature beer that lacked the rounded and slightly lactic flavours of a well-matured stale ale with which it was blended. Mild developed as an ale in its own right as the result of several factors. City brewers in the eighteenth century started to baulk at the high prices charged by country brewers who had cornered the market in maturing strong ales for blending. The city brewers started to brew their own mild. Mild had also become a stop-gap brew during summer months. Usually brewing did not take place in hot weather before refrigeration because of the risk of infection. But if supplies of spring-brewed beer ran out, a rapid batch of mild would be produced and sold quickly before it went off. In the nineteenth century consumer tastes changed and mild became popular, no doubt as a reaction to the widespread adulteration of porters and stouts.

The early milds would have been harsh to the taste with a powerful

aroma and flavour of green apple that is common to immature beers. At first brewers blended in some well-matured ale to take away the harshness and in so doing laid the origins of porter. In the nineteenth century, brewers countered the harshness of mild by moving away from brown malt, with its slightly scorched and acrid flavour as a result of curing over wood fire, to pale malt blended with chocolate malt, torrefied barley and oatmeal for a smoother, more palatable appeal. New strains of hops, such as the Golding, were also far less harsh than older varieties. Mild remained the drink of the working class when pale ale convulsed the brewing industry in the last century. Pale ales, heavily hopped and using the finest malting barley, were more expensive and pandered to the snobberies and social niceties of a new lower middle class determined, above all else, to keep clear of the social mores of the hoi-polloi.

Mild should not be a synonym for weak, though the modern version of the style is all too often low in alcohol. The term has gone through several stages. At first it meant an ale that was served as soon as fermentation was finished and had not acquired an acetic or lactic flavour as a result of long conditioning. By the turn of the twentieth century it stood for a beer less heavily hopped than pale ale. Today, with only a few exceptions, it is the lowest gravity ale produced in a brewery.

RIGHT: *The tap room in the Beacon Hotel in Sedgley, home of Sarah Hughes' dark mild.*

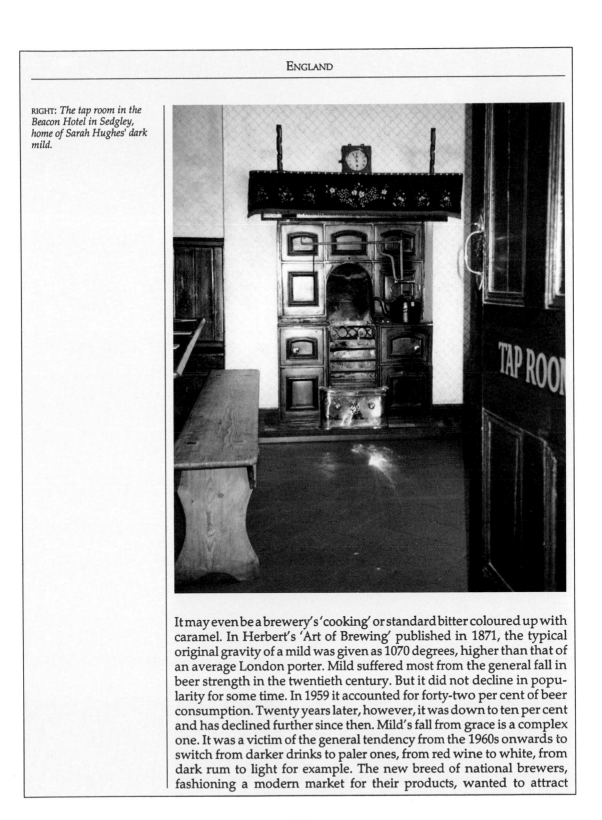

RIGHT: *The tap room in the Beacon Hotel in Sedgley, home of Sarah Hughes' dark mild.*

It may even be a brewery's 'cooking' or standard bitter coloured up with caramel. In Herbert's 'Art of Brewing' published in 1871, the typical original gravity of a mild was given as 1070 degrees, higher than that of an average London porter. Mild suffered most from the general fall in beer strength in the twentieth century. But it did not decline in popularity for some time. In 1959 it accounted for forty-two per cent of beer consumption. Twenty years later, however, it was down to ten per cent and has declined further since then. Mild's fall from grace is a complex one. It was a victim of the general tendency from the 1960s onwards to switch from darker drinks to paler ones, from red wine to white, from dark rum to light for example. The new breed of national brewers, fashioning a modern market for their products, wanted to attract younger people into their pubs and attempted to do so with keg beers and ersatz lagers that were pale in colour as well as character. Mild was dismissed as 'cloth cap', an outdated image that became a self-fulfilling prophecy with the de-industrialisation of Britain in the 1980s. Publicans had not helped mild's cause by the habit of pouring beer slops into their mild casks and hoping the darkness of the beer would disguise the practice.

Mild is still drunk in large quantities in one region of England. It is that part of the West Midlands centred on Wolverhampton and known as the Black Country. It would be tempting to think that the curious name comes from the popularity of dark ales but the area was once the powerhouse of the Industrial Revolution, with thousands of factory chimneys and furnaces pumping black smoke into the skies. Industrial workers, after eight long hours at the work face, needed instant refreshment. Ales rich with unfermented malt sugars fitted the bill. The biggest producer of mild in the Black Country today is Wolverhampton and Dudley Breweries. It is England's biggest regional brewer. It owns 850 pubs and produces half a million barrels of beer a year and sixty per cent of that is in the form of mild. It brews two milds, Banks's, which represents the Wolverhampton part of the company, and Hanson's, a brewery in Dudley run for many years by a legendary woman named Julia Hanson. Her brewery has closed and Hanson's ales are now brewed in Wolverhampton. Great care is taken to keep Banks's and Hanson's ales apart to avoid any cross-fertilisation of yeast strains. The Wolverhampton brewery is one of the most impressive in England, bursting with gleaming copper mash tuns and brew kettles. The company is equally punctilious about the ingredients it uses. Maris Otter barley is contract grown and floor malted in W&D's own maltings. Hops are the whole flowers of Fuggles and Goldings with some Bramling

ABOVE TOP: John Hughes of Sarah Hughes Brewery.

ABOVE BOTTOM: Sarah Hughes Dark Ruby Mild

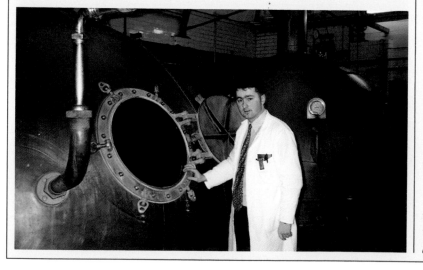

LEFT: Burnished coppers at Banks's Brewery in Wolverhampton where mild ale outstrips bitter.

ABOVE: *A Bardic touch at Batham's Black Country brewhouse and tap.*

Cross from British Columbia. The ales are late hopped during the copper boil but are not dry hopped in cask. Hanson's Mild has fifty units of colour and twenty-five units of bitterness. The colour comes from crystal malt. W&D has reduced the strength of the ale from 3.6 per cent alcohol to 3.3 in order to sell it for around £1 a pint in the Dudley area, where unemployment is distressingly high. It is an admirable, socially-responsive attitude but it does mean that the clean, nutty and quenching character of the beer has been diminished. Banks's Ale, 3.5 per cent alcohol, forty units of colour and twenty-five bitterness units, uses caramel rather than crystal malt for colour. Caramel is a contentious ingredient. W&D's head brewer, Richard Westwood, maintains that it is flavourless. I find, on the other hand, that it gives a slightly vinous, port-wine character to his ale. I much prefer the grainy, nutty flavour that crystal malt gives to beer. As brewers frequently tell me that adjuncts today are no cheaper than barley malt I see no reason for using them.

The Vine pub in Brierley Hill is a shrine for lovers of Black Country ale. The much-photographed façade bears an inscription from Shakespeare's The Two Gentlemen of Verona: 'Blessings of Your Heart, You Brew Good Ale'. The simple, homely pub with regular live jazz concerts in the spacious back bar, also houses Batham's Delph Brewery, which supplies a tiny estate of nine pubs. The brothers Tim and Matthew Batham are the fifth generation of the family to run the company. The

Bathams are Black Country stock. The brewery was founded by Daniel Batham when he lost his mining job in 1881 and became landlord of a brew pub. In 1912 the Bathams took over the Vine, which became the centrepiece of a thriving brewing and pub-owning venture. A butcher's shop and slaughterhouse were part of the premises of the Vine for many years and were the reason for the pub's nickname, the Bull and Bladder.

Batham's had been in business for seventy years before it first brewed a bitter beer. Its success had been rooted in dark mild. It brewed a tiny amount of bitter in the 1950s for just one pub in Worcestershire, well outside its traditional trading area. Sales soared in the 1970s when the bitter was named the best in Britain in a Daily Mirror competition. Today bitter accounts for ninety per cent of Batham's six thousand barrels a year output but sales of mild, after years of decline, are now rising again. Tim is refreshingly open about his brewing methods and describes his mild as 'a dark pale ale'. The brew house is run along traditional 'tower' lines, with production flowing logically from floor to floor. The hot liquor tank feeds the mash tun with water from the public supply that has been Burtonised with gypsum. Malt is made from Maris Otter barley. From the mash tun the wort is pumped to the copper where brewing sugar is added to the boil along with Herefordshire Northdown and East Kent Goldings hops. The hopped wort is clarified in a hop back and then pumped to wooden fermenting vessels, some of them more than one hundred years' old. They are now lined with polyproplene. Mild and bitter are parti-gyle beers. Additional liquor is blended with the 1043 gravity bitter to reduce it to 3.6 per cent alcohol for mild. Caramel is added to the fermenter and Tim Batham puts in twice as much yeast for mild than for bitter. The acidity of the wort is lower in the mild as a result of the breakdown liquor and it is vital to get a vigorous fermentation going as quickly as possible, using the Whitbread B strain. At the end of primary fermentation the mild is racked into casks and heavily primed with sugar to ensure a strong second fermentation. The beer is dry hopped with Goldings and has an unusually big hop character for the style. There is a dark winey fruitiness on the palate with blackcurrant predominating. The finish is bitter-sweet and becomes dry and quenching.

Edwin Holden's brewery in Woodsetton on the outskirts of Dudley is just a couple of miles from Batham's. In common with Batham's, Holden's started life as a brew pub, the Park Inn, where Edwin's grandparents started the business. They brewed in the pub cellar but as business expanded a separate brewery was built next door. It produces nine thousand barrels a year, of which around thirty per cent is the 3.6 per cent Black Country Mild. When Edwin took over from his father in 1966 mild accounted for eighty per cent of production. It fell to around twenty per cent and is now rising again. Edwin Holden is another keen supporter of Maris Otter barley, floor malted for him by Crisps of Norfolk. For colour he uses crystal, amber and black malts with some torrefied wheat that helps filtration in the mash tun. No caramel is used.

ABOVE: *Tim Batham ... keeping the family tradition alive.*

ABOVE: *Edwin Holden ... mild-mannered Midlands brewer.*

Fuggles hops are grown for Holden's by farmer Mike Hancocks in Malvern, Worcestershire. The mild has twenty-five units of bitterness. The yeast strain came from the now closed Wem Brewery in Shropshire. The beer is primed with three pints of liquid sugar in each cask for secondary fermentation. I enjoyed a glass with Edwin in the Park Inn. The beer has a rich and fruity aroma underpinned by an earthy whiff of Fuggles. It is refreshing and fruity in the mouth with a finish that begins sweet but becomes dry.

In Walsall the giant Bass group has allowed a dark ale to continue to see the light. The Highgate Brewery produces only dark ales, is well below its 100,000 barrel capacity and would, if the accountants had their way, have been closed years ago. But Bass has kept faith with the red-brick Victorian tower plant and in the early 1990s started to promote Highgate Mild nationally, renaming it Highgate Dark. Dark is parti-gyled with Highgate Old. The recipe calls for two tonnes of Halcyon pale malt, sixty-five kilos of black and fifteen to twenty kilos of crystal for every one hundred barrels brewed. Brewing liquor, rich in iron, comes from a bore hole on the site. Hops are Fuggles and Goldings. Liquor breaks down the Old to 3.25 per cent alcohol for Dark. Mashing is in two ancient tuns, originally made from wood and re-lined with stainless steel but retaining hand-raised wooden lids. Boiling takes place in two burnished coppers with internal calandrias topped by funnels known as Chinese hats. The splendid fermenting room is packed with a variety of round and square vessels, once made just from wood but now lined to keep bugs at bay. The Highgate yeast strain is described by the brewer as 'a beast'. It is, unusually in modern brewing, a four-strain type, each strain attacking elements of the brewing sugars at different times. The finished Dark, with maltose syrup and caramel added to the malts, has sixty-three units of colour and twenty-two of bitterness. It has a complex aroma and palate, with powerful hints of dark fruit, chocolate and liquorice and a dry, nutty finish with good hop character.

A glimpse and a taste of a genuine Victorian mild can be marvelled at in the Beacon Hotel in Sedgley. The hotel was built in 1850, complete with a tiny tower brewery in the yard at the back. Sarah Hughes bought the hotel in 1921 and ran it for thirty years, handing it on to her son and daughters when she died in 1951. The brewery produced a strong (1060 degrees), dark mild but the Hughes family closed the plant in 1958. Sarah Hughes' grandson, John, decided to begin brewing again in 1987. All the old wooden vessels had rotted away and had to be replaced by stainless steel ones, faced with wood. John discovered the recipe for his grandmother's ale in a cigar box locked in a bank security vault. To watch the brewing process, you have to clamber up narrow wooden stairs to the top of the building. Maris Otter pale malt is blended with ten per cent crystal. After mashing and sparging, the wort is dropped a few feet into a tiny underback and from there into an original, open-topped copper where the wort is boiled with Fuggles and Goldings. It drops to a hop back for clarification and then into five fermenters converted from cellar tanks from the closed Ansells Brewery in Birmingham. John Hughes won't reveal the source of his yeast but says it comes from another Black Country brewery, which narrows the field.

He has lovingly restored the hotel and turned in into a shrine to Victoriana, complete with tap room, smoke room and snug, all with open fires and tiled floors. Each room is supplied with beer from a central servery, with glasses pushed through hatches. Every item is Victorian, including gas lamps, wallpaper and an out-of-tune piano. There is nothing tuneless, though, about Sarah Hughes' Dark Ruby Mild, six per cent alcohol. It has a rich and fruity nose where blackcurrant dominates, laced with an earthy Fuggles aroma. The palate is deeply complex, summoning up every dark fruit imaginable. The finish becomes stunningly dry with a lot of Fuggles character. People travel long distances for a taste of genuine mild. One man came all the way from Hong Kong, proving that the style still has considerable pulling power.

ALE UNDER GLASS

Bottle-conditioned ale is enjoying a sudden and welcome revival. For years there was just a handful of beers that matured in bottle and threw a slight sediment. But as both an indication of the real ale revival and, in the case of some regional brewers, as a nose-thumbing response to high-tech and misleadingly marketed 'draught beers in cans', the numbers have grown. For years the biggest-selling bottle-conditioned beer in the British Isles was Guinness's Original Stout but, with the exception of the Irish Republic, this was phased out in the early 1990s in favour of a pasteurised version. Worthington White Shield, brewed by Bass following the merger with its Burton neighbour in 1927, has fared better. Widely available in pubs, it is now on sale in supermarkets and off-licences complete with a neck label that tells the story of the beer and advice on how to pour it without getting the sediment in the glass. At 5.6 per cent alcohol, White Shield is closest to a true India Pale Ale. It is brewed from Halcyon and Pipkin pale malts and a touch of black malt for colour. Hops are Challenger and Northdown. The beer has 20.5 units of colour and an impressive forty units of bitterness. It has an enticing aroma of spices, hops and light fruit, is bitter and fruity in the mouth and has a deep, nutty finish with a big hop presence and delicate fruit notes, including a hint of apple.

John Smith's Brewery in Tadcaster produces another ale with deep, historic roots. Courage Imperial Russian Stout was first brewed for the Russia trade in the nineteenth century. It became a cult beer at the Czar's imperial court and was so popular that a brewery was built in Estonia by Barclay Perkins agent, a Belgian named Le Coq, to supply the local trade. The brewery was nationalised in 1917 by the Bolsheviks. In 1971, after decades of bitter dispute, the Soviet government finally agreed to pay £240,000 in compensation for the loss of the brewery. Today, the stout is brewed in small batches every few years. The recipe is made up

of pale ale, amber and black malts and a little Pilsner malt, with brewing sugar. An enormous amount of Target hops, around twenty-four pounds per barrel, are used. It is ten per cent alcohol, has an aroma of fresh leather and liquorice, has bitter black chocolate in the mouth and an intense finish packed with bitter dark fruit and hops. There is a slightly oily, tarry note to the beer that is a hallmark of the style. When the stout was brewed by Courage in London it was matured for a year in oak casks. Now it is sold after a short conditioning in the brewery. The beer will improve with age. In 1992, when I mentioned Imperial Russian Stout on BBC Radio's Food Programme, I received a phone call from a listener in Newmarket, Suffolk, who said he owned a 1969 bottle which I was welcome to have. The beer was in remarkable condition and was softer and silkier than a younger version.

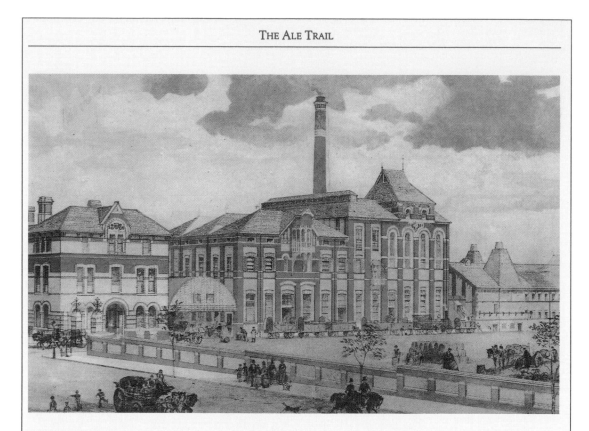

ABOVE: *Classic 19th-century Eldridge Pope brewery in Dorchester ... 'Casterbridge' in the Wessex novels of Thomas Hardy.*

In Burton-on-Trent the Burton Bridge micro produces its four per cent Porter in a hand-painted bottle. It is brewed from Pipkin pale, crystal and chocolate malts and is hopped with Challenger and Target varieties. It has hops and chocolate on the nose, warm biscuity malt in the mouth and a dry finish with strong hops and dark malt characteristics. A second Midlands micro, Titanic of Stoke-on-Trent, brews a Christmas Ale, a strong ale called Wreckage and a stout, all in bottle-conditioned as well as cask versions.

In the Thames Valley, the Chiltern Brewery in Aylesbury brews a 4.9 per cent Three Hundreds Old Ale and an 8.5 per cent Bodger's Barley Wine. Both use Maris Otter pale malt and invert sugar, with a healthy fifteen per cent crystal malt in the Three Hundreds. Both beers are complex, fruity and hoppy. In Lewes in Sussex, Harvey's magnificent Victorian tower brewery produces a 4.8 per cent bottled Porter meticulously brewed to an original recipe. Another Sussex brewery, King and Barnes of Horsham, puts its 4.8 per cent premium bitter Festive into bottle with great hop character from Challenger, Goldings and Whitbread Goldings (41.5 units of bitterness) and an eight per cent Christmas Ale, rich in crystal malt and generously hopped with Goldings fresh from the autumn's harvest. In Faversham, Kent, Shepherd Neame has produced a bottle-conditioned version of its 4.7 per cent Spitfire Ale. With a complex recipe of pale, crystal, amber and wheat malts, torrefied wheat

RIGHT: *Thomas Hardy's study in the Dorchester Museum. Hardy praised the ales of the town.*

and glucose syrup and four hop varieties, the beer has a powerful and peppery hops character underscored by rich fruit.

Eldridge Pope's resplendent Victorian brewery produces one of the best-known bottle-conditioned beers in the world, Thomas Hardy's Ale. It commemorates the life and work of the great novelist and poet, who praised the ales of 'Casterbridge' [Dorchester] in his work. The brewery produced the beer for a Hardy festival in 1968. It proved so popular that it is now brewed on a regular basis in numbered editions. Thomas Hardy's Ale, with an original gravity of 1125 degrees and 12 per cent alcohol by volume, is meant to be laid down for at least three years and will stay in drinkable condition for twenty-five. It is made from Pipkin pale ale malt only. The ruby colour comes from the strength of the beer and some natural caramelisation of the malt sugars during the copper boil. Challenger, Goldings and Northdown hops are used and produce a massive seventy-five units of bitterness. It is pitched with yeast several times during fermentation and is then matured for three months in the brewery. In 1992 I took part in a fascinating tasting of several vintages of the ale, led by the chairman of the brewery, Christopher Pope. The differences from year to year were remarkable, with winey and sherry notes dominating in the older vintages. When I reported the tasting in What's Brewing, some CAMRA hackles were raised by such descriptions as 'rich tobacco' and 'a library of old leather-bound books' but this ale is not to be lightly dismissed with such hand-me-down descriptions as 'a bit hoppy and malty'. Thomas Hardy did it better when he described the ale of Casterbridge as 'brisk as a volcano, full in body, piquant ... luminous as an autumn sunset'.

Southern England is rich in bottle-conditioned ales. Gale's of Horndean brews a Prize Old Ale of nine per cent alcohol in hand-corked bottles. It is brewed from Maris Otter pale malt, two per cent black malt and Fuggles and Goldings whole hops. It has 47.5 units of bitterness. The stunning aroma is rich in hops and ripe fruit, including apple notes. The palate and finish are dominated by dark fruits, spices and resiny hops.

To mark 250 years of brewing in 1992, Whitbread brewed a 12.5 per cent Celebration Ale in corked and sealed bottles. Brewed from pale, amber and crystal malts, Goldings and Whitbread Goldings hops and the company's Z strain of yeast perfected for strong beers, Celebration Ale will improve over twenty-five years. In 1992 it was understandably rather harsh and tannic but two years later it was altogether smoother and silkier with a luscious red-brown colour, great hop character and a port-wine intensity in the mouth. It should be quite interesting by the year 2017.

Greene King's Strong Suffolk Ale is not naturally conditioned in the bottle but is one of the few contemporary ales that is blended like one from the eighteenth century. The six per cent beer is a blend of BPA (Best Pale Ale, five per cent alcohol) and Old 5X, 12 per cent. The stronger ale is matured in two untreated oak vats for two years. The enormous casks, each one holding sixty barrels, are tucked away at the back of the brewery and are reached by a daunting clamber up narrow ladders and across catwalks. The lids of the vats are covered in Suffolk marl, the local chalky soil, to stop wild yeasts attacking the beer. Nevertheless, Old 5X, tasted straight in the brewery before blending, does have a slight lactic sourness that is still noticeable even when mixed with the malty BPA. The finished beer has a rich, fruity, oaky aroma and palate and good peppery, spicy hops. It is yet another fascinating link with the glorious past of English brewing.

Chapter Two
Scotland and Wales

The Celtic regions of Britain have their own distinctive ales. A powerful temperance movement in Wales coincided with the needs of miners and steel workers to refresh themselves with copious amounts of sweet, weak ale. The Scots, perhaps because of the indignity of being dubbed 'North Britons' by the English following the Act of Union of 1603, stubbornly persisted with dark, heavy ales. Both countries came late to the hop and continued to use other plants — notably heather — long after English brewers had become addicted to the climbing weed. Scotland succumbed to a taste for lager beer much earlier than the English. It seemed the Scottish ale heritage would disappear but it is now flourishing again.

The earliest brewers in Scotland were not Celts but the Picts, the hardy, cave-dwelling race of people who raided Roman Britain but were exterminated in a terrible series of pogroms in the fourth century by marauders from Ireland. The Picts brewed a heather ale, the fame of which spread far beyond the borders of the remote, mountainous country. The navigator Pytheas, when he visited Scotland, recorded that the Picts brewed a potent drink. According to legend, the last Pict threw himself from the cliffs into the sea rather than pass on the secret of heather ale to the High King of Ireland, Niall of the Nine Hostages, great-great-grandfather of St Columba, who had been bloodily exterminating the entire Pictish people. According to Robert Louis Stephenson, the brave Pict's last words:

BELOW: *Copper at Maclay's.*

> But now in vain is the torture
> Fire shall never avail
> Here dies in my bosom
> The secret of heather ale.

But heather ale survived and was commemorated in the same poem:

> From the bonny bells o' heather
> They brewed a drink langsyne
> Was sweeter far than honey
> Was stronger far than wine.

A visitor to Islay in 1774 noted that ale was made there from malt, hops and 'heath'. In the nineteenth century, B.J. Williams, writing in the

LEFT: *Coppers at the Caledonian brewery in Edinburgh ... fired by direct heat.*

Gallovidian, the journal of the Galloway area, said that 'Contrary to other legends, down to comparatively recent times it [heather ale] was brewed locally in pear-shaped kilns, notably in the parishes of Minigaff and Kirkmabreck'. He added that darnel [corn weed] and bere [a pre-historic variety of barley] were also used in the brew. Remains of Pictish breweries can still be found in Galloway. They are pear-shaped enclo-sures built by streams, roughly sixteen feet long, three feet wide and three feet high. Heather ale existed in the Orkney islands until the early twentieth century. An attempt to brew it between the two world wars by Marian McNeill and Neil Gunn was not successful. They boiled the heather with the wort. David Johnstone, former head brewer of Tennent Caledonian in Glasgow, in a paper 'In search of Scotch Ale' presented to Irish brewers in 1984, commented, 'It seemed surprising that they adopted this method when they were aware of John Bickerdyke's nineteenth-century description in Curiosities of Ale and Beer of the way the heather was used: "The blossoms of the heather are carefully gathered and cleansed, then placed in the bottom of the vessels. Wort of the ordinary kind is allowed to drain through the blossoms and gains in its passage a peculiar and agreeable flavour known to all familiar with heather honey'." Just as many modern brewers add additional hops to the hop back or collecting vessel after the boil, it seems that the Picts adopted the same method with heather. Stephenson's reference to the sweetness of heather ale suggests that honey may have been used. The Scots are known to have made a type of mead known as bee ale, spiced with ginger, cinnamon or cloves. It was also known by a name derived from Pictish, bragwort. It is possible that heather ale and bee ale were blended together to produce a sweeter drink. It is unlikely that any type of early Scots ale was 'stronger far than wine' as ale yeast finds it hard to produce high levels of alcohol. The strongest beer I have ever tasted,

ABOVE: *Clan-destine ale ...*
Fraoch heather ale uses a
Gaelic recipe handed down
from Pictish and Celtic times.

a 17.5 per cent triple bock from the Samuel Adams brewery in Boston, Massachusetts, started with conventional brewer's yeast but fermentation was completed by a champagne wine yeast.

The key question, what did heather ale taste like, was answered in 1993 when Bruce Williams, who runs a home-brew supply shop in Glasgow, produced a version following years of painstaking research. A recipe for heather ale had been translated from Gaelic by a woman from the Western Isles. Williams called his beer Leann Fraoch, Gaelic for heather ale. The first cask-conditioned brew was 3.6 per cent alcohol and was made from bell and ling varieties of heather, myrica [bog myrtle], honey, barley malt, water and conventional ale yeast. The ale had a delicate but decided perfume from the heather but was otherwise rather thin but refreshing. Since then Bruce Williams has refined the recipe several times. By the autumn of 1994, the beer, renamed simply Fraoch, was four per cent in cask and five per cent in a bottled version. Williams uses Scotch ale malt (90 per cent), carapils (five per cent) and wheat malt (five per cent) with 200 grams per barrel of six per cent alpha hops, 100 grams of fresh ginger root, and twelve litres per barrel of heather flowers: heather is calculated as a quarter of the volume of the grist. Half of the heather is put into the copper with hops and ginger, the whole boiled for an hour and a half, and the remainder of the heather lines the hop back. He brews the ale at Maclay's of Alloa. Fraoch caused considerable interest and by 1994 was available to both Albannach and Sasunnach people — Scottish and English — in specialist pubs as far from Glasgow as Canterbury. In the autumn of 1994 the five per cent bottled version had an earthy heather and herbal aroma with a hint of liquorice, a dry herbal palate with orange fruit and finish that becomes dry and minty. For up-to-date information about the ale, call 0141-339 3479.

Dr Keith Thomas of Brewlab carried out research into heather as a fermentable material. He discovered that heather contains a white powder known as fog, composed of a variety of micro-organisms. Heather that grows on wet uplands, as in Scotland, would have a high level of microbes and wild yeasts that would have led to spontaneous fermentation in times when cultured strains of brewer's yeast were unknown.

Ale brewed in a more conventional way, from barley malt, had a poor reputation in Scotland. In 1598 Fynes Morrison wrote that the local ale would 'distemper a strange body' while an English traveller, Thomas Kirke, described it as 'sorry stuff' in the early eighteenth century, 'tunned up in a small vessel, called a cogue [mash tun]; after it has stood a few hours, they drink it out of the cogue, yest and all'. Imports of ale from England reached such proportions that in 1625 the Scottish Parliament passed an Act forbidding the 'Hamebringing of Foreyn Beir'. Nobody paid any attention to it. The probable reason for the superiority of English ale was the use of the hop, which gave it better keeping qualities. The Scottish climate was not conducive to the development of a hop industry. A few hops were grown in the Lowlands in the sixteenth century but even that small industry faded out as the climate became colder. The only ale considered to be worth drinking was the strongest, made from the first runnings of the mash. In England it was the convention to produce three ales from the same mash. In Scotland they were determined to get as many brews as possible from one mash. The 'Guidewife of Lochrin' in Kinross made the following from one peck [quarter of a bushel] of malt:

> Twenty pints o Strong Ale
> Twenty Pints o Sma'
> Twenty Pints o Hinky Pinky
> Twenty Pints o Plooman's Drinkie
> Twenty Pints o Splitter Splatter
> and Twenty Pints Was Waur Nor Watter.

Hinky Pinky was an even weaker beer than small, a plooman was brewed for agricultural workers [ploughmen], splitter splatter was weak and watery while the final brew was no better than water. In this context Scottish small beer would have been of reasonable strength. Strong ale, if it was stored for a couple of years, was potent and drinkable. John Leslie, the Bishop of Ross, noted in 1578 that 'In the opinions of strange natiounes it is thought baith [both] be the colour and be the taste of Malmsey'. Strong ale was often called 'Scots wine'. French aristocrats who escaped the guillotine in the nineteenth century by settling in Edinburgh, referred to the local ale as 'Scottish Burgundy' while 'malt wine' or 'Scottish Malmsey' was strong ale fortified with whisky. As a result of the 'Auld Alliance' with France, wealthier Scots drank large amounts of real wine, mainly claret from Bordeaux. It was during the Napoleonic wars, when supplies of French wine were cut off, that a truly entrepreneurial commercial brewing industry in Scotland was consolidated. Before 1700, brewing had been confined to inns and farms. From 1730 a few commercial brewers set up in business to satisfy a demand for ale from emigrants in the West Indies and North America. Export became a definitive brewing style and McEwan's Export remains a major product from the Scottish and Newcastle group. As a counter to the harsh climate, Scots ale was rich, warming and heavy, lightly hopped because of the cost of importing hops from England, and made from black and chocolate malts and roasted barley as well as pale malt. Scots ales were in great demand throughout the world, exported to North America, the Caribbean, India and Australasia. Beer even crossed the border and a 'Scotch' became a cult beer in the North-east of England: the Lorimer and Clark brewery in Edinburgh was built next to the Caledonian railway in order to send ale by train to Newcastle. The industry settled in the Lowlands, around the cities of Alloa, Edinburgh and Glasgow. Fascinating names are given to Scottish ales: 'light' for mild even when dark in colour, 'heavy' for stronger ale, 'wee heavy' for a powerful ale sold in nip bottles. They are also sold as sixty, seventy,

eighty and ninety shilling ales from a nineteenth-century system of grading beers according to the price of a barrel. But the names should not detract from the more important fact that they are brewed in a quite different way to English ales. The copper boil lasts for a much shorter time than in England. As fewer hops are used, it is important not to boil away the delicate aromas and flavours of the plant. Fermentation is at a much lower temperature of 10° C/50° F, compared to 20° C/70° F in England. As a result the yeast works slowly, does not create a great head, need not be skimmed and eventually settles at the bottom of the fermenter. Fermentation lasts for around three weeks and the green beer is then stored for several more. The similarities with lager brewing are obvious. David Johnstone thinks it happened empirically, before the Industrial Revolution, when brewing only took place in winter. It was the exceptionally cold weather in Scotland that created slow ferments and the system continued when refrigeration appeared. It is not hard to see why lager brewing took off so much earlier in Scotland than in England. Hugh Tennent's Wellpark Brewery started to produce bottom-fermented lager beers in 1885. Scotland is close to Scandinavia and lager would have been exported from Denmark and Sweden. And as Scots sought work in other countries to escape unemployment at home they would have returned with a taste for the 'new beer'.

The finest malting barley grows in the Lowlands, though the brewers have to share it with the powerful whisky distillers. As late as the 1960s there were sixteen breweries in Edinburgh alone and the aromas belching from their chimneys gave the city its nickname of Auld Reekie. But Scottish brewing was devastated by mergers and takeovers even more effectively than in England. Scottish Brewers, created from two former rivals, Younger and McEwan, merged in 1960 with Newcastle Breweries to form Scottish and Newcastle, while Tennent of Glasgow joined forces with Caledonian Breweries to create Tennent Caledonian, a subsidiary of Bass. The Alloa Brewery was bought by Allied Breweries, now Carlsberg-Tetley, while Whitbread bought and closed the legendary Campbell, Hope and King brewery in Edinburgh. The S&N-Tennent duopoly accounts for around eighty per cent of beer brewed in Scotland. The driving force for the spate of mergers was lager, which demanded large capital outlay beyond the means of smaller brewers. Lager and keg ales threatened to wipe out cask-conditioned ale completely in the 1970s and 1980s. But an alliance between CAMRA — a small but highly active force in Scotland — and a handful of determined small brewers has saved the day. Cask ale started to revive in the 1990s. It is still a tiny proportion of the total market but it is growing and in Edinburgh and Aberdeen the only busy pubs are the real ale outlets.

The Caledonian Brewery in Edinburgh is one of the finest in the whole of Britain. It was formerly the Lorimer and Clark plant owned by the Vaux group of Sunderland. When Vaux announced the closure of the brewery in 1987, a rescue bid was launched by Russell Sharp, a former executive in the whisky industry. Caledonian is now revered for the quality of its ales, which include a malty Eighty Shilling, an organic Golden Promise and the remarkable R&D Deuchar's IPA. The last-named uses the recipe of the long-defunct Deuchar's brewery and is a fascinating example of the Scottish interpretation of the style. It is 3.9 per cent alcohol and has around thirty-five units of bitterness, high for a Scottish beer. The grist is Golden Promise pale malt — the classic Scottish malting barley — crystal and a little wheat malt. Whole Fuggles and Goldings hops are used in the open coppers, once fired by coal and today by direct gas flame (Russell Sharp says wort and hops in his coppers are boiled properly, not 'stewed'). The ale has a fine peppery Goldings aroma with citric fruit notes, there is a quenching balance of malt, hops and tart fruit in the mouth and the finish has a long, delicate hop character. The beer has won many awards, including the accolade of Beer of the Year three times from the Glasgow branch of CAMRA. As Russell Sharp commented, when Glaswegians give an award to an Edinburgh beer, it must be exceptional.

Traquair House near Peebles in the Scottish Borders is the oldest inhabited stately building in Scotland. Mary Queen of Scots stayed

BELOW: *Catherine Maxwell Stuart and her staff in front of Traquair House.*

there and Prince Charles Edward Stuart, 'Bonnie Prince Charlie', the leader of the Jacobite rebellion, visited. The house is owned by the Maxwell Stuarts, members of the aristocratic clan, and they keep the main Bear Gates to the house locked until a Stuart reclaims the throne of England and Scotland, a forlorn hope. The former laird [lord] of the estate, Peter Maxwell Stuart, discovered a disused Elizabethan brew house in the grounds of this striking building. He lovingly restored it, added a copper, and started to brew a house ale. Traquair House Ale is exported to the United States and Japan, is widely available throughout Britain and can be bought and consumed on the premises. It is seven per cent alcohol, thirty-five units of bitterness, and made from pale malt with the slightest touch of black. East Kent Goldings are grown and supplied by the specialist grower Tony Redsell. The ale has a rich spicy and hoppy aroma with a hint of chocolate, there is ripe vinous fruit in the mouth, while the finish is dominated by hops, fruit and chocolate. The estate and brewery are now managed by Mr Maxwell Stuart's daughter, Catherine.

In the historic town of Dunbar, close to the English border, the Belhaven Brewery is based in fine old buildings that once included its own maltings. Its version of the Eighty Shilling style is the classic, brewed with pale, black and crystal malts, and Fuggles and Goldings hops. It has thirty-three units of colour, twenty-nine of bitterness and has an enticing aroma of tart gooseberry fruit underscored by gentle hops. Another Borders brewery, Broughton, is based in the home town of John Buchan, author of *The Thirty-Nine Steps*. Another of his novels, *Greenmantle*, is also the name of Broughton's flagship ale, 3.9 per cent, with a little roasted barley alongside the malt. The ale is remarkably fruity, with strong hints of orange and lemon on the nose and palate. The brewery, owned by David Younger of the brewing dynasty, also produces a strong Old Jock (6.7 per cent) and has recreated a traditional Oatmeal Stout.

Maclay's of Alloa has also brought back an Oatmalt Stout (4.5 per cent) with a fine bitter-sweet character. The ancient brewery was bought in the early 1990s by Evelyn Matthews, a former director of Tennent-Caledonian. He is investing heavily in the site, which has a wide portfolio of ales, running the whole gamut of shillings, from sixty upwards, and including a Porter, a Summer Ale and a Scotch Ale. Alloa's ales are noticeably hoppy by Scottish standards. The Summer Ale (3.6 per cent alcohol) reaches fifty units of bitterness and has a stunning aroma and palate of fresh hop flowers.

The most northerly brewery in the British Isles is run by an Englishman, Roger White, at Quoyloo on the main island of the Orkneys. The Orkney Brewery stresses the Viking traditions of the islands with a powerful 8.5 per cent Skullsplitter, a richly fruity beer brewed from Golden Promise, crystal and chocolate malts and Goldings hops. He also brews a fruity Raven Ale (3.8 per cent), a dry, chocolatey and bitter Dragonhead Stout (4.1 per cent) and a ruby-coloured, complex Dark

BELOW: *Keeping Alloa ales independent ... Maclay's Thistle Brewery.*

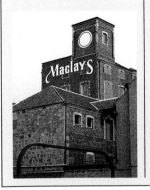

Island (4.7 per cent). White experimented with a Bere Ale, using the pre-
historic type of barley still grown on Orkney for milling and used in
bannocks, a local oatcake. Bere has a small amount of sugary extract and
had to be blended with modern malt. The result was a thin, rather cidery
drink. Roger White can lay claim to be a member of that rare club,
teetotal brewers. Like Beethoven, he is sadly unable to enjoy the beauty
of his creations.

Welsh ale has long enjoyed a fine reputation beyond the boundaries
of the principality. During the Saxon invasion of the British Isles, the
Celtic Welsh retreated to their heartland, built barricades and brewed an
ale that was distinctively different to the style imposed on the English
by the invaders. The quality and reputation of Welsh ale was sufficiently
high for it to be demanded as part payment for rents and other services.
Such payments were not confined to Wales. In the twelfth century, the
Abbot of Medeshamstede [Peterborough] granted land to a tenant
named Wulfrud in return for an annual payment of thirty shillings plus
'a horse, fifteen mittan of clear ale, five mittan of Welsh ale and fifteen
sesters of mild ale'. The powerful King Offa, builder of the famous dyke
that marked the boundary between Wales and England, was not against
Welsh ale crossing his self-imposed barrier. When he granted land at
Westbury and Stanbury to the church of Worcester he accepted payments that included 'two tunne full of clear ale and a cumbe [sixteen
quarts] of Welsh ale'. Some agreements specified that the Welsh ale
should be sweet. As the Celts were great producers of mead made from
honey it seems likely that honey was also used to both sweeten ale and
to encourage a second fermentation.

In The Curiosities of Ale and Beer, John Bickerdyke said: 'Welsh ales
were in Saxon times well known and highly esteemed. In the laws of
Hywel Dda [Howell the Good] two kinds of ale are mentioned —
Bragawd or Bragot, which was paid as tribute to the king by a free
township, and Cwrwf, which was more common and was paid by the
servile township in cases where the former kind ran short ... It may be
hence gathered that in early times the highly-flavoured Bragawd was
held in greater estimation than the Cwrwf [common ale].' In modern
Welsh, cwrwf is known as cwrw, the word for ale. The difference
between this common ale and bragawd or braggett is that the former
was brewed for quick consumption while the later was stored for some
time, acquired a lactic character and was flavoured with herbs and
spices.

In 1994 Iain Turnbull, who studied brewing at Heriot-Watt University in Edinburgh and has worked for Courage and Brain's of Cardiff,
launched a scheme to brew braggett on a commercial scale in a replica
of a medieval brewery based in a Welsh manor house at Llancaiach
Fawr. His research shows that while common Welsh ale was produced
by a single fermentation, braggett was 'staled' and then refermented
with honey and spices. In all braggett would have three fermentations

— in the brewery, in wooden casks as a result of attack by wild yeasts, and then by the addition of honey. In order to achieve authenticity, Iain Turnbull used both a standard ale yeast and Belgian lambic yeasts (Brettanomyces Bruxellensis and Dekkera Bruxellensis) obtained from the National Collection of Yeast Cultures in Norwich. His recipe was complex. The palest barley malt used was amber, with wheat malt, black malt, roasted barley, crystal, chocolate, oatmeal, and peated malt. The original gravity of the wort was 1064 degrees. This would rise to 1080 degrees when honey was added, along with ginger, cloves, nutmeg and other spices.

The history of modern brewing in Wales is one of conflict between brewers and the needs of drinkers on one hand, and the powerful temperance influence of the Nonconformist church. The 'chapel' was an ever-present force in the lives of Welsh people. Drinkers were not allowed to enter the chapel on the Sabbath. From the 1830s the church had successfully encouraged — or threatened with hell-fire — thousands of drinkers to 'sign the pledge' and give up alcohol. Many areas of Wales were 'dry' on Sundays when the church demanded that pubs

BELOW: *When Wales had pits, miners - seen here in Cwmbach - drank large amounts of low-strength beer.* (Photo courtesy Brian Glover)

167

should shut. As a result brewers felt restrained to concentrate on low gravity ales as though this might spare them from the wrath of the church. In 1892, Frederick Soames of the Nag's Head Brewery in Wrexham told Alfred Barnard, author of Noted Breweries of Great Britain and Ireland, that he was determined to brew a light beer as opposed to the common heavy ale as such an ale would 'assist the cause of real temperance'. When the Wrexham Lager Brewery was founded in 1892, its owners claimed that their beer was 'almost non-intoxicating' and 'when more generally known and consumed, it will diminish intoxication and do more for the temperance cause than all the efforts of the total abstainers'. The brewers were understandably frightened. A Bill in Parliament in 1891 sought to impose total prohibition on Wales and only failed at the final vote.

The brewers kept their heads down. They concentrated on low gravity ales and this did not entirely displease miners and other industrial workers who needed large amounts of weak beer. The two most popular types of beer were PAs [pale ales] and XX dark milds, both around three per cent alcohol. As late as 1960 the Fernvale Brewery in the Rhondda brewed just one draught beer, SPA with a gravity of 1031 degrees. The Rhymney Brewery, closed by Whitbread in the late 1970s, brewed two draught beers, Golden Hopped Ale (1036) and Pale Mild Ale (1030). PMA was easily the biggest seller of the two, averaging 1,750 barrels a week compared to 250 for GHB. Strong bottled ales were a misnomer. Hancock's of Cardiff made a Strong Ale with a gravity of 1030. Today the two biggest-selling ales in Wales, both keg beers, are Welsh Brewers' Allbright (1033) and Whitbread's 1032 Welsh Bitter.

But times—and ales—are changing. The influence of the church has waned and so has heavy industry. Characterful beers are now in demand though one of the finest ales brewed in Wales, Brain's Red Dragon Dark (3.5 per cent alcohol) is a reminder of the past. Brewed from pale and chocolate malts and hopped with Fuggles and Goldings, it has a delicious aroma of chocolate, malt in the mouth and a light, quenching finish. Brain's 4.2 per cent SA is a superb, malty-fruity ale, known to devotees as 'Skull Attack' and evidence of the growth of quality products in the country. Two breweries in Llanelli, Buckley's and Felinfoel, both produce dark milds of 3.4 per cent, good quaffing bitters and stronger ales of considerable character. Felinfoel's five per cent Double Dragon is a rich and slightly vinous ale with a low twenty-five units of bitterness for the strength. With one eye still nervously on the church, Buckley has introduced a 4.5 per cent bitter called Reverend James Original, brewed with Maris Otter pale malt, torrefied wheat and invert sugar, and hopped with Fuggles and Goldings. It is an aromatic and spicy ale, fruity and with good hop presence.

The biggest brewery in the principality, Welsh Brewers of Cardiff, is a subsidiary of Bass. Its cask-conditioned ales are a tiny proportion of its production but Worthington Best Bitter (3.8 per cent) has been turned by the parent company into a major brand throughout Britain. With twenty-two units of bitterness it is a rather bland offering. Micros are beginning to offer greater choice. Bullmastiff in Cardiff has a four per

RIGHT: *New brews in Welsh Wales ... the Bragdy Dyffryn Clwyd Brewery in Denbigh.*

cent Ebony Dark packed with hops and chocolate, two hoppy bitters (3.5 and four per cent) and a powerful 6.5 per cent Son of a Bitch — named after a dog, it must be stressed — with a massive blast of Goldings hops, ripe fruit and sweet malt. North Wales, for long dominated by the Wrexham Lager Brewery, now owned by Carlsberg-Tetley, has Plassey Brewery's five per cent Cwrw Tudno (the ale of St Tudno, the patron saint of Llandudno), spicy and hoppy, a vinous, six per cent Dragon's Breath and a hoppy four per cent Bitter. In Denbigh, where Welsh speaking still dominates, the Bragdy Dyffryn Clwyd (literally the Denbigh Brewery in Clwyd) produces a 3.6 per cent Cwrw Comfort (Comfort Ale) and 4.2 per cent Cwrw Castell named in honour of Denbigh's thirteenth-century castle. Owner Ioan Evans brews both beers in Denbigh's old Butter Market from Halcyon pale malt, crystal and chocolate with Challenger hops. They are highly distinctive, hoppy and fruity. Castell in particular has a tempting aroma of orange and pear drops fruitiness. The Snowdonia Brewery has a delicately fruity Mel y Moelywyn (Honey of the Mountains) 3.7 per cent bitter, a fruity five per cent Snowdon and a hoppy-fruity bottle-conditioned Celt.

BELOW: *Welsh members of CAMRA at a beer festival in Denbigh.*

Chapter Three
Ireland

Founder of a dynasty ... Arthur Guinness.

It would be deeply insulting to the Irish to suggest that they live in a time warp. Yet their love of a beer style that originated in the eighteenth century gives credence to the view. Perhaps a more sensitive approach would be that a people who struggled for centuries for their independence understandably have a deep attachment to a beer they feel is their own. Stout is rooted in the Irish way of live to such an extent that Guinness stamps the Irish harp, the national insignia, on its products. While porter and stout are enjoying a small renaissance in Britain and craft brewers are carefully concocting them in the United States, in Ireland stout is and was the dominant beer style. It has even seen off the challenge of lager and won fresh support from a new generation of drinkers in the 1990s.

Whisper it quietly in the bars of Dublin and Cork, but stout was an English invention. But the Irish took it to their hearts, refashioned it and branded it so indelibly and inextricably with their nationhood that it is now thought of as their enduring contribution to the world of beer.

And Irish stout is different. To be precise, *dry* Irish stout is a beer style in its own right. Others may try to copy it or emulate it but few succeed. Before porter and stout, the Irish brewed in the Celtic tradition, producing sweet, dark, heavy and unhopped ale. Ale has been brewed in Ireland for some 5,000 years and St Patrick is thought to have employed his own brewer. As in European countries, monasteries dominated brewing for centuries. The hop seemed to make an even later appearance in Ireland than in Britain and when Arthur Guinness began work as a brewer in the middle of the eighteenth century he made an unhopped ale. Hops are difficult to grow in Ireland's damp climate — a few are grown in Kilkenny — and they were expensive to import as the English rulers of the country placed every possible tariff and barrier in the way of the development of an indigenous Irish brewing industry, to such an extent that it was cheaper to buy imported English ale than home-brewed Irish. English ale poured without let or hindrance into Ireland and from the 1730s an increasing proportion of it was made up of London porter and stout. The struggling Irish brewers who, like the Scots, enjoyed a poor reputation for their ale, decided to brew porter to survive.

The records are vague but it is thought that Richard Guinness, father

of Arthur, brewed ale in County Kildare. Richard was born in the 1690s and was the land agent for the rector of Celbridge. He brewed ale for the rector's family. The benevolent rector left £100 in his will to Arthur Guinness who bought a brewery in Leixlip in 1756. By 1759 he was in Dublin where he took a 9,000 year lease on a disused brewery in St James's Gate at an annual rent of £45. He agreed to such a long lease as the water on the site came free. Guinness was outraged when the city council later forced him to pay £10 a year for water. The brewery had been on the market for ten years and was in a bad state of disrepair. 'The underback is quite decayed,' Guinness complained and noted that there were only the remains of the coppers. As a safeguard, he also bought an adjacent flour mills to provide him with raw material and as a second business in case he failed as a brewer. By 1787 Guinness was brewing porter as well as ale and in 1799 he took the momentous decision to brew only porter. It is not certain that Guinness went to London to study porter brewing but he did employ a London brewer who had moved to Dublin to offer his porter skills to the highest bidder. Guinness's business expanded rapidly. He joined the establishment, becoming both the appointed brewer for Dublin Castle, the seat of colonial power, and Master of the Brewers' Guild. He lobbied successfully to have taxes on beer lowered to combat the evils of gin drinking. While other Irish brewers remained small, satisfied to supply their local communities, Guinness used first the canals and later the railway to dominate the island. Rail track was laid from the brewery to link up with the public

ABOVE: *Barges being loaded with Guinness stout by the River Liffey in Dublin.*

RIGHT: *Guinness was famous in Dicken's time even though the name was mis-spelt. The company says half the world can't spell the name, the other half can't pronounce it. A sketch by Phiz from The Pickwick Papers.*

system. When Arthur Guinness died in 1803 he was worth £10,000. His company concentrated on two strengths of porter, marked X and XX. The XX was renamed Extra Porter Stout in the 1820s while an export version was known as Foreign Extra Porter Stout. Eventually the word porter was dropped from the titles, though Guinness continued to brew single X until the 1970s, mainly for the Belfast market.

The power of the Guinness family can be gauged by the fact that Arthur's son, also called Arthur, became Governor of the Bank of Ireland. More important for the history of brewing, it was Arthur II who laid the foundations for the distinctive style of Irish stout. At the time brewers paid duty on malt, not on the alcoholic strength of beer. Arthur Guinness II, eager to cut costs and to avoid paying any unnecessary taxes to the English, decided to use some unmalted and untaxed roasted barley with his malt. The acrid flavour of the charred barley added bitterness and an unmistakably dry character to the beer that marked it out from its English rivals. Roasted barley may also have allowed Guinness to use fewer expensive imported hops for domestic beer. It was Arthur II who developed the recipe for Foreign Export Porter Stout. In common with the English brewers of India Pale Ale, he doubled the hop rate of the stout to enable it to withstand long sea journeys to the colonies. By the 1860s, Guinness porter and stout, no doubt to the chagrin of English brewers, were the most popular beers of their type in Britain. Prime Minister Benjamin Disraeli frequently dined, after a late-night session of parliament, on chops and Guinness while Guinness and oysters became part of the staple diet of London's Cockneys. The Irish beer was commemorated in illustrations in the novels of Charles Dickens, though it was misspelt as 'Guiness'. The company says ruefully that it has a name one half of the world cannot spell and the other half cannot pronounce.

Benjamin Guinness, the first member of the brewing dynasty to become a millionaire, expanded the business further. The appalling famine of the 1840s forced a third of the Irish population to emigrate, mainly to North America. By 1858 Benjamin Guinness had an agent in New York and he also discovered a substantial market for stout in Belgium, a market that has never gone away. By the end of the century Guinness was the biggest brewery in Europe. By the end of World War One it was the biggest brewery in the world, a remarkable achievement for a company based in a country with a population of five million. Its fortunes had been boosted when the British government forced brewers to cut back on the use of highly roasted grain to save energy during the war. With Home Rule fever mounting in Ireland, the government did not dare impose such restrictions on Irish brewers. Porter and stout went into sharp decline in Britain, leaving Ireland as the sole defender of the brewing faith.

ABOVE: *The Real McCoy ... Guinness Foreign Extra Stout, a blend of young and old beers, recalls the early days of Porter.*

In spite of the massive growth of lager in the twentieth century, Guinness remains one of the world's biggest brewing groups. Since the 1930s it has had a separate brewery at Park Royal in London to supply the British market. Its success in Britain was aided by the clever advertising designed by the S H Benson agency, one of whose copywriters was the crime novelist Dorothy L Sayers, creator of the upper-class sleuth, Lord Peter Wimsey. Benson's used the slogans 'Guinness is Good for You' and 'Guinness Gives you Strength' to enormous advantage. Posters showing men carrying giants girders and other challenging burdens gave the stout great credibility. Invalids and nursing mothers were advised by doctors to drink a glass every day. Any suggestion that beer might be beneficial is banned in Britain today but the goodness of Guinness is still extolled in Africa, where the stout is considered to be an aphrodisiac. In the United States, where Guinness had to rebuild its market after Prohibition, it was forced to adapt its advertising slogan to 'My Goodness, My Guinness'. In 1947 Guinness built a brewery on Long Island but closed it in 1954. Irish-Americans, who claim, with more romance than logic, to total forty million, preferred to get their dark stuff from the Emerald Isle. The benefits of drinking Guinness were exalted by the Irish writer Flann O'Brien in his dissertation on A Pint of Plain in *At Swim-Two-Birds* (Plain was the popular name for single X Guinness or Porter):

> When your health is bad and your heart feels strange,
> And your face is pale and wan,
> When doctors say that you need a change,
> A PINT OF PLAIN IS YOUR ONLY MAN.

There are more than nineteen versions of Guinness stout brewed world-wide today — but, sadly, no Plain — and the remarkable Foreign Extra Stout is sold in fifty-five countries and brewed under licence in

forty-four. Ten million pints of Guinness in all its forms are drunk everyday throughout the world. Foreign Extra Stout, FES for short, is a palpable link with the early days of porter brewing. Tucked away in the vast modern, stainless steel Dublin brewery, which produces two and a half million pints a day, are two old oak vats. Stout is stored in the vats for one to three months where it picks up lactic flavours from the action of wild Brettanomyces yeasts. This is stale beer in the historic meaning of the word. It is blended with young stout and the bottles are then stored for a further month before they are released for sale. FES is made from pale malt, twenty-five per cent flaked barley and ten per cent roasted barley. Hops are a blend of several varieties, including Galena, Nugget and Target. The finished beer is 7.5 per cent alcohol, with bitterness units in the sixties. The complex stout has a toasty, roasty, winey and woody aroma, a full bitter-sweet palate with great hop character, and a finish that becomes dry and bitter with hints of sour fruit. There are further hints of liquorice, and dark and mysterious fruits, including banana. On the nose there is the musty aroma that brewers call 'horse blanket' from the action of wild yeasts.

In African countries where FES is brewed under licence the Dublin brewery sends what it calls a 'secret ingredient' in the form of either powder or syrup. The local breweries use sorghum and maize to make a pale beer as barley is not available. The pale beer is then blended with the Dublin concoction which I believe to be hopped wort that has been boiled and evaporated. I tasted a sample of FES brewed on Mauritius. It was six months old, had no lactic notes, but was rich, rounded and fruity, bitter-sweet in the mouth and had a surprisingly delicate, bitter finish.

All the Dublin stouts are brewed with water from the Wicklow Mountains and hardened with gypsum. Arthur Guinness's original multi-strain of yeast survives but this has been cultured down to just one, flocculant strain. It works at a high temperature of 25° C/77° F and

BELOW: *Dublin powerhouse, the modern Guinness plant.*

fermentation lasts for just two days. It stays in solution, neither rising to the top nor sinking to bottom of the vessels. It is not skimmed but is removed by centrifuge. Stout destined to become the classic, bottle-conditioned Guinness Original is blended with some wort — the Germans call this kräusening — and a second fermentation takes place in the bottle. This sumptuous beer, 4.1 per cent alcohol, forty-three to forty-seven units of bitterness, intensely dry, bitter and hoppy with ripe, dark fruit, is now only available in the Irish Republic. There was much anguish among stout connoisseurs when Guinness withdrew it from the British market.

The Irish draught, also 4.1 per cent and the same bitterness units, is less assertive today as the company seeks to attract younger drinkers weaned on lager. It has a gentle malt aroma, dark fruit in the mouth and a light, dry finish with some delicate hop. The Export Draught for Europe (five per cent, forty-five to fifty-three units of bitterness) has a pronounced hop aroma with dark and bitter malt in the mouth and a big dry finish. When sold in Germany, unmalted roasted barley is replaced by dark malted barley to meet the requirements of the Reinheitsgebot purity law. Bottled stout sold in North America is 5.4 per cent, with forty-five to fifty-three units of bitterness. There is dark fruit on the nose and the palate and a good hoppy finish. It is more heavily carbonated than other Dublin-brewed stouts. Dublin still produces stout for the Belgian market. The eight per cent beer, with forty-five to fifty-five bitterness units, has massive dark fruit on the nose, great hop attack, burnt raisins in the mouth and a big, bitter-sweet finish packed with dark fruit and hops.

There is no cask-conditioned stout in the Irish Republic. It disappeared in the 1960s when Guinness moved from cask to a filtered beer served by a mix of carbon dioxide and nitrogen gases. Such is the daunting power of Guinness in the republic that its two smaller competitors, Beamish and Murphy, followed suit. Stout now accounts for fifty-five per cent of beer sales in the country. Ale takes nineteen per cent, with the rest lager. Guinness owns the major lager producer, Harp, and fought a battle with itself to wrest market share back from lager in the 1980s. To attract young drinkers, the serving temperature of draught Guinness has been dropped to 9° C/48° F. There is little chance of cask stout being introduced while Guinness and rival brews are served at that sort of chilly temperature.

The old Guinness hop store off St James's Gate has been turned into a museum. It is open daily and has a replica of an ancient brewhouse as well as a small theatre where the story of the company is told.

Cork is the home of the other two brewers of Irish stout and is also the centre of the finest malting barley region, with limestone soil. Beamish and Crawford claims to be the oldest brewer of porter and stout in Ireland and was certainly producing porter by 1792. Messrs Beamish and Crawford, of Scottish Protestant descent from the north of Ireland, came south to export butter and beef and bought an old ale brewery near

the River Lee. The half-timbered, Tudor-style façade, built in the 1920s, leads into a reception area where the plates from an old mash tun are built into the floor. The brewhouse is a modern and functional Steinecker plant that can brew lager as well as stout. Beamish made porter until the 1960s but had stopped using the name. In common with Guinness it branded its beers with Xs to denote strength. In 1962 the company was bought by Carling O'Keefe of Canada which in turn was bought by the Foster's Lager group of Australia. This has given Beamish's main brand entrée into Britain through Foster's Courage subsidiary. It has had a turbulent if brief history in the United States where the giant Jim Beam whiskey group has attempted to stop its sale on the mystifying grounds that the names Beam and Beamish would cause consumer confusion. By 1994 it seemed that the dispute would be settled in Beamish's favour.

Beamish Stout (4.3 per cent alcohol, thirty-eight to forty-four units of bitterness) is the most assertive of the modern Irish draughts. It is made from pale and dark malts, malted wheat, roast barley and wheat syrup and hopped with Irish Northdown, German Hallertau Perle and Styrian Goldings. The aroma is hoppy and chocolatey, grainy and fruity in the mouth with a deep, bitter-sweet finish underscored by generous hop bitterness.

Murphy's address is the Lady's Well Brewery on the north side of Cork. The well is a religious shrine to which pilgrims still flock and once supplied water for the brewery, though the town's supply is now used. The brothers James, William, Jerome and Frances, as staunchly Catholic

ABOVE: *The Counting House ... entrance to Beamish's handsome Cork brewery.*

as Beamish and Crawford were Protestant, built the brewery on the site of an orphans' hospital in 1856. The Murphys brewed porter but, in common with Beamish and Guinness, eventually concentrated on stout alone. In the mid-1980s the brewery was still traditional, including a coal-fired copper. But the brewhouse is now modern and made of stainless steel. Murphy's was bought by Heineken and the brewery is multi-functional, able to make lager as well as stout. The main stout, 4.3 per cent alcohol, thirty-five to thirty-six units of bitterness, is brewed from pale and chocolate malts and roasted barley, with all Target hops. It is a quenching, lightly fruity and roasty stout, less demanding than its competitors' brews. Outside Ireland it is strongly branded as Murphy's *Irish* Stout. It has enjoyed considerable success in the United States. In Britain it is marketed by Whitbread, though most of the stout for sale is brewed by Whitbread's Welsh brewery in Magor. An Irish stout brewed in Wales? At least it keeps the Celtic connection.

There are three ale breweries in the republic, all owned by the omnipotent Guinness. The brewing giant bought Cherry's of Waterford, Macardle of Dundalk and Smithwick's of Kilkenny in the 1960s as a response to the British Watney group, which had launched its Red Barrel keg bitter in Ireland. Guinness need not have worried because Red Barrel flopped and Watney's retreated back to Britain. Perhaps Watney's thought a beer with red in the title would appeal to drinkers of Irish ales, which are traditionally of a reddish hue.

John Smithwick founded his brewery in Kilkenny in 1710. This handsome city, dominated by its castle and the River Nore, was once the seat of the Irish parliament. Smithwick built his brewery, the oldest in Ireland, amid the ruins of St Francis Abbey where Franciscan monks had brewed since the fourteenth century. The tower and nave of the thirteenth-century abbey still stand, surrounded by the modern brewery. The abbey is used on brewery labels. Smithwick's brewed porter and stout as well as ale until 1918 but, somewhat perversely given Ireland's modern brewing preferences, then concentrated on ale. The modern Steinecker plant produces one million hectolitres a year. Pale malt is augmented by a small proportion of roasted barley, a Celtic tradition, and twenty per cent high maltose syrup. Challenger, Golding, Northdown and Target hops are used in three additions in the copper. Fermentation takes place in conicals. The brewing liquor is Burtonised with gypsum. All the ales are made by high-gravity brewing and reduced with liquor to the required strength. The main brand and second only to Guinness Draught in popularity, is Smithwick's Draught, 3.5 per cent alcohol with twenty-two units of bitterness. It has a creamy, malty, estery aroma with a hint of dark fruit in the mouth and bitter-sweet finish. An export version is four per cent while a special, all-malt brew for Germany is 5.2 per cent and has an exceptionally fruity nose and palate. A five per cent Barley Wine, with a ripe, Dundee-cake fruitiness and good hop bitterness, is brewed by Macardle's, but using Smithwick's yeast. All draught Irish ales are filtered and pasteurised and

served cold at 7° C/44° F. My tour of Kilkenny bars was slow as I had to wait for my pint to warm up to a drinkable temperature at each stop.

An 'Irish ale' that has a considerable following in other countries is no longer brewed in Ireland. George Killian Lett's Enniscorthy brewery closed in 1956 but Lett licensed the name to Pelforth in France and later Coors in the United States and more recently Heineken in the Netherlands.

In Northern Ireland Bass has a brewery in Belfast that produces only processed beers. The only cask-conditioned ales in the whole island come from the Hilden micro in Lisburn, which brews a 3.8 per cent Hilden Ale, malty and fruity, a 3.9 per cent Porter and a four per cent aromatic and hoppy Special. The Kitchen Bar in Belfast city centre is planning to brew on the premises.

BELOW: *The last Guinness barge being towed down the Liffey to retirement. In spite of the myth, Guinness is not made from the Liffey but from water flowing out of the Wicklow hills.*

Chapter Four
Belgium and the Netherlands

The ale heritage of the Low Countries laid low for years. Pilsner-style lagers still dominate Belgium and the Netherlands, with their intertwined geographies, histories and shared language in the Flemish areas. But ale has emerged from lager's shadow. In so doing it has revealed in Belgium in particular a wealth of ales, an astonishing profusion of styles. With spontaneously-fermented lambic and gueuze beers, Belgium has one of the oldest and certainly most idiosyncratic styles. The boundaries between wine and beer are blurred by the use of fruit in both lambic and conventionally-fermented ales. Wheat or 'white' beers are another bond with ancient methods, using spices as bittering agents. The sour red beers of Flanders have links with the staled porters and stouts of the British Isles while pale ales have great depth of flavour and an explosion of hop bitterness. Best known to the outside world, Belgium and the Netherlands are home to the only working breweries owned and run by Trappist monks. The ale revival in the Netherlands is on a much smaller scale but the enormous interest shown in Belgian ales and the growth of home-grown micros is encouraging even giants like Heineken to rediscover its roots.

LAMBIC AND GUEUZE

The staunchest ale lovers have been known to blanche at the thought of drinking beers made from wild yeasts, especially when fruit is added to them. I have seen even hardened CAMRA members refuse a second glass of lambic in the Cantillon brewery in Brussels. These beers may not be to everyone's taste — and many Belgians prefer them with the addition of sweetener — but they are a potent symbol of brewing's past. Their vinous and cidery palate underscore the absurdity of building false barriers between beer and wine. Their long ageing process helps destroy the myth that beer is a rough and ready drink. And even though the act of turning sweet wort into alcohol is left to nature, the production of lambic demands the highest skill.

Lambic beers have been made for four hundred years or more. There is only a handful of producers left, grouped in the valley of the River Senne (Zenne in Flemish). The river runs through Brussels and two lambic brewers, the large Belle-Vue and the small Cantillon, are based there. This is Brueghel country and the stolid peasant folk carousing

181

through the paintings of the three Brueghels, Pieter the Elder in particular, were drinking lambic, not wine, from their earthenware pots. The term lambic is lost in history and has as many interpretations as the origins of porter. One theory is that the name is taken from the town of Lembeek, which has had a guild of brewers since the fifteenth century and an annual pilgrimage to the shrine of the patron saint of lambic brewers, Saint Veronus. One of the principal lambic producers, Frank Boon, is based in the town. Another theory is that the conquering Spanish in the sixteenth and seventeenth centuries called the farmhouse breweries and gin distilleries in the Senne Valley *alembics*. One thing is certain: lambic is the oldest beer style still made commercially. It is an agricultural beer that was once the only type drunk in Brussels and its environs. It declined in step with rural life and the rise of heavy industry. Lambic's cause was not helped when a type of prohibition in Belgium at the turn of the century stopped gin and other spirits being sold in cafés and bars. Drinkers turned to strong ales rather than the lower gravity lambics. The rapid spread of Pilsner beers did little to help lambic either. Lambic and gueuze have been protected by Belgian law since 1965, by a European Union ordinance of 1992 and an appellation contrôlée from the European Beer Consumers Union. But such backing will only keep them in production if they are supported by consumers.

The method of production is still slow, ruminative and bucolic, even when carried out in Anderlecht, a district of Brussels likened to Liverpool because of the tough environment and the local passion for soccer. Brewing does not take place in the summer months. In centuries past, farmers would not have brewed in summer as they needed to devote all their energies to the harvest. And even spontaneous fermentation is too

ABOVE: *Gambolling with gueuze ... the peasants in the paintings of Breughel the Elder were drinking lambic not wine.*

BELOW: *Checking the condition of lambic in the Belle-Vue brewery.*

RIGHT: *Belgian still life - lambic gueuze, the `wine' of the country.*
(Photo: Mike Benner)

unpredictable and uncontrollable in hot weather. The biggest brewer of lambic beers (350,000 hectolitres a year), including kriek (cherry) and framboise (raspberry) fruit versions, is Vandenstock's Belle-Vue brewery. It was family-owned until 1991 when it was bought by the Belgian giant Interbrew, best known for its mass market lagers, Stella Artois and Jupiler. The size of the company and its owners gave it a poor reputation among lambic connoisseurs, especially as Belle-Vue (which also brews under the De Neve label) tended to produce extremely sweet and sticky versions of the style. The brewery claimed it was merely meeting consumer demand and it does blend beers to meet the requirements of individual bars. But its reputation improved overnight in 1993 when it launched a Sélection Lambic, a bottle-conditioned blended gueuze that was quickly awarded an appellation from EBCU. It is 5.2 per cent alcohol, has a hazy copper colour, an appealing aroma of roast chestnuts, is mouth-puckeringly sour with some spiciness and has a dry, fruity finish. I had visited Belle-Vue twice and had never seen brewing taking place, though I marvelled at the many rooms packed with oak casks full of maturing beer. The absence of brewing tended to fuel the belief that Belle-Vue was merely a repository for other brewers' lambics. But in the winter of 1993 the doors of the brewhouse were finally opened and I was able to see production in full flood.

Lambic is a type of wheat beer. In fact, its protective laws and ordinances state that at least thirty per cent wheat must be used in the mash. The wheat is unmalted. The reasons are probably empirical: farmer-brewers had limited time at their disposal and knew that sufficient extract and enzymes could be provided by barley malt. It may have been a cost-cutting exercise if barley malt was bought in from specialist maltsters. Most important, the use of wheat gave a tart, quenching and spicy character to the beer. At Belle-Vue the grains are mashed in two separate vessels and then clarified in a lauter tun. The barley malt is extremely pale like a Pils variety. As a result of the presence of wheat, the wort run-off is turbid and milky-white. A lambic will normally have an original gravity of around 1050 degrees and a finished alcohol by volume of 4.5 to five per cent. This can rise to six when fruit is added during maturation. The copper boil is a long one, often lasting for three hours. The wort is heavily hopped, using Belgian, German or English varieties. But the hops are four years old, have lost much of their aromatic qualities and have a pronounced cheesy smell. They are used solely for their preservative qualities. After the boil, the hopped wort goes to the attic of the brewery. This is common to all lambic producers, for it is under the roof that alcohol is produced. The wort is pumped into a shallow open fermenter known as a cool ship, made either of copper or stainless steel. The room fills with steam as the wort runs into the ship and begins to cool. The louvres on the window are left open and during the night wild yeasts come in and attack the sugars in the wort once the temperature has fallen below 18° C/66° F.

In conventional brewing, every effort is made to keep wild yeast at bay and to allow fermentation to be carried out by carefully cultured top or bottom yeasts. In the Senne Valley, brewers are like Jiminy Cricket: they give a little whistle and welcome in a huge range of wild yeasts. Research at the University of Louvain (Leuven in Flemish) has identified two main types of Brettanomyces yeast, bruxellensis and lambicus. But when all the yeast strains in the atmosphere, the cellars and inside the casks are added together they number as many as thirty-five. When the beer reaches the maturation halls and is stored in oak casks, it is attacked by both microflora in the wood and in the atmosphere. The casks are left open to the atmosphere. To the horror of many visitors, cobwebs abound, often linking casks. The brewers are reluctant to disturb the natural environment and also welcome the presence of spiders, which kill fruit flies. The wild organisms create a flor on top of

the maturing beer similar to the flor in sherry casks that prevents oxidation. Belle-Vue has 15,000 casks, all of them bought from the Portuguese port industry and ranged on five floors. They come in different sizes, 250 litre tuns, 650 litre pipes and thirty hectolitre foudres. They are made mainly of oak, with a few from chestnut. The oldest cask is 250 years, the average age is fifty.

The wort is left in the cool ship for ten hours by which time fermentation is well under way. The beer will stay in cask for several years. Some of the Belle-Vue lambics are more than six years old. I walked down the dimly-lit, cool avenues between the casks — each chalkmarked to indicate the year and month it was filled — every so often tasting a small glass tapped for me. A lambic that was just a month old had a yeasty aroma and a bready taste. A year-old beer was sour on the nose, sweet and sour in the mouth and with a cheesy finish from the hops. At eighteen months the beer had taken on a delightful sherry colour, a musty Brettanomyces nose, a vinous palate and a dry finish with still a hint of cheesy hops. At six and a half years the beer was much paler, had a sour, winey aroma, a sharp, tangy palate with a pronounced sherry character and a sour, lactic finish. The cheesiness had disappeared. It takes some time for Brettanomyces yeasts to dominate the other wild strains.

A straight lambic, tart, cidery and served flat, is usually on draught. The most popular form of the beer is gueuze (also spelt geuze), a blend of young and old lambics in bottle. The young lambic causes a fresh fermentation in the bottle. The result is a spritzy, foaming beer served from a bottle that has been corked with a wire cage like Champagne. The blending requires enormous skill. The blender must decide how much young lambic to marry with the old: usually sixty per cent young, but the beer will have more character if as much old lambic as possible is used. The bottles will be stored on their sides in cellars for between six and eighteen months. Gueuze beers tend to be around 5.5 per cent alcohol and are dry, tart and wonderfully refreshing. And the name? Again, no one is certain but it is possible that it is a nickname derived from geyser, as the beer tends to rush and foam when released from the bottle. The Bruxellois certainly pronounce it with great force: gur-zer.

The most exotic versions of lambic are those in which a further fermentation is caused by the addition of fruit. The two basic fruits used are cherry and raspberry. The sudden popularity of fruit beers has created some commercial beers that use peach, banana and even peppermint but they are not true to the style or are even serious beers. The use of cherries and raspberries is similar to the use of juniper at a time when hops were not part of brewing. The fruit increased fermentability and added a tartness to the finished beer that blended well with the malt. And fruit seems to fuse especially well with beers in which wheat, with its fruity, apple-like flavours, is used. Small, hard cherries grow in abundance in the Brussels area. The preferred variety is the Schaarbeek though the Gorsem is also used. The cherries are picked late so that the

LEFT: *Cherry ripe ... specially-grown fruit used for Kriek beer.*

fermentable sugars are well concentrated. As soon as they are harvested they are added to casks — usually at the rate of one kilo of cherries to five litres of beer — with the addition of some young lambic. The sugars in the fruit and the young beer create a new fermentation. The tannins on the skins add to the dryness of the finished beer while the pips impart further dryness and an almond-like character. A bunch of twigs is placed in the bung hole of each cask to stop the cherries blocking it. Some producers of fruit lambics use syrups rather than the whole fruit. This is frowned on by purists. At Belle-Vue they use whole cherries in kriek but raspberry juice in framboise: they say that whole raspberries disintegrate and block filters. A young kriek (the Flemish word for cherry: the French word is not used) or a framboise/frambozen (raspberry) beer may be bottled and released in the autumn following the harvest: Belle-Vue has a 'Kriek Nouveau'. Brewers will allow other casks to mature for much longer and will blend and top up casks in order to marry young and old beers.

Many people approach fruit beers with a fear of trying them. Once they get over the initial shock they are often hooked for life, marvelling at the tempting pink colour in the glass, the heady aroma of sour fruit, the quenching palate and dry fruity finish. At Belle-Vue I tasted a young kriek just a few months old with a light cherry aroma, bitter fruit in the mouth and a pronounced cherry finish. A year-old kriek made with the classic Schaarbeek fruit had an appealing ruby-red colour, a sour palate and finish packed with desperately dry fruit. An eighteen month-old kriek had a superb dry, earthy aroma reminiscent of the Gamay grape used in Beaujolais, with bitter cherries in the mouth and a dry and winey finish. A framboise of nine months had a delightful perfumy aroma, with bitter-sweet fruit in the mouth and a petillant finish with sweet fruit.

The craft brewery and museum of Cantillon is tiny compared to Belle-Vue but is respected as the greatest exponent of lambic. It has regular opening days for visitors (56 rue Gheude, Anderlecht, 1070 Brussels: phone 02 521 4928). Even the name of the street seems imbued with the thought of gueuze. Because of a surfeit of Hoegaarden the previous night, I failed to wake to the dawn chorus on my allotted visit and found the cramped reception area packed with visitors sampling lambic and kriek long before the sun was over the yard-arm. Cantillon is owned by Jean-Pierre Van Roy, a descendant of the Cantillon family that brewed in Lembeek from the eighteenth century and moved to Brussels in 1900. Van Roy is a fanatic — in the best sense of the word — about the lambic style and heritage and tends to be dismissive of other brewers' efforts. He brews with a cast-iron mash tun, copper brew kettle and a copper cool ship under the eaves. Several hundred giants casks hold the gently slumbering and fermenting beer. Van Roy, unusually, produces on an occasional basis a bottled lambic that has been kept in the wood for three years. His five per cent Brabantiae is a blend of three different ages of lambic and is shockingly dry, the kriek (five per cent) is dry, aromatic and fruity while perhaps the classic Cantillon, Rosé de Gambrinus, a blend of cherry and raspberry, has a delicate fruity, aromatic quality. Van Roy is pushing back the frontiers between wine and beer still further with a Gueuze Vigneronne, made from grapes and blended lambics. Cantillon also from time to time produces faro, a sweetened lambic that was much in vogue between the two world wars.

BROWN ALE

Cherries and raspberries are added to a classic brown ale from East Flanders, but the addition of fruit should not obscure the basic style. The Old Brown [Oud Bruin] ales of Oudenaarde, a waterside city steeped in Flemish culture and history, are highly complex beers that form the beery basis for the famous Flemish beef and onion stew, carbonade flamande. The major producer of brown ale in the region is Liefman's, which dates from 1679. The fame of the brewery was built with great flair and élan in the 1970s and eighties by Rose Blancquaert. She was the brewer's secretary and took over the running of the company when he died. Madame Rose, as she is known with affection and deference, has now retired to run a restaurant in Oudenaarde, De Mouterij, the Maltings. Brewing and general management is now in the hands of her equally energetic son, Olav, though the company was bought by the large Riva group in the early 1990s.

Oud Bruin is made from a blend of Pilsner malts, with Munich and Vienna darker malts and some roasted barley. Whitbread Goldings for bitterness are joined with Czech and German hops for aroma. The water is specially treated to be low in calcium and high in sodium bicarbonate, which must make the beer good for the digestion. Five per cent alcohol by volume, Oud Bruin is fermented in open vessels for seven days ('two Sabbaths') and then matured for four months. A stronger version of the beer, six per cent, is the result of blending the basic Oud Bruin with beer

LEFT: *In a brown study ... Liefman's Brewery in Oudenaarde where Oud Bruin classic brown beer is made.*

ABOVE: *Yeast running into a fermenter at Liefmans.*

that has been matured for six to eight months. The two beers are centrifuged, primed with sugar, re-seeded with yeast and stored for three months before leaving the brewery. The blend is known as Goudenband — Gold Riband. The multi-strain yeast came originally from the Rodenbach brewery, which may account for the hint of sourness in the beers, balanced by rich malts and dark, raisiny fruit. Goudenband will improve over the years and take on a rich sherry-like quality. Once a year, Liefman's adds cherries and raspberries to the stronger beer, which referments for up to two months. The kriek is 7.1 per cent by volume, with a tart fruitiness, the raspberry, 5.1, has a magnificent aroma and is sweet on the palate. All the Liefman's ales are sold in bottles that range in size to a Champagne magnum and are attractively wrapped in coloured tissue paper. Since the arrival of Riva, wort is produced at its main plant at Dentergem and then sent to Liefman's for fermentation and maturation.

Riva has bought another brewery producing a classic dark brown ale. Het Anker is in Mechelen (Malines in French) and brews a dry Bruynen and the complex, aromatic Gouden Carolus, a 7.8 per cent alcohol, bottle-conditioned ale that improves with age and has a rich chocolate and dark fruit character. After a long day of beer tasting in Belgium, I found a glass of Gouden Carolus a wonderfully soothing nightcap.

RED ALE
I approached my first-ever glass of Rodenbach in a restaurant in Ostend with extreme caution. I knew its reputation as the sour, red beer of West Flanders. Now, in bars and restaurants in several countries, I will call for a Rodenbach if it is available for I delight in its tart and refreshing character. The brewery is in the canalside town of Roeselare (Roulers in

RIGHT: *Rodenbach is the result of long maturation in these huge unlined oak tuns.*

French) and the beer is the result of long maturation in unlined oak tuns. Here is yet another link with the past, a beer that is deliberately allowed to stale from the action of wild yeasts and other micro-organisms. The Rodenbachs are German in origin from near Coblenz. Ferdinand Rodenbach was stationed in the Low Countries as a military surgeon when the region was under Austrian rule and he decided to settle there. The Rodenbachs threw themselves with great energy into all aspects of Belgian life, including the struggle for independence. In 1820 Alexander Rodenbach, who was blind, bought a small brewery in Roeselare. In the 1870s Eugene Rodenbach went to England to study brewing and his experience encouraged him to develop the stale, aged beer that is the hallmark of the company. There has been considerable speculation over which breweries Rodenbach visited. It has been suggested that he might have gone to Greene King in Bury St Edmunds, Suffolk, which is geographically close and where a soured Strong Suffolk Ale is brewed. Neither brewery has any records to support this. (I took some bottles of Strong Suffolk with me to Rodenbach for a comparative tasting. Rodenbach is considerably sourer, but Strong Suffolk is blended with a conventional ale and the 12 per cent 5X tasted 'straight' in the Suffolk brewery is far more tart.) Rodenbach brewery believes that Eugene went not to Suffolk but to the Tyneside area of North-east England. My research suggests that he probably visited the large brewery of John Barras, which was founded in Gateshead in 1770 and moved to Newcastle in 1860. Barras, later part of the Newcastle Breweries group, now Scottish and Newcastle, produced a renowned porter that was stored for a full twelve months in wooden tuns to 'ripen'. As the early porters were tawny or brown rather than black, I feel there is a strong possibility that the inspiration for Rodenbach's beer was English porter.

Rodenbach's St George's Brewery is a handsome one, its grounds dominated by an old malt kiln that is now a museum. Well water comes from underground springs beneath a lake on the other side of the road, where the brewer lives in some style in a chateau provided by the company. The beer is made from a blend of pale malts from both spring and winter varieties and a darker malt that gives a reddish hue. It is known as Vienna malt in mainland Europe and is similar to English crystal. Malts make up eighty per cent of the grist, the rest comes from corn grits. Brewers' Gold and Kent Goldings hops are used. They are aromatic hops, low in bitterness. Rodenbach uses them for their preservative quality. The brewery does not want too high a level of bitterness, which would not marry well with the tartness of the beer. A multi-strain top-fermenting yeast carries out primary fermentation over seven days, after which the beer has a second fermentation in metal tanks. The beer destined for the regular Rodenbach is ready to be bottled after six weeks but beer for ageing is stored in ceiling-high oak tuns for at least eighteen months and often as long as two years. There are more than ten halls of giant, red-hooped tuns that stand on raised brick bases. The smallest holds 120 hectolitres, the biggest six hundred. The staves

RIGHT: *Plus ça change ...*
Rodenbach brewers and vats
before World War Two.

of each tun are numbered and a small army of coopers is kept busy repairing the vessels. The insides of the tuns are regularly scraped in order to keep a correct balance of tannins and caramels in the oak. During the long rest in wood, lactobacilli and acetobacters are busy adding a sour, lactic quality to the beer. Matured beer is blended with young to produce the regular beer, 4.6 by volume. It has a sour, winey aroma, is tart and quenching in the mouth with more sour fruit in the finish. Grand Cru, with between fourteen and eighteen units of bitterness, is 5.2 per cent alcohol, and is bottled straight from the tuns. It is bigger in all respects, oaky, woody, tannic, sour and fruity. Both beers have some sugar added to them to take the extreme edge off the sourness. To mark one hundred and fifty years of the brewery, a version of Grand Cru was made with a dash of cherry essence. This is known as Alexander Rodenbach. All the beers are flash pasteurised. They are undoubtedly world classics but many admirers of the style, myself included, would like the brewery to consider a version of Grand Cru that is bottle-conditioned without sweetening. The beers are not only superb with food but make a formidable contribution to cooking. I had a memorable meal in Roeselare at the restaurant Den Haselt (Zuidstraat 19, tel 225240) where every course was cooked with a version of Rodenbach.

WHITE BEER
The style of wheat beer known as 'white' in Belgium has become a cult drink. The name (bière blanche/witbier) comes from the pale, lemony colour of the beer and the dense white head created during serving. The classic of the style, Hoegaarden, is brewed in a small town of that name in the region of Brabant near the great brewing and university city of Leuven/Louvain. The rich soil is ideal for growing

LEFT: *Charge of the white brigade ... Hoegaarden Brewery that revived `white' beer in Belgium.*

barley, oats and wheat. Monks were brewing there from the fifteenth century and naturally turned to the grains from the surrounding fields for their raw ingredients. Herbs and spices were added to blend with the malts and give tartness to the flavour. When the region was part of the Netherlands, brewers started to use the spices and other exotic ingredients which the Dutch brought back from their travels. The wheat beers

ABOVE: *Forbidden Fruit - a bold libidinous beer like its label.*

of Brabant became famous for their use of coriander and Curaçao orange peel. But their fame was not enough to help them survive. The area around Hoegaarden had thirty white beer brewers in the nineteenth century but they had all disappeared by the 1950s. In the 1960s Pierre Celis decided to revive the style which he had known and loved. He moved into the site of one defunct brewery and brought in equipment from another. He called the brewery De Kluis, the Cloister, in honour of the monastery that had started the white beer tradition centuries before. The success of Hoegaarden prompted others to enter the market, notably Riva's Dentergems creamy, apple-fruity Witbier, the dry and spicy Blanche de Namur from du Bocq, De Gouden Boom's lemony Brugs Tarwebier/Blanche de Bruges in the beautiful canalside city, and an uncompromisingly tart and spicy beer from the Silly Brewery near Tournai called Titje.

Hoegaarden dominates the market, all the more so since Interbrew bought out Celis. (He has moved to the unlikely setting of Texas where he brews Celis White with considerable success.) The De Kluis brewery is now polished and modern and some drinkers feel the beer has lost some of its character since the arrival of Interbrew. This may be due to the phasing out of oats, which added a delectable creamy grain note. But the beer is still marvellously good. The grist is made up of fifty-fifty barley malt and unmalted wheat. Hops are East Kent Goldings for aroma and Czech Saaz for gentle bitterness. The bitterness units are around twenty: the brewer is not aiming for a big hop character. Coriander seeds and orange peel are added during the boil. Following fermentation, the beer is warm conditioned for up to a month and then primed and re-seeded with yeast before bottling. The draught comes from kegs, which I found alarming as the beer is going through a second fermentation and, unlike a vented cask, the carbon dioxide cannot escape. But I was assured there was no risk of exploding kegs as the second ferment produces only a small amount of extra gas and alcohol. The beer is 4.8 per cent by volume. It has an appealing spicy nose with clear evidence of the orange peel, it is tart and refreshing in the mouth with quenching citric fruit, and the finish is bitter-sweet and clean on the tongue. The brewery also produces a Grand Cru (8.7 per cent) which has a similar spicing but is made only from barley malt: it is hazy in the glass and has a lingering, complex, fruity palate. Forbidden Fruit (Le Fruit Défendu/De Verboden Vrucht) has achieved some notoriety as a result of a bottle label depicting Adam and Eve in their bare essentials. It is certainly a bold, libidinous beer, nine per cent, with a fine coriander spiciness balanced by rich fruit and chocolate. Julius, 8.7 per cent, is a strong pale ale while Benedict is an Abbey-style, 7.3 per cent, powerful and chocolatey ale.

TRAPPIST ALES

It is one of the most fascinating of all the great ale experiences, to hear th-e poignant plain song of monks at their devotions in the austere surrounding of their monasteries while you revel in the magnificence of their brews. Once monasteries were at the heart of brewing. But dissolution, political hounding and the doubtful attractions of the secular life have combined to reduce monastic brewing to an historic fragment. In Austria and Germany a few monasteries still brew but the torch is held aloft most proudly by the Trappists of Belgium and the Netherlands. The Trappists came from France. They were a strict order that had broken away from the Cistercians, who had in turn left the Benedictines on the grounds that the followers of St Benedict were guilty of theological backsliding. The Trappists founded an abbey at La Trappe in Normandy. The French Revolution and the Napoleonic period forced them to seek fresh pastures as their abbeys were sacked and the land confiscated. The monks headed north into the Low Countries and settled down afresh to live off the produce of the fields they tended. In France they had made liqueurs from wine. In a land where the grape could not grow, they brewed beer to offer to guests and pilgrims, to drink with their simple vegetarian meals and to sustain them during Lent. Today there are five monastic breweries left in Belgium and one in the Netherlands that still produce ales. The number of monks is declining alarmingly as fewer young people are attracted to monastic life. Principles have been relaxed. The Trappists are no longer quite so famously silent and they have entered the world of business with considerable flair and diligence, though they employ secular people to run their commercial affairs. When Sainsbury's, the giant British supermarket chain, approached several of the breweries in 1993 with a view to selling an 'own label' Trappist beer, one of the best-known Belgian producers sternly said it would need a special dispensation from the Pope if it were to contemplate such a move. Supermarket bosses are not used to having to wait for white smoke to appear from the Vatican before making commercial decisions. Fortunately for Sainsbury's, the Schaapskooi brewery in the Netherlands felt the Pontiff need not be troubled and agreed to supply the supermarket.

Brother Tarcissius, a young monk, showed me round the abbey and the brewery at Koningshoeven near Tilburg in Dutch Brabant. Koeningshoeven means the King's Gardens and the land was given as a gift to the monks by the monarch. The Schaapskoi (Sheepfold) brewery was set up in the 1880s to raise funds for the restoration of the abbey. Brother Tarcissius leaves his bed for his devotions at four-thirty every morning and then hurries to the brewhouse next door. Brewing now takes place in a modern, stainless steel plant complete with lauter tuns and is run by secular employees, though Brother Tarcissius looks after the brew on their days off. If Schaapskoi has a reputation as the most hard-nosed and commercial of the Trappist breweries, it may be a result of its struggle for independence. After World War Two, the brewery was bought by Stella Artois, which wanted to establish a bridgehead in the Netherlands. It produced an unlikely 'Trappist Pils' and installed a small lager plant. The lager was not a success and the brothers raised the

RIGHT: *Brother Antoine in the Rochefort brewery. Trappist ales were used as `liquid bread' when the monks were fasting.*
(photo: Paul Hoggart)

funds to buy the brewhouse back from Stella, the only known example of a monks' management buy-out. The three main beers, La Trappe Dubbel, Tripel and Quadrupel, are notably fruity and hoppy. The 6.5 per cent Dubbel is brewed from pale, Munich and other coloured malts and is hopped with Northern Brewer from the Hallertau region. It is tawny in colour with an orange Muscat aroma and palate, overlain by peppery hops. The eight per cent bronze Tripel bursts with Goldings hops and spicy fruit. The ten per cent Quadrupel is brewed every autumn as a vintage beer. It is reddish in hue and has a deceptively smooth palate with delicate fruit and a deep, spicy/fruity finish. The brewery is experimenting with a lower alcohol Single.

Chimay is the best-known and biggest by far of the Trappist breweries. Its beers can be found throughout the world and can have an odd effect on people. I once witnessed a group of British beer writers dancing down the main road in Ostend while singing 'I wish I could Chimay like my sister Kate' after a too-long liquid lunch. The Kate in question has no known connections with a nunnery. The Abbaye de Notre-Dame de Scourmont is near a tiny hamlet called Forges but takes the name of Chimay from a nearby small town in the Hainault region near the French border. The brothers are firmly in charge of brewing, though they do employ some secular help. I was delighted to meet Paul Arnott, a young Scot and a graduate of the Heriot Watt brewing university in Edinburgh, who is the quality control manager at Chimay. The monks began to brew in the 1860s and were the first to use the term Trappist ale and sell them commercially after World War Two. The head brewer at the time, Father Théodore, worked with the Belgian brewing scientist Jean De Clerk and they isolated a yeast strain that is responsible for the distinctive blackcurrant fruit character of the beers. Chimay's debt to Jean de Clerk is marked by his burial site in the grounds of the abbey. The local water is untreated and is soft and acidic. The brewers admit to using Hallertau hops but are otherwise disappointingly Trappist about the ingredients used. I believe, but cannot confirm, that they use an extremely pale, possibly Pils malt with caramalt for colour and flavour. Some American Yakima hops may be added to the Hallertau. All the beers are given a *dosage* of sugar for priming the bottles. The brewhouse was once highly traditional with copper kettles. The modern one is functional, with most vessels hidden behind tiled walls. Fermentation temperature is high and lasts for only a few days. The beers are known by the colour of their caps. The original is Chimay Red, also known as Première when bottled in a large Bordeaux-style bottle, seven per cent alcohol by volume. It has a fine copper colour and rich, fruity nose and palate with great hop bitterness. Chimay White is quite different and may have been introduced in 1968 to counter the success of the beer from the nearby Trappist brewery of Orval, though the brothers at Chimay deny this. It is more fully attenuated than the other Chimay beers, is an enticing pale, orange-peach colour and is notably dry and hoppy. Chimay Blue or Grande Réserve in large bottles is nine per cent alcohol and has an enormous depth of fruit, giving it a port wine or, according to the brewers, Zinfandel character. There is plenty of spice from hops and yeast. Each year's Blue is vintage-dated and will improve in bottle after two years and will stay in condition for five. All three beers will improve with laying down. The monks plead with drinkers not to

chill their sublime beers and ask that they should be served at room temperature. Chimay also makes some excellent cheeses, one of which has beer blended into it.

The Abbaye de Notre-Dame d'Orval is in the Belgian province of Luxembourg. Orval is a corruption of 'golden valley'. According to local legend, a princess from Tuscany lost her golden ring in a lake in the valley. She said that if it were restored to her she would build an abbey there. A trout broke the surface of the lake with the ring in its mouth and the image is used as the brewery's logo. In reality, the first abbey was founded in 1070 by Benedictines, was rebuilt by Cistercians, and was sacked in the seventeenth century. Its replacement met a similar fate during the French Revolution. The present abbey was constructed in the 1920s and 1930s. Unlike the other Trappists, Orval concentrates on just one beer, a remarkable orange coloured ale made from a blend of pale malts, including Beauce and Gatinais, and caramalt for colour. Candy sugar is added in the copper with German Hallertau and East Kent Goldings hops. The beer has forty units of bitterness and the hops give both a splendidly aromatic bouquet and great bitterness to the palate and finish. The brewing method is fascinating. After primary fermentation using a top yeast, the beer undergoes a secondary one with several strains of bottom cultures at 15° C/59° F, on a bed of dry Goldings hops. The second fermentation lasts for six to seven weeks. The beer is then bottled and the original top yeast is added to force a third fermentation. The beer should not be chilled. It has a complex aroma and palate of spices and tart fruit allied to earthy hops, with an extremely dry finish. The brothers also make bread and cheese which are on sale with their beer in a brewery shop.

Rochefort Trappist ales are brewed at the Abbaye de Notre-Dame de Saint-Rémy in rolling Ardennes country. The monks produce three beers, using Pils and Munich malts and dark candy sugar in the copper, along with Hallertau and Styrian Goldings hops. Rochefort Six — the strength comes from an old Belgian system of measuring alcohol — is 7.5 per cent by volume in modern terms. It has a pale brown colour with a gentle, fruity, slightly herbal palate. Rochefort 8 (9.2 per cent) is a big beer, copper-brown, with a rich fruity aroma and palate reminiscent of raisins and dates. Rochefort 10 (11.3 per cent) has enormous depth, as the strength indicates. Gentle hops blend with dark fruit, nuts and chocolate. The malty, fruity character of the beers is connected with their original basic use, as 'liquid bread' for the monks who were fasting.

The two remaining Trappist breweries are in Flemish-speaking areas. Westmalle comes from the Abdij der Trappisten north of Antwerp and its most famous product is the palest of all Trappist brews. The brothers use French and Bavarian pale malts, with German, Czech and Styrian Goldings hops added in three stages. Candy sugar is added in the copper. The nine per cent Tripel has just thirteen units of colour with thirty-five to thirty-eight units of bitterness. The beer has a secondary fermentation in tanks lasting from one to three months and is then primed with sugar and yeast added for bottle conditioning. It has a tart, citric fruit aroma with good resiny hops, is fruity again in the mouth and finish with a rounded, warming character from the yeast. The brewery's Double, 6.5 per cent by volume, is a russet brew due to the use of dark malts and sugar. It is chocolatey, fruity and nutty. The monks also produce a Single for their own consumption.

ABOVE: *Brotherly beer love ... a monk at the Westvleteren Trappist brewery.*

When I arrived at the Abdij Sint Sixtus in the hamlet of Westvleteren, cowled monks hurried out and pulled the main gates shut. I got the message, though I was able to chat by a side entrance to a pleasant monk, Brother Mattias, who spoke excellent English. Fortunately the Westvleteren ales can be sampled across the road in the homely Café De Vrede. Westvleteren is in West Flanders and is handy for the channel ports and the famous city of Ypres (Ieper). The monks brew malty and spicy ales, starting with a green-topped Double (four per cent), a Red (6.2 per cent) with dark fruit and peppery hops, and the Blue Extra (8.4 per cent) with an enormous attack of tart fruit and alcohol. A 10.6 Abbot may explain why the monks don't want too many visitors: the top of the range ale has an explosion of fruit (raspberries and strawberries) and malt allied to a soft, silky and alluring creaminess. The St Sixtus beers are described as 'Flemish Burgundy' and a sign in the café, written by a brother thirty years ago, says, 'The Good Lord has changed water into wine so how can drinking beer be a sin?' There was no need to add the question mark.

ABBEY BEERS

It is curious that in a country that prides itself on its speciality ales and the great Trappist heritage in particular that tradition is muddled by abbey beers. Many people, even beer connoisseurs, are confused by the designations Trappist and abbey. Even though I understood the distinction I assumed that brewers and monks worked hand-in-hand. 'Where is the abbey?' I asked at the Mont St-Guibert brewery owned by Interbrew. About three hundred kilometres down the motorway, I was told. Interbrew produces a range of beers under licence from the Abbey of Leffe, which has not brewed since Napoleonic times. The labels carry a striking stained-glass illustration of an abbey, to prolong the illusion. Another Belgian giant, Alken-Maes, a subsidiary of Kronenbourg of France, produces abbey beers for the Grimbergen monks north of Brussels. The monastery at Corsendonk licenses its name to two breweries. There is no specific abbey beer style but the number of brands — and confusion — proliferate. Stick to Trappist ales.

BELGIAN ALES

When the public sale of spirits, especially the prized genever, was banned at the turn of the century, drinkers turned to strong pale and golden ales. The modern classic of the golden style, even though it was only introduced in the 1970s, is the renowned Duvel. Like Guinness, people struggle over the pronunciation. It is not French, though many say 'Du-velle'. The word is the Flemish for devil and is pronounced 'Doo-vul', with the emphasis on the first syllable. While few would confuse Guinness with lager many assume that Duvel, with its superb golden Pilsner colour, must be bottom fermenting. On the contrary, it is one of the world's finest and most aromatic and complex ales. It is made by the Moortgat Brewery in Breendonk north of Brussels, founded in 1871 and which originally made dark, top-fermenting ales. With the help of brewing scientist Jean De Clerk, Moortgat managed to select a strain of yeast ideal for producing dark beers similar to the Scotch Ales imported from Britain. When the first Moortgat version was produced, a brewery worker is alleged to have said, 'This is a devil of a beer!' and the name stuck. As Pilsner lagers started to dominate the market after World War Two, Moortgat responded, again with De Clerk's help, to produce a golden ale that would protect and build its market. Two-row summer French and Belgian barleys are specially malted for Moortgat. Duvel has a colour rating of seven to eight, only fractionally higher than a Pilsner. The beer is infusion mashed and the wort has a gravity of 1056 degrees. Saaz and Styrian Goldings are added to the copper boil in three stages. The beer will have twenty-nine to thirty-one units of bitterness. Dextrose is added before primary fermentation to encourage full attenuation by the yeast. This lifts the gravity to 1066. Two strains of yeast are used for primary fermentation and the hopped wort is split into two batches, to be attacked by the different yeasts. Primary fermentation lasts for six days, followed by three days secondary fermentation at cold temperature. The beer is then cold conditioned for a month, filtered with dextrose and given a *dosage* of one of the original yeasts. The gravity is once again boosted, this time to around 1073 degrees. The beer is bottled and held for two weeks, during which time it undergoes its third fermentation. The finished result is a beer with a remarkable 8.5 per cent alcohol by volume. It is poured into a special tulip-shaped glass to contain the vast, fluffy head created. The aroma has an unmistakable and powerful hint of pears. Aromatic hops and delicate fruit dominate the palate while the finish is perfumy from the hops.

Many Belgians like to drink Duvel chilled but it expresses its sublime character best at cellar temperature. Make sure you drink it from a bottle with a red cap: the green cap version is filtered and the devil has lost his bite. There are several competitors to Duvel, often with similar names, such Joker, Rascal and Judas. But the Devil still plays the best tunes.

The biggest-selling ale in Belgium is Palm, brewed by a family-owned brewery in the hamlet of Steenhuffel. Spéciale Palm, 5.2 per cent volume, has a tart and citric aroma and palate and a refreshing fruit-and-hops finish. The brewery also produces a bottle-conditioned, 7.4 per cent Aerts 1900, designed to replicate a typical turn-of-the-century Belgian ale.

De Koninck means 'the king' and the ale of that name from Antwerp can with some justification claim to be part of the royalty of beer. The brewery began life as a humble brew-pub in 1833 and has remained true to the style of beer of the city, resisting moves to switch to Pilsner production. Its copper colour comes from Pilsner and Vienna malts with no sugars or adjuncts. The hops are all Saaz though some of the variety are grown in Belgium and they are added at three stages during the boil in a copper heated by direct flame. Fermentation lasts for up to eight days and then the green beer has two weeks' cold conditioning. The beer is filtered but only the bottled version is pasteurised. It is five per cent alcohol and has such a peppery hop aroma that it is like liquid snuff. The yeast strain that goes back for decades imparts a gentle fruitiness to the beer, which has a long hoppy finish. In the bars and cafés of Antwerp the beer is drunk traditionally from a goblet known as a 'bolleke'. The name amuses visitors from Britain especially when they are urged by the waiters not to drop one. In the café Pelgrim opposite the brewery drinkers are in the habit of adding live yeast to their beer and the brewery supplies a bucketful from the fermenting room.

BELOW: *La Binchoise Brewery in Binche, Wallonia.*

THE BEERS OF WALLONIA

In French-speaking Wallonia they feel their beers, with the exception of the Trappist ones, are overlooked and underrated. They complain that no one in Flanders has heard of their ales. Neglect can lead to decline and it would be a tragedy if the beers of the region were to disappear, especially the style known as saison. Clearly they are seasonal beers. They were brewed — in some cases are still brewed — by farmers who would make them in the winter months and store them for drinking during the hot summers, though they are now made all year round. The style, the brewers and the methods have links with the bières de garde across the border in the Nord-Pas de Calais region of

France. Saisons are top fermenting, often have dark malts, have generous hop rates and a big, fruity character. I have stayed twice in the fine city of Tournai, with its awesome cathedral, as a base for visiting the local breweries, all of them tiny. The classic brewer of saison is Dupont at Tourpes, based on a farm with its own spring. The brewery was founded in 1850 and has been run by the Dupont family since the 1920s. Marc Rosier, grandson of the original Duponts, is now in charge. The small, charming, steam-filled and traditional brewhouse produces five to six thousand hectolitres a year, using pale and caramalts with Kent Goldings and Styrian hops. The 6.5 per cent saison is called Vieille Provision. 'Old Provision' is a term that dates from the time when these stored seasonal beers were an important part of the farmers' nutrition and diet. It has an intense peppery hoppiness from the use of East Kent Goldings, a hazy golden colour and a dense head when poured. Avec Les Bons Voeux de la Brasserie is a mouthful in every way, a 9.2 per cent Christmas seasonal bursting with hops and citric fruit: it gives you the best wishes of the brewery. Dupont also produces beers under the Moinette label, named after Marc Rosier's farm. Moine means 'monk' and the farm estate is thought to have once been an abbey. The 'little monk' beers are both 8.5 per cent, a blonde and a brune. The pale version is hoppy and aromatic, the brown fruity and sweet. There are also organic versions of some of the beers: Moinette Biologique and Saison Dupont Biologique.

The Brasserie à Vapeur, the Steam Brewery, in the village of Pipaix, dates from 1785 and uses equipment from the 1920s, though much of the original copper was stripped by the Germans during World War Two. The site was saved and revived in the 1980s by two local schoolteachers who loved the traditions of the area. The tiny plant, powered by a coal-fired steam engine, produces a 6.5 per cent Saison de Pipaix spiced with anis, black pepper, medicinal lichen and other 'botanicals'. It is orange fruity and spicy on the nose and aroma. There are two eight per cent ales, Vapeur Rousse and Vapeur en Folie. The mash tun is cast iron with a wooden surround and the coppers are also cast iron. After fermentation the beers are conditioned for three weeks then primed in the bottle and warm conditioned for up to a month. The Rousse, which includes ginger, has a russet colour, a hoppy and orange fruit aroma, is tart, slightly vinous and sour in the mouth.

The Silly Brewery causes amusement to English speakers but merely takes its name from its village which in turn is named after the local river, the Sil. It is a farm brewery dating from the 1850s that once had a windmill to grind the grain. Silly has achieved recognition outside Wallonia due to the tireless enthusiasm of its marketing manager, Charles Fontaine. Its 5.4 per cent Saison Silly is brewed from French malts plus Belgian caramalt for colour, with English Goldings. In the manner of several saison brewers in cramped brewhouses, the mash tun doubles as a hop back, with the wort returning to the tun for filtration after the copper boil. Fermentation lasts for fifteen days in small conicals using a top yeast. The beers are matured in tanks for two weeks and then

BELOW: *Serious Silly brewer ... Charles Fontaine at Silly Brewery.*

201

filtered. The Saison is copper coloured with peppery hops and winey fruit on the nose, dark fruits in the mouth and a dry and hoppy finish. Silly also brews a pale and brown Double Enghien — Enghien is a nearby village that used to have its own brewery — a Silly Scotch in the style of Scotch ales exported to Belgium (and even the ebullient Charles Fontaine might have trouble selling it in Glasgow), a well-named Divine (9.5 per cent) described as an 'artisanal beer' with a big peppery hop aroma, hops and dark fruit in the mouth and a bitter fruit and hops finish. The bottle-conditioned five per cent Titje wheat beer has a tempting lemon jelly aroma, tart citric fruit and spices in the mouth, and a quenching finish. The Silly beers can enjoyed in the restaurant and bar La Titien Bassilly (Lower Silly). The bar has a remarkable version of bar billiards called 'cork billiards': the stoppers on the table look like Champagne corks.

The Du Bocq brewery in the small village of Purnode near Namur brews a highly regarded 6.1 per cent Saison Regal and the widely-distributed Blanche de Namur wheat beer (4.5 per cent). Sadly, Purnode was cut off by snow when I attempted to reach the brewery. I did manage, despite the snow, to find La Binchoise micro-brewery in the old walled town of Binche near the industrial city of Charleroi. It does not claim to brew a saison as such but many of its products are strictly seasonal, including a nine per cent Christmas Beer with a vast spicy hop aroma with orange fruit in the mouth and on the finish, a five per cent September festival beer, an 8.5 per cent Honey Beer (Bière au Miel) with sixty kilos of honey per brew added after the boil. The nine per cent Marie is named in honour of Marie de Hongrie, sister of Charles Quint, the king of Burgundy in 1549.

The strongest beer in Belgium comes from Wallonia. Bush Beer is a mighty twelve per cent alcohol and would be classified as barley wine in Britain. The handsome brewery and former farm, with its attractive

green-shuttered buildings fronting the main road to Mons at Pipaix, is owned by the Dubuisson family: buisson is French for Bush. The brewery was founded in 1769 and the name of the beer was Anglicised in 1933 as a result of the popularity of English ales in Belgium. Annual production is around 15,000 hectolitres. The beer is sold in the US under the name Scaldis (the Latin for Belgium's major river, the Scheldt) to avoid a clash with Anheuser-Busch, brewers of the ubiquitous Budweiser. The amber beer is made from pale and cara malts with Styrian and Kent Goldings hops. The Goldings dominate the aroma and palate along with delicious winey fruit and nuts. The beer has forty-two units of bitterness. Primary fermentation lasts a week in enclosed vessels and the beer is then cold conditioned for four to six weeks. Dubuisson also produces a Christmas beer, darker than the regular Bush, with an aroma like Dundee cake, rich and sultana-fruity in the mouth and a big vinous finish.

MAD ABOUT BEER

There cannot be a style called 'mad beer' but the De Dolle Brouwers, the Mad Brewers, do not fit into any other category of Belgian ales. It is a micro driven by eccentricity, passion and enthusiasm, open to the public at weekends. It is in Esen, near Diksmuide, West Flanders, not far from Ostend. The bar and reception area has an enormous open fire, a welcome sight in winter. The small brewery dates from the 1840s and seemed certain to close in 1980 when the owner was taken ill. But a group of keen home-brewing brothers, who had started with a beer kit from Boots the Chemist while on a visit to England, bought the site and started to brew at weekends. The driving force is an architect, Kris Herteleer, and his mother. She often leads the brewery tours and expands on the joys of beer: 'Water is medicine, malt is medicine, hops are medicine, therefore beer is medicine' though she does warn about 'savage yeasts'. The Dolle Brouwers' yeast is supplied by Rodenbach, which may explain 'Mutti' Herteleer's concern. The brewhouse is tiny, cramped and filled with antique equipment: a pre-World War One mash tun, a copper fired by direct flame, and an open wort cooler (a cool ship). Untreated water comes from six wells in the town. The main brew is Oerbier, 'original brew', first made in a wash-tub in the Herteleer home. It uses six malts, including caramalt and black malt, with Belgian hops from Poperinge and East Kent Goldings. It has a sour plums aroma (showing its Rodenbach connections), and is bitter-sweet in the mouth with a fruity finish. The eight per cent Arabier is a summer ale: the name comes from a Flemish joke incapable of translation, though a parrot is involved: perhaps Monty Python could fathom it. It is a hazy bronze colour with a Damson jam and spicy hops aroma, with rich fruit and hops in the mouth and a big fruity finish. It is dry hopped with Goldings. Boskeun (Easter Bunny: eight per cent) is another seasonal ale and is sweetened with honey. Stille Nacht is a Christmas beer with a big marmalade fruit aroma and palate with a dry finish and a hint of

BELOW: *Mad Brewers' seasonal ale.*

sourness. The brewery may be a mad house but the beer is brilliant. If you get the chance, make a weekend visit to Roeselarestraat 12b, 8160 Esen-Diksmuide, phone 051 502781.

DUTCH ALE

The Dutch have a saying 'When beer is in the man, commonsense is in the can', can being a jug. The Netherlands (call it 'Holland' if you must, but that is just a province of the country) has a long and noble ale brewing heritage. But most of the records are lost and the heritage is now largely confined to dark paintings of stolid Dutch brewers in their guild meetings. Frustratingly, as a great seeker after the truth about nineteenth-century ales exported to the English and Dutch colonies, I was both fascinated to hear that the Dutch East Indies Company, like its English counterpart, had exported a 'strong, rich beer' to Indonesia and horrified to be told that no records exist. In earlier centuries, the main cities were bursting with ale breweries. In 1480 the combined annual production of Haarlem, Gouda and Delft, the major brewing centres, was 925,000 barrels, each barrel holding 155 litres. By 1545 the figure had risen to 1.1 million barrels. Spices from the Indies were used by brewers

ABOVE: *Mother love ... Mutti Herteleer at De Dolle Brouwers.*

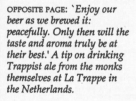

OPPOSITE PAGE: `*Enjoy our beer as we brewed it: peacefully. Only then will the taste and aroma truly be at their best.' A tip on drinking Trappist ale from the monks themselves at La Trappe in the Netherlands.*

LEFT: *A happy Dutch drinker by Frans Hals.*

LEFT: *IJ, IJ ... idiosyncratic Amsterdam brewpub.*

throughout the Low Countries to flavour their ales, a habit that survives in the white beers of Belgium. Ale came under sustained attack in the last century from several sources. Tea and coffee drinking became popular with the upper and middle classes, while the working class developed a dangerous taste for strong gin — genever. As beer consumption slumped, brewers lowered the strengths of their ales in an attempt to survive. They were further undermined by the spreading popularity of Pilsner lagers. Gerard Adriaan Heineken opened his first small brewery,

the Haystack, in Amsterdam to provide an antidote to the evils of gin drinking. Lager beer, dominated today by Heineken, which includes Amstel and Brand, and Grolsch, with several other smaller producers, today accounts for ninety-nine per cent of beer production.

So what price an ale revival? Better than the lager production figure might suggest. Belgian ales are popular and easy to obtain and a handful of local brewers are attempting to blow on the flame. If the crowds of young people in the t'IJ brew pub in Amsterdam are any gauge, then the prospects are good. The brew pub was opened in 1984 by songwriter Kaspar Peterson in an old public bath house topped by a windmill at Funenkade 7, 1018 AL Amsterdam, phone 020 228325, open Wednesday to Sunday, 3-8pm. The name of the enterprise and its beers are all punny. The IJ is the name of the waterway on which Amsterdam harbour stands and the pronunciation of the word — 'ay' — is almost identical to the Dutch for an egg. Hence the ostrich on the pub sign. There is a windmill in the desert in the background to the sign, indicating that Amsterdam was a beer desert until Kaspar opened shop. Ten brews are available but not all at one time. Natte, meaning 'wet', is a 6.5 brown ale in the style of a Belgian dubbel. It has a luminous ruby-red colour and intense peppery hop aroma, with nuts and blackcurrant fruit in the mouth and a bitter-sweet finish becoming dry. Zatte, eight per cent, means, simply, 'drunk' and is in the tripel style, pale in colour and with a spicy, hoppy character. Columbus's Egg, nine per cent, is cloudy bronze with a big winey aroma, citric fruit in the mouth and more fruit in the finish. Struis, also nine per cent, is the Dutch for ostrich and is spicy, fruity and dry. There are also an autumn bock, a New Year beer, a spring beer, an English style bitter called Mij (mosquito) and Vlo, flea beer. I had to fight my way in to the bar. They had to force me to leave. I shall return.

The Gulpener brewery in Gulpen, near Maastricht, is best known for its Pilsners but in the 1980s recreated a speciality of the region, an old ('aajt') ale fermented by wild yeasts. The style had disappeared in the 1930s. The wort from the mash is taken to a secret place and exposed to the atmosphere until it is attacked by Brettanomyces yeast and lactobacilli. The wort is then stored in unlined wooden casks for a year or more for secondary fermentation. It is filtered and blended with Gulpener's dark lager. The result is a sweet-and-sour, tawny 3.5 per cent beer with a refreshing, tart flavour. The beer is available in Ze Zwarte Ruiter (the Black Knight), 4 Markt, Gulpen.

The De Ridder brewery in Maastricht uses a medieval warrior as its emblem. It stands proudly on the waterfront of the Maas (Meuse). It has been owned by Heineken since 1982 but has been allowed to brew in a traditional fashion in a handsome old tiled brewhouse dating from 1852. Wieckse Witte is the main product, a top-fermenting wheat beer (five per cent) with lots of tart, lemony, spicy character. Wiecske comes from the same Saxon root as the English wick, meaning a settlement. Ridder also produces a robust, fruity, toffeeish ale in the Dortmunder style

ABOVE: *De Ridder brewery in Maastricht, Heineken outpost on the banks of the Maas.*

called Maltezer (6.5 per cent).

Grolsch may be small in Heineken terms but it is an international company with some clout, best known for its Pilsner with the fresh mown grass aroma in the famous swing-top bottle. But it also produces a top-fermenting five per cent Amber, similar to a German Alt, with a big malty aroma but lots of hop in the finish, and a 6.5 per cent Bok packed with sweet malt and fruit.

Dutch Boks or Bocks tend to be top-fermented even though they follow the style of German Bocks, strong, seasonal lager beers. The Sint Martinus micro brewery in Groningen brews the medieval-style Cluyn (see The History section) and a 6.5 per cent Bok brewed for the autumn called Bommen Berend. The label shows a goat but the beer is named after the much-hated Bishop Bommen Berend of Munster, who held religious sway in the area but was kicked out by the Dutch in 1628. The goat is traditional: Bock, the German for a male goat, is a corruption of Einbeck, the German town where the style originates. Nico Derks's Bock has a fruit gums and hops aroma, hops and dark fruit in the mouth, and a vinous, bitter finish. It is brewed from pale, crystal, amber and Munich malts and is hopped with Northern Brewer and Perle varieties. Nico claims that, at four hundred hectolitres a year, his plant must be the most micro-ish in the world. The Lilliputian mash tun and copper were once the developing and fixing machine for the local hospital's X-ray department. The beers ferment in plastic vessels at the front of the beer shop, which has a bar attached (Stadsbrouwerij St Martinus, Oude Kijk in 't Jatstraat 16, Groningen, tel 050 182188). Nico Derks also brews Noorder Blond, a 5.5 per cent bottle-conditioned beer made from eighty

RIGHT: *Call up yesterday ... Nico Derks of Sint Martinus who has recreated a medieval Dutch ale.*

per cent barley malt and twenty per cent malted wheat, hopped with Tettnanger. It has a strong hint of bubblegum and lemon jelly on the nose, and a tart and quenching palate. The saucy label shows an Art Deco-ish lady who seems to have mislaid her bodice. A 7.5 per cent spiced beer uses coriander, woodruff, aniseed and cloves and is refermented in the bottle with honey. It has a powerful spicy aroma with woodruff dominating, citric fruit in the mouth and a dry finish with a hint of cloves. St Martinus also brews extremely occasional beers, such as Mistletoe at Christmas and Valentine's in February.

The Raaf Bierbrouwerij (Raven Brewery) started life as farmhouse, brewery and maltings at Heumen near Nijmegen in the 1700s, closed in the 1920s and reopened in 1984. It was bought by Breda-Oranjeboom, the Dutch subsidiary of Allied Breweries of Britain, which busily promoted its wheat beer, Raaf Witbier. The five per cent beer is tart and spicy, a good example of the style. Raaf brews several other beers, including a dubbel, a tripel and a bok but the future of all the beers is in the melting pot as Allied (now Allied Domecq) announced it was selling all its Dutch companies in the autumn of 1994. Sherry clearly has more appeal.

Back in Amsterdam, an enterprising brew-pub was opened in 1992 by the brothers Albert and Casper Hoffman. The Brouwhuis Maximiliaan, with a nice touch of historic irony, is in a former convent on the edge of the red light district (Kloveniersburgwal 6/8, tel 020 6242778). It took a Dutch firm one and half years to build the attractive copper brewing vessels, which are on view in the bar. The mash tun also acts as the copper after the wort has been clarified in a lauter tun. Fermentation using a top yeast is in conical vessels at the rear of the building. None of

BELOW: *Love in a cold climate ... Sint Martinus sexy brew.*

the beers is filtered or pasteurised. They include a 7.5 per cent Kloosterbier (cloister beer), a Belgian-style white, Waags Wit (five per cent), a Cologne-style Kölsch (4.5 per cent), a 7.5 per cent Tripel, a Winter Warmer and a spring Märzen. The Hoffmans have collaborated with Derek Walsh, a Canadian CAMRA member now living in the Netherlands, to brew a 4.5 per cent ruby-red Porter with a dark malt, hops and spices aroma, a spicy and bitter palate, and bitter chocolate on the finish.

The giant Heineken now realises there is more to life than light versions of Pilsners. It is marketing Van Vollenhoven Stout (six per cent), a rare link with the Netherlands's brewing past. Van Vollenhoven was founded in Amsterdam in 1733 and brewed until World War Two. It was bought jointly by Heineken and Amstel when they were separate companies. The stout is now bottom-fermented, so does not classify as an ale but is a delicious beer with a rich coffee and chocolate aroma, an oily and perfumy palate, and a bitter, hoppy finish with more coffee and chocolate. Heineken also offers some bottom-fermenting versions of bok beers and has launched George Killian's Irish Red Ale, brewed by its French Pelforth subsidiary, under the name of Kylian (6.5 per cent). The copper-coloured ale uses Vienna malt and has twenty-two units of bitterness. If Heineken could overcome a fear of top-fermenting yeasts, it could brew some good ales itself.

ABOVE: *Red light for a good beer ... the Maximiliaan Brouwhuis in Amsterdam is on the edge of the city's notorious brothel area.*

Chapter Five
France

Classic beer in France? Surely this is a printing error: replace beer with wine. But the French, in common with other Latin people, are cutting back on wine consumption and switching to 'healthier' beer. Most of the beer consumed in France comes in the shape of the unremarkable lagers of the Strasbourg area. But many are discovering that in the flatlands between Calais and Lille there is a different tradition of farmhouse ales called bière de garde. Translated into English, 'beer to keep' is almost identical to the German lager, meaning 'store'. But the stored beers of northern France, in the Nord-Pas de Calais, have different roots that pre-date the Industrial Revolution. Like the Saisons of neighbouring Wallonia, they were beers brewed in the winter and stored in wooden casks for summer-time drinking by farmers, their families and their workers. In both Pas de Calais and Wallonia, farm labourers were once paid in kind, with potatoes and beer.

Beer is taken seriously by the French in an area that not only shares a common border with the Belgians but where Flemish names abound. The best-known of the bière de garde brewers, Duyck, stresses that this may be France but it is French Flanders. Every summer the people of Douai take to the streets for a festival celebrated with beer. The two giants that lead the procession, Les Enfants de Gayant, have given their name to the local brewery. This enterprising company produces a large portfolio of beers, including an Abbey beer, a 12 per cent perfumy lager Bière du Démon, and an interesting Lutèce Bière de Paris, a malty brown beer based on an extinct style developed in the capital centuries ago, when beer was stored in icy caves alongside the Seine. As a result, Lutèce is a bottom-fermenting beer and I suspect the brewers are happy to have found historical justification for using lager yeast. Several producers of bières de garde have also switched to bottom fermentation. It would be tragic if, just as the outside world has discovered this fascinating contribution to the ale family, the producers start to dilute the style. I hope the energetic Les Amis de la Bière, who champion traditional brewing in the region, will lobby brewers hard to stay with top fermentation.

Beer was brewed not just for farm labourers but for coal miners as well. The Lille area was once the great mining region of France, scene of Zola's heroic novel *Germinal*, but all the pits have shut and the miner

with his lamp on the label of Ch'ti beer is a ghostly figure, disappearing into the background. Ch'ti is brewed by the Brasserie Castelain at Bénifontaine near Lens. The curious name for the beer is Picardy dialect for 'c'est toi', literally 'it suits you'. The brewery, part of a farm, was built in 1926 and was bought by the Castelain family in 1966. Yves Castelain, the young member of the family running the brewery today, told me that in 1900 there were two thousand breweries in the Nord-Pas de Calais region. Now there is just a handful. Castelain used to brew a special two per cent alcohol beer for miners but the last pit shut in 1991. The brewery, with gleaming copper vessels, produces 28,000 hectolitres a year. Yves Castelain uses Flemish and French hops and barley, and has developed his own recipes for a pale and a brown version of Ch'ti as well as an organic Jade, Christmas and March beers, and an abbey-style Sint Arnoldus. In common with most brewers in the region, Yves Castelain is looking for malty, fruity aromas and palates in his beers and hops, from Flanders and Germany, are used with restraint. Around ten per cent brewing sugar is added during the boil. Yves uses a lager yeast but ferments at 15° C/60° F. Lager yeast gives him greater control over production, he says firmly. The beers are fermented for ten to twelve days and then conditioned for up to two months. Ch'ti Blonde is made from four malts, the brune from eight, including Munich, cara-Munich and torrefied malt. The 6.5 per cent alcohol beers are rich and fruity, with

ABOVE: *Les Enfants de Gayant, giant figures paraded through Douai every year at the start of the town's festival. The giants give their name to the local brewery.*
BELOW: *Prolier than thou ... Ch'ti Brewery once wore its workers' heart on its label.*

RIGHT: *Guard them well ... range of Bières de Garde.* (Photo: Mike Benner)

RIGHT: *Guard them well ... range of Bières de Garde.* (Photo: Mike Benner)

the brown in particular having a strong hint of raisins in the mouth. The 4.6 per cent organic Jade allows the hops to express themselves more. It has a good earthy and perfumy hop aroma, sweet malt in the mouth and a fruity finish that becomes dry.

In the hills of French Hainaut, up against the Belgian border, the Bailleux family runs the Café Restaurant au Baron in Gussignies and also brews on the premises. All the products are true top-fermenting, bottle-conditioned bières de gardes, though one is called a saison in the Walloon tradition. The Cuvée des Jonquilles, despite the name, does not use daffodils in the brewing process but it has a delightful golden colour and flowery-fruity appeal. The seven per cent ale is brewed in the spring, hence the daffodil associations. Four malts and four hop varieties are used. The Saison Saint Médard, also seven per cent, has a tempting cherry colour and a fruity aroma not unlike a Kriek but without the lambic sourness. There is also a chocolatey and spicy Christmas beer.

The Brasserie d'Annouellin in the small, spick-and-span town of the same name between Lille and Lens, is 'fuelled by optimism' according to its owner, Bertrand Lepers. Typical of the region, the brewery, founded in 1905, was once a farm and Bertrand's wife, Yvonne, comes from farmer-brewers at Flers. When they married they merged the two breweries: whom Bacchus has joined, let no man put asunder. The mash tun doubles as the copper after the wort has been clarified. The beer ferments in horizontal tanks in cellars that were once cattle byres. Primary fermentations last a week, followed by two weeks of conditioning. Yeast comes fresh each week from the Jean d'Arc brewery. Local malt and hops are used: the Lepers used to grow hops. Bernard Lepers, as if mirroring his dryish ales, has a deadpan sense of humour. He once brewed a bière de table for families and a two per cent beer for schools. 'They stopped that twenty years ago and truancy increased'. His humour is best seen on the label of his bière de garde. It is called Pastor Ale and posters announce, with a nod to Beethoven, 'c'est une symphonie'. It is certainly a most harmonious brew, an ode to joyous drinking. It is 6.5 per cent alcohol and is made only from pale malt: Monsieur Lepers avoids brewing sugars, except in a Christmas ale. Pastor Ale has a gold colour, pronounced orange fruit and earthy hops on the nose, more tangy fruit in the mouth and a big dry, fruity, hoppy finish. The 7.3 per cent L'Angelus, with a painting by Millais on the label, is even more outstanding. It is a wheat beer, using thirty per cent buck wheat in flour form. It is bronze coloured and has a powerful citric tangerine aroma backed by spicy hops, with more tart fruit in the mouth and a long, bitter-sweet finish. With its pronounced orange fruit character, this is the Grand Marnier of the beer world.

ABOVE: *Tuneful brewer ... Bernard Lepers of Annoeullin.*

Bernard Leper's humour is catching. The St Sylvestre brewery at Steenvoorde, in the heart of the hop country, produces a gold bière de garde called 3 Monts (8.5 per cent). It is named after three local hills: in the flat lands of the region even three small hillocks are worthy of commemoration. The beer is noticeably dry and winey and with good hop character from local Brewers' Gold and German Tettnang.

Brasserie Duyck is based in the hamlet of Jenlain, which gives it name to the most famous bière de garde. It is south-east of Valenciennes and began life as a farm. The farmer brewed and eventually concentrated on brewing. Félix Duyck, of clear Flemish stock, took over the brewing in 1922, which is now run by his son Robert and grandson Raymond. Production has grown to an impressive 90,000 hectolitres a year but brewing remains firmly traditional in copper vessels. Malts from Flanders, Champagne and Burgundy are used along with four hop varieties from Belgium, France, Germany and Slovenia. Jenlain, 6.5 per cent alcohol, is a russet coloured, spicy, malty ale of great depth and character, now widely available outside France and bottled with Champagne-style corks and cradles. The Duycks did fall into the temptation of using a lager yeast but latest information is that they have returned to an ale strain. They also brew a Christmas ale and a paler spring (Printemps) beer.

Beer is celebrated in the bustling city of Lille in Les Brasseurs at 22 Place de la Gare (phone 20 06 46 25). This brew pub specialises in cuisine a la bière, including a type of local pizza. The beers are all malt and unpasteurised, brewed in a tiny but immaculate brew house. You can order La Palette du Barman, four taster glasses of each beer. The Blonde has a malty, perfumy aroma with a bitter-sweet palate. The Ambré has

a dark toasty character, the Brune has hints of sweet nuts and bitter chocolate, while the Blanche cloudy wheat beer has a sharp, tangy apples-and-cloves aroma, citric fruit in the mouth and a dry finish with a powerful hint of apple.

I also enjoyed local beers in the town of Carvin, deep in the heart of the old mining region. The Café Belle-Vue offered a sweetish Bière de Noel while the Café de Paris sold a bière flambé, with liqueur added to beer and then set ablaze. The result was smoky and warming on a cold winter's day. Both cafés are on the town square where the main street is called Avenue Jean Jaurès and another is the Avenue Salvador Allende. This was once staunch French socialist territory: Jaurès was the founder of the Socialist Party. Now only the beer remains, the political inspiration as ghostly as the miner on the label of a bottle of Ch'ti.

Chapter Six
Germany

To say that ale is the classic brewing style of Germany is to invite the men in white coats to usher you away to a safe house and keep you under lock and key. Germany is, after all, *the* great lager brewing nation. Lagering, storing beer at a cold temperature, was turned in the nineteenth century from a simple country technique for keeping beer fresh in hot weather into a commercial method that revolutionised brewing world-wide. And yet the types of beer that pre-dated commercial lager brewing refused to go away. Today it is ales that show the only growth in Germany as people look for greater character and variety in their beers. In Bavaria wheat beers have boomed to such a extent that Spaten, the Munich brewery famous for developing modern lagering, now finds that half its production is given over to top-fermenting ale. In Cologne and Düsseldorf golden Kölsch and copper-coloured Alt beers generate great support and affection while in Berlin the sour style of wheat beer helps celebrate the end of walls and divisions that once split that great city.

Bavarians are famous not only as the world's greatest consumers of beer but as the people who have kept faith with the Reinheitsgebot, the sixteenth-century 'Purity Pledge' that laid down that only barley, water and yeast could be used in brewing. Hops were added later. You will notice that the word 'wheat' is missing from the pledge. The reason is simple. It was the Bavarian royal family, the House of Wittelsbach, that drew up the terms of the Reinheitsgebot and its reasons were not altruistic. The Bavarian royals drank wheat beer. They were determined that no one else should sample it. The masses could make do with brown beers made from wood-cured malts but the princes and their families would enjoy the paler delights of wheat beer. As the monarchy had a monopoly over the supply of both barley and wheat you could say it had the people over a barrel. The mystique that surrounded wheat beer was broken in 1850 when the royal family licensed a Munich brewer named Georg Schneider to brew the style. He brewed first in the renowned Hofbräuhaus (royal court brewhouse) in Munich and later moved to Im Tal (the Dale) just off the main square. Schneider (the German for Taylor) was successful to such an extent that he bought a second brewery in Kelheim in the heart of the great Hallertau hop region. The brewery at Im Tal was destroyed by allied bombs during World War

ABOVE: *Immaculate decoctions ... fermenting room at Schneider's plant in Kelheim.*

Two and brewing is now confined to Kelheim, though the tavern on the site of the Munich brewery remains Schneider's showplace. Photographs of the effects of allied bombing raids line the walls down to the cellar and British visitors are advised not to be too enthusiastically Union Jack the Lads.

The Kelheim brewery, a curious but pleasing blend of Spanish and Gothic architecture, was built in 1607 and is almost certainly the oldest continuous wheat beer plant in the world. It is managed today by the jovial Georg Schneider V, his elegant wife Margaret and their son, also named Georg, who is being groomed for the succession. They own a beautiful brewery, with sparkling vessels and tiled surrounds, impressively clean as only a German brewery can be.

It also has open fermenters, a rare sight in Germany where fear of wild yeasts and contamination keeps most beers under wraps. Schneider makes 300,000 hectolitres a year and ninety per cent of that is a 5.4 per cent Weisse. The remaining ten per cent goes to Aventinus, an eight per cent doppelbock — double strong — and a new, lighter beer called Weizen Hell. Hell in Bavaria means a light beer (in terms of strength). Weisse (white) and weizen (wheat) are interchangeable terms in wheat beer labelling. Schneider uses half a million tonnes of local barley and wheat a year. Both grains are malted — raw grain cannot be used under the terms of the Reinheitsgebot. They are blended in the proportion of

217

sixty per cent wheat malt to forty per cent barley. Some Vienna and dark malts are added to give the Weisse its appealing bronze-copper colour. Hersbrücker hops from the Hallertau are used in pellet form with a little hop extract. Weisse has just fourteen to fifteen units of bitterness. Hops are wanted primarily for their preservative quality and too overpowering a hop aroma would destroy the classic spicy, fruity character of a true wheat beer. 'No hop merchant would get rich on Schneider,' Georg VI laughed. Water comes from local wells. It is too hard and is softened by osmosis to remove some of the natural salts.

The modern brewhouse was installed in 1988. It has stainless steel mashing vessels and kettles standing on marble floors. A double decoction method is used, with portions of the mash pumped from one vessel to another, heated to a higher temperature and then returned to the first vessel. Decoction mashing was introduced in mainland Europe when malts there were not well modified — the proteins in the grain were not sufficiently degraded to allow the enzymes to turn starch into sugar. As modern malts are usually well modified, decoction mashing is probably unnecessary to break down the cell walls of the grain. But Schneider is determined to stay true to tradition. Mashing begins at a far lower temperature, 38 degrees C, than is customary in an English brewery using an infusion mash. As the wort is pumped from one vessel to the next, the temperature rises to 43, 48 and 56 degrees, reaching a final 65 degrees. The spent grains are sparged at 75 degrees. The hops are added in two stages during the copper boil and the wort is then pumped to the fermentation hall containing sixteen stainless steel vats, each one holding 350 hectolitres. The atmosphere is ripe with superb fruity aromas as the yeast goes to work on the sugars. Banana is the most obvious of the aromas, with powerful wafts of apple as well. The single strain yeast culture has been used for as long as anyone can remember and the brewers stand in awe of it, refusing to allow anything to upset it. The shape of fermenting vessels cannot be altered, neither can the specification of the malt. Twice a day, the yeast is skimmed from the top of the fermenters, cleaned and pitched back into the wort. Fermentation lasts between three and five days at 20 degrees C. The beer is not filtered and is bottled at a warm temperature. Yeast, with some unfermented wort to give the right balance of yeast to sugar, are added. The beer is matured at 20 degrees for a week. This produces a lively carbonation as a second fermentation begins. The beer then has fourteen days of cold conditioning at eight degrees to stabilise it.

Schneider is at pains to stress that bottle conditioning uses the house top yeast. It is critical of other Bavarian wheat beer brewers who have responded to the surge in demand for the beer by cutting corners. They use a lager yeast in the bottle, which adds to stability and shelf life but flattens some of the rich fruity and spicy flavours. Some even filter and pasteurise the beer after primary fermentation before re-seeding with lager yeast and adding some sediment to give an impression of natural cloudiness.

The unfiltered Schneider Weisse ('mit Hefe' on a wheat beer label means 'with yeast', 'kristall' is filtered) has a pronounced banana, cloves and nutmeg aroma with a tart and slightly acidic flavour in the mouth and a creamy, fruity finish. The bubblegum characteristic that many drinkers find in wheat beer is due to the phenols and guaicols produced by a true wheat beer yeast that are similar to the compounds found in tropical tree sap used to make chewing gum, Juicy Fruit in particular. The magnificent Aventinus is bronze-red in colour thanks to the generous use of caramalt, has a rich spices and chocolate aroma and palate, and more spices, fruit and cloves in the finish. It is a wonderful nightcap or winter warmer. Schneider prefers its beers to be drunk within eight months but says they will remain in drinkable condition for eight years if they are kept cool and dark. Georg Schneider VI says Aventinus tastes like port wine after twenty-five years: it would be tempting to lay some down.

In the small town of Miesbach in the Obberbayern mountains Hans Hopf is another brewer who has seen his business grow spectacularly thanks to the wheat beer revival. The German for hop is hopfen and Herr Hopf has a marketing department's dream name for a brewer. His family-owned company started brewing in the famous town of Garmish-Partenkirchen — where the arena for Hitler's Winter Olympics has been left as a grisly reminder of the times — but moved to Miesbach in the 1930s. Hopf produces only wheat beers and has seen production grow from a thousand hectolitres in 1958 to 45,000 by 1994. Hans Hopf thinks demand will take production to 70,000 but he wouldn't want to go beyond that figure. He has a horror of getting too big. He has had to extend his brewhouse to cope with demand. Splendid older copper vessels now nestle with stainless steel ones. His brewmaster, Dr Andreas

LEFT: *Wheat beer ready for delivery at Spaten in Munich.*

Wideneder, has access to plenty of pure Alpine water. He uses German and French malt, with wheat malt accounting for sixty-five per cent of the mash. Hops are Hallertau and Spalt varieties. The intriguing fermenting vessels look like a cross between Michelin men and the motorised Dalek robots of the long-running British TV sci-fi series Dr Who. The stainless steel vessels are closed save for openings like visors at the top where the top-fermenting yeast can be seen vigorously at work. After primary fermentation the beer in bottles and kegs is cooled to 10 to 15 degrees C to allow a second fermentation to start, encouraged by kräusening with some wort from the brewhouse. The beer is kept at 12 degrees for a week to purge diactyl — toffee flavours — and the temperature is then raised to 15 for three weeks. A blend of both top and bottom yeasts is used for secondary fermentation. Dr Wideneder would much prefer to use just a top yeast but he says his beer has to stand on supermarket shelves and lager yeast gives greater stability. The main Hopf beer, a 5.3 per cent Export with twelve units of bitterness, has a vast peppery and spicy aroma overlain by banana and bubblegum. It is tart and spicy in the mouth with a big fruity finish. Dr Wideneder has to balance aromas and flavours to suit conflicting consumer demands. 'Some drinkers think there is too much banana. In Miesbach they prefer the beer clear, fifteen kilometres away they want it cloudy. I'm like a preacher — my sermon has to please everyone.'

In Munich the Spaten brewery has seen its world turned upside down. It is famous throughout the world as the brewery where Gabriel Sedlmayr, a member of the controlling family, developed commercial

BELOW: *Old wooden lagering tank at Spaten.*

ABOVE: *Cult beer ... Spaten's wheat beer now accounts for half the brewery's production.*

lager brewing in the nineteenth century. But Spaten's range of lagers is under attack from its wheat beers. The Franziskaner brands now account for more than fifty per cent of the brewery's production. The success of the wheat beers has even outstripped the market share for the style in Bavaria, which grew from thirteen per cent in the early 1980s to twenty-four per cent ten years later and is predicted to reach thirty per cent. For years wheat beer was such a side line in the brewery that it was sold under the general Spaten label (spaten is German for shovel and the company logo is a malt shovel). But today, in order not to take too much attention away from the lagers, Spaten's wheat beers are all sold as Franziskaner. The labels show a cheerful Franciscan monk contemplating a tankard of ale. The original wheat beer brewery, bought by the Sedlmayrs, was the oldest in Munich and stood next to a Franciscan (Franziskaner) monastery. The Bavarian name for Munich, München, is a corruption of Monchen, 'place of the monks'.

The main Spaten wheat beer, Franziskaner Weissbier, five per cent alcohol, has an unusually high wheat malt content, 75 per cent to 25 per cent barley malt. The other brands, Hell (light), Dunkel (dark), a filtered Kristall and a strong Bock, are made more conventionally from a fifty-fifty blend of malts. French and German malts are used with a complex and subtle blend of Hallertau, Tettnang, Spalt, Perle and Orion hops. Fermentation for the wheat beers is kept separate from the lagers, to avoid any cross-fertilisation of yeast strains. Even so, the top yeast used for wheat beer production sediments to the bottom of conical fermenters. After primary fermentation, the beer is centrifuged to remove the yeast and is bottled and re-seeded with a lager yeast for the second fermentation. The beer then has a diactyl rest period at 20 degrees before moving to a cool storage area. Frankiskaner, which accounted for 570,000 of Spaten's one million hectolitre production in 1993, is massively popular but for me it lacks some of the rounded fruit and spices of the traditional style.

Among the many wheat beer brewers of Bavaria, Erdinger is the major producer. It is based in the town of Erding, twenty miles to the North-east of Munich. The brewery has all its malt, barley and wheat, contract-grown in the locality. The water is soft and the hops used are Perle and Tettnang. Primary fermentation takes place in unusually shallow horizontal tanks. For secondary fermentation, the beers are re-seeded with a bottom yeast. The Erdinger beers, the biggest-selling wheat beers in the world, seem a little coy to me, lightly fruity but lacking attack and bite. The basic brands are a mit Hefe and a Kristall at 5.3 per cent alcohol and a fractionally stronger Dunkel. The Pikantus Weizenbock, 7.3 per cent, has greater character, with chocolate and liquorice on the palate.

My first ever taste of Berliner Weisse was in a bar in Amsterdam. I found it so eye-wateringly tart that I succumbed and allowed the waiter to add a dose of woodruff syrup in the Berlin fashion. The beer turned green but stopped me going the same colour. The acidity of the beer is memorable. Like a Belgian lambic or gueuze, you have to work at it to acquire the taste but it is worth the struggle. You may end up agreeing with Napoleon's troops in Berlin, who described the beer as 'the Champagne of the North'. The description is apposite, for the grapes of the Champagne region produce such a tart wine that it becomes acceptable only after the long, slow process of producing a sparkling version, which involves some lactic activity. Berliner Weisse could not be more different to the wheat beers of the south. It is low in alcohol, around three per cent, is extremely pale in colour, has a light fruitiness and little hop aroma. The origins of the style are unknown — one theory is that Huguenots picked up the skill of brewing sour beer as they migrated north from France through Flanders. What is certain is that at one time there were seven hundred Weissbier producers in the Berlin area. Now there are two.

The lactic cultures that work with a conventional top yeast to ferment Berliner Weisse were isolated early in the twentieth century by scientists who created Berlin's renowned university research and brewing school. The culture is named Lactobacillus delbrücki after Professor Max Delbrück, the key research scientist. The Berliner Kindl Brauerei, the bigger of the two producers, had to rebuild its brewhouse in the 1950s. The original vessels were confiscated by the Russians at the end of the war (one of Stalin's lesser-known crimes). Commendably, Kindl designed the new brewhouse in 1930s Bauhaus style, still using copper. The well water is softened. The wheat malt percentage is thought to be around thirty per cent and the finished alcohol is a modest 2.5 per cent by volume. Bitterness units are ten from Northern Brewer. After mashing and boiling, the lactobacillus is added first to start acidification, followed by the top yeast. Fermentation lasts a week, followed by several days of cold conditioning. The beer is then filtered and bottled with some conventional top yeast and kräusen.

The Schultheiss brewery blends equal amounts of wheat and barley malt in the mash to produce a three per cent beer. Hallertau hops achieve just four to eight units of bitterness. Top fermenting yeast and lactobacilli are blended together with wort that is between three and six months old to encourage a lively fermentation, which lasts for just three or four days. The beer is warm conditioned for three to six months and is then kräusened and lactobacillus added for bottling. The result is an astonishingly complex, fruity, sour, quenching drink. Both breweries produce standard lagers and wheat beer production is only a fraction of their output. Unlike Bavaria, the wheat beers of Berlin are under threat and need urgent consumer support. Pick up your woodruff and depart.

The Kölsch beers of Cologne (Köln in German) show no sign of losing favour. The city and surrounding districts have some twenty breweries all dedicated to the one style of pale, perfumy, top-fermenting ale. In terms of numbers, it is the greatest brewing city in the world. The beer style has been given the equivalent of an appellation: no one outside Cologne can brew a Kölschbier. The brewers are rightly proud of the parchment signed in 1985 by their trade association and the German government that guaranteed the sanctity of the style. Brewing has been

RIGHT: *Impressive façade at Berliner Kindl.*
(Photo: Michael Jackson Collection)

223

a major occupation in Cologne, capital of the Rhineland, since Roman times. Monasteries dominated production and in turn were replaced by commercial brewers and tavern-brewers. The modern Kölsch beers are pale in colour but the malt is likely to have been darker in previous centuries. But in the twentieth century the style is often referred to as 'Wiess', a Cologne spelling of white, which refers to the colour of the beer rather than the use of wheat malt, though some brewers add a proportion of wheat to the mash. The style came under enormous pressure before and after World War Two from the growth of Pilsner beers. To their eternal credit, the brewers of Cologne decided to stick with tradition and top fermentation though concessions were made with paler malts and cold conditioning.

The style of Kölsch today is around five per cent alcohol with a malty aroma, some light fruit, soft in the mouth from the local water and with delicate perfumy hops. Bittering units are normally in the high twenties but extreme bitterness is avoided. Hallertau and Tettnang are the preferred varieties. The yeast busily attenuates the sugars and the beers tend to be dry in the finish. The biggest producer of Kölsch today is the Küppers brewery. It was founded just twenty years ago and is still considered something of an upstart. It has built market share through adroit advertising but its beer is easy-drinking and unexceptional. An unfiltered version, called Wiess, is not a wheat beer but has a more distinctively fruity and hoppy character. The best-known of the taverns offering Kölsch is P J Früh at 12-14 Am Hof. The beer used to be brewed on the premises but a separate brewery has been built away from the

town centre. The bar is extremely busy and the beer (all barley malt, no wheat) is dangerously drinkable with delicate fruit on the nose and light, slightly tart hops in the finish. Gaffel, at 20-22 Alter Markt in the Old Town, has a nutty, spritzy version of the style that throws a big fluffy head when poured. The Heller brewpub at 33 Roon Strasse has a fine vaulted cellar bar with intriguing stained-glass windows. The beer comes in two versions: a malty, sweetish Kölsch and an unfiltered, fruitier, slightly acidic Ur-Wiess.

The great industrial city of Düsseldorf, not far from the Dutch border and Maastricht, was once a major coal-mining area. This may explain some similarity between the Alt beers of the city and the bières de garde of northern France: they were made to refresh people after a hard day's labour at the pit face or in the fields. With their copper colour, Alt beers are closer to a British bitter or pale ale but the similarities should not be exaggerated. Alt means old but the growing popularity of the style both in its heartland and throughout Germany suggests that young people do not regard it as a beer for wrinklies. For them Alt or Altbier indicates not something old fashioned but a distinctive, flavoursome beer made by top fermentation. The most characterful Alts are found in the famous brew pubs of the city where enormous amounts are knocked back in small glasses not much bigger than a chaser, accompanied by vast plates of local food. The biggest commercial brewer is Diebels, a family-owned concern established by Josef Diebels in 1878 in the hamlet of Issum a few miles outside the city. It has been in the family for four generations and is now run by the young Böskens Diebel who is both chairman and chief executive. His brewery produced 1.6 million hectolitres in 1991, twice as much as in the previous year. Diebels is now the sixth biggest brewing group in Germany: the other five are all Pilsner producers. The Issum company has emerged at the expense of other Alt brewers. The biggest brewer in Düsseldorf was Hannen but its production fell when it was bought first by a tobacco company and then by Carlsberg of Denmark. Schlösser, part of the Dortmunder Union Brewery group, has also lost market share.

Diebels Alt has a gravity of 1045 degrees and is 4.8 per cent alcohol by volume. It is copper coloured with a pronounced peppery hop aroma balanced by rich malt. It is bitter in the mouth with a dry and nutty finish and a hint of orange fruit. Malt is blended from six suppliers. Ninety-eight per cent of the grist is pale Pils malt, with two per cent roasted malt, a nice 'Scottish' touch. Other brewers use a dash of Vienna or black malt for colour and flavour. Hops are mainly Northern Brewer for bitterness and Perle for aroma, producing thirty-two to thirty-three units of bitterness. Brewing liquor comes from the brewery's own wells. Calcium hydroxide ('lime milk') is added to soften it. The modern Steinecker brewhouse has tiled walls with a mosaic showing the old brewery at the turn of the century. Four mash kettles feed four wort kettles, where the hops are put in in one addition. Mashing is the decoction system which thoroughly turns all the starches into sugar. The fifty year-old yeast strain is a top worker but is cropped from the bottom of conical fermenters. It is noticeably less fruity than a typical British ale yeast and

ABOVE: *Young man in a hurry ... Dr Paul Bösken-Diebels has seen his family firm become the leading Alt brewery.*

BELOW: *Impressive modern brewhouse at Diebels.*

226

fully attenuates the wort. (A brewer at Diebels earnestly wrote in my notebook that he used Saccharomyces cerevisiae 'unlike you British who use Brettanomyces': he must have had a vinegary pint in a London pub at some time.) Primary fermentation lasts just two days. The green beer has a short diactyl rest and is stored in tanks for between ten days in summer and three weeks in winter. It is still a shock to hear Germans say they lager their beer when they are talking about ale.

For the real taste of Altbier you have to go out into the taverns of Alt Stadt, Düsseldorf's charming Old Town with cobbled streets and gas lamps. Im Füchschen, the Little Fox, in Ratinger Strasse is a vast, rambling building with tiled walls, red-tiled floors and wooden benches. It has an enormous food menu specialising in pork dishes. But the main interest is the house beer, tapped from casks on the bar. It is maltier than Diebels with a toasty flavour and a sweet, fruity finish that becomes dry. It costs around two marks a glass, about fifty pence in British money.

Zum Uerige in Berger Strasse means at the place of the cranky fellow. It attracts crowds cranky about it splendid beer, brewed in copper kettles and fermenters viewed from one of the many rooms. The place is a maze and a hive of activity, with beer served at crackerjack pace. The beer is dry hopped and uses roasted malt. It is fruity, aromatic and hoppy. There is a take-away service in flip-top bottles. Zum Schlüssel, the Key, is in Bolker Strasse, birthplace of the poet Heinrich Heine. It is a less frenetic place than Uerige, light and airy, with a tiled floor, long tables for diners and copper brewing kettles seen through a window at the rear. The beer has an appealing, perfumy hop aroma, is bitter-sweet in the mouth and has a dry finish. A local at the bar confided in me: 'After the fifth one you start to taste it'. It is not just the British who under-estimate their greatest achievements.

Chapter Seven
United States and Canada

Ale brewing in the United States is at last emerging from the long shadow of Prohibition. The total ban on the manufacture and sale of alcohol ran from 1920 until 1933 but its ramifications lasted far longer. Prohibition not only gave frightening power to the mob, which controlled the sale of illicit booze with murderous success, but it produced a distorted brewing industry when the ban was lifted. The United States was rich in breweries before 1920, many of them brewing ale. But thousands fell by the wayside during Prohibition. The bigger brewers survived by diversifying — many switched to making soft drinks and a cynic might say they never stopped doing so — able to ride out the barren years on the back of accumulated wealth. A slimmed-down industry emerged in 1933, made slimmer still by the economic depression that gripped the country in that decade, followed by World War Two. Prohibition, recession and war fashioned new beer styles. Giant breweries dominated the market and flooded it with brands that were identical in flavour (or lack of it) from the Canadian border to the Gulf of Mexico. Light lagers became ever lighter as brewers mixed cheaper adjuncts, such as corn and rice, with their malt. With vast numbers of men abroad during the war, the brewers wooed women with even blander concoctions. The use of skilful mass marketing, sponsorship of both minor and major sporting events, and an adroit manipulation of supply, helped Anheuser-Busch, brewers of Budweiser and Michelob, Miller, Coors and Pabst to dominate brewing and drinking with frightening effect. Budweiser, the world's biggest beer brand, accounts for almost half the beer consumed in the US, with Miller Lite taking another huge slice. Manufacturers of alcohol are not allowed to own bars but there are more ways than one to skin the brewery cat. The beer giants own the wholesaling companies that supply beer to bars. Smaller companies cannot get on the trucks or into the outlets. And huge discounts are offered to bars to take supplies only from one company.

It seemed that the country's great brewing heritage — of fine lagers as well as ale — had been lost. The Founding Fathers brought an ale culture with them from England. George Washington loved London porter to such a degree that he had it specially imported until the revolution. The second wave of immigrants from central Europe brought with them the ability to produce quality lager beers. Ale and lager

BELOW: *Send your lawyer a crate!*

enjoyed equal popularity until Prohibition and even in the 1950s such famous ales as Ballantine's were among the biggest brands in the country. But the onward march of light lagers seemed inexorable, sidelining other styles and traditions. Today, even though the brewing worm has turned, the giants seem ubiquitous. Many people tell me they have visited the US, failed to find anything drinkable and turned in desperation to imported Bass and Guinness. They are unaware that some four hundred micro, craft, new wave or 'specialty' brewers now operate, many of them concentrating on ales of remarkable quality. All the new-wave brewers together account for around one per cent of total beer production. That share is expected to double by the end of the century. In some regions, such as the Pacific North-west, the share is already around two per cent. And two per cent of the American beer market is not, as they say, small potatoes. Brewers the size of Anchor, Samuel Adams and Sierra Nevada can no longer be termed micro. They each brew more than a large English regional brewer. Their impact is now considerable. Using their own distributions networks, the micros have won greater appreciation for their beers. In New York City, San Francisco, Chicago, Houston, Dallas, Philadelphia, Portland (Oregon) and Seattle, to name just a few urban areas, good beer is no longer an underground drink. To mix a metaphor, it is out of the closet and on to the bar. Backed by the energetic work of the American Homebrewers' Association, beer lovers hankering for good tasty products now have a focus and direction. A growing number of beer guides and beer newspapers point people in the direction of quality and taste. When I visited the small Pike Place brewery in Seattle in the summer of 1994 a young couple arrived from Florida to taste the beer. In a country the size of the United States that shows remarkable dedication.

Two men are largely responsible for the upsurge in interest in good beer in the US. One was born to wealth. He used it to save a brewery and create both a legend and revive the country's only indigenous beer style. The second is of Scottish/Canadian immigrant stock and started to brew ales not only of great quality but strictly to style in an isolated town in the mountains of Washington state. The impact of both men has reverberated throughout the country and inspired a legion of other would-be brewers to follow in their steps.

Fritz Maytag is a member of the washing-machine manufacturing family. He was a student at Stanford University and enjoyed a San Francisco speciality known as Steam Beer. In 1965 he ordered a glass in his local bar and was told it would be the last as the maker, the Anchor Steam Brewery, was about to close. Maytag wrote his own chapter of the American Dream. He cashed in some of his shares in the family business, bought the brewery and created a legend. Steam beer is unique to San Francisco. It is a style that dates from the California Gold Rush of the 1890s. When prospectors poured into the small town they found a largely Mexican population drinking wine or tequilla. The gold diggers wanted beer and in particular they wanted the lager beers they enjoyed

BELOW: *Mould-breaking beers from the Anchor Brewery, where the American revival started.*

ABOVE: *Conditioning room at Anchor Brewery, San Francisco, built on the site of a former coffee-roasting factory.*

back east. The handful of ale brewers in the area were desperate to meet the demand. But refrigeration had not yet arrived and the Californian coast, unlike Bavaria, does not have icy caves in which to store beer. The brewers tackled the problem by fermenting their beers with lager yeasts at ale temperatures. They developed shallow vessels — a cross between fermenters and cool ships — that exposed more of the beer to the atmosphere and encouraged it to cool rapidly. The beer continued a lively fermentation in casks in the bar, producing a high level of natural carbon dioxide. As a result, when a cask was tapped it let off such a hiss of escaping gas that drinkers called it steam.

The brewery Maytag inherited in the 1960s was literally on its last legs, so strapped for cash that it used baker's yeast for fermentation and had just one employee. Maytag slowly nursed it back to success, though it took ten years for the Anchor Brewery to become profitable. Eventually he was able to move the brewery from its dilapidated site under a freeway to an imposing 1930s Art Deco building in Mariposa Street, San Francisco, formerly the offices of a coffee-roasting company. Over the years, Maytag has immersed himself in the art, science and history of brewing. He has recreated a Sumerian beer from the Old World (see The History) and has toured breweries throughout the world. His visits to

ABOVE: *All steamed up ... the Anchor copper brewhouse.*

such great ale breweries in England as Marston's, Timothy Taylor's and Young's deepened both his love of fine beer and his determination to brew to the highest possible standards. In San Francisco he has built a brewery that is a shrine to the art of brewing. The reception area is like a comfortable club, with deep chairs, fascinating prints of old San Francisco and its brewing history, and a large bar where all the Anchor beers are tapped. Plate glass windows allow visitors to look into the brewhouse. To describe it as beautiful sounds like a blend of hyperbole and over-indulgence at the bar but how else to describe this symphony of burnished copper mash kettles, wort kettles and lauter tuns, hand-built for Maytag by a German company? Anchor now has a small portfolio of ales, though Steam Beer remains its flagship and it is fermented well away from the ales to prevent cross-fertilisation of yeast strains. If Steam Beer is not by strict definition an ale, it deserves recognition here as a result of its significant role in encouraging the growth of the American micro revolution. Fermentation takes place in open vessels just two feet deep, using lager yeast but a warm temperature of between 16 to 21 degrees C, 60-70 F. It has a finished strength of five per cent alcohol by volume or four per cent by weight under the American system. The grist is a blend of pale and crystal malts with no brewing sugars. Hops are Northern Brewer which are added three times in the kettle. After fermentation, the green beer is warm-conditioned for three weeks and is then kräusened by adding some partially-fermented wort to encourage a strong secondary fermentation. It is a complex, bronze-coloured beer, with a rich, malty-nutty aroma, malt and light fruit in the mouth and a finish in which the hop slowly dominates. It has thirty to thirty-five units of bitterness. It is clean, quenching and, as Americans say, 'hits the spot' like a lager, but those qualities are overlain by a decidedly ale fruitiness.

The genuine ales in the brewery are fermented in conventional six-feet deep vessels. It was Maytag's visit to English ale breweries that encouraged him to develop Liberty Ale in 1975. The English brewers would have been less impressed by the choice of name, for it commemorated the ride two hundred years earlier by Paul Revere from Boston to Lexington to warn the American revolutionaries that the British army was on the march. His ride signalled the start of the War of Independence. Liberty is one of the world's classic ales, six per cent by volume, 4.8 by weight. It is brewed from pale malt and is hopped with American Cascades. American hops take no prisoners. Like Californian grapes, they are big, bold, assertive and perfumy. Cascades are added not only to the kettle but also to the maturation tank and the finished ale has an intense lemon-citric aroma and palate and a big dry, hoppy finish. The other Anchor beers are a rich Porter (five by weight, six by volume) with a Cappuccino-coffee character, a tart, refreshing Wheat Beer made from seventy per cent wheat with delicate apple fruit hints, the staggering Old Foghorn barley wine (seven by weight, 8.75 by volume), fruity and vinous with eighty-five units of bitterness from Cascade hops, and Our

231

Special Ale, brewed every year for the Thanksgiving and Christmas periods. It has a different specification each year and always uses a 'secret' ingredient: in the past this has been cloves, coriander, cinnamon and nutmeg.

If, like an ice-skating judge, I had to hold up cards to mark Anchor beers, the only mark less than ten would be for 'presentation'. Fritz Maytag is a firm believer in pasteurisation, both in bottle and keg. In a country devoid of tied trade, he does not trust bar owners to look after living beer. I appreciate the problem but other new wave brewers are experimenting with cask-conditioned ale (on an admittedly localised basis) and bottle-conditioning is becoming the hallmark of some of the better ales. It would a cruel irony if Anchor were eventually to be seen as a conservative force in the brewing industry, left behind as the new waves crash on to the beach. But I am looking at the American experience through British eyes and I am anxious not to detract from Maytag's enormous achievement. Pasteurised they may but his beers are of the very highest quality and they have helped to transform the perception of beer in the US.

To find Bert Grant's brewery I had to fly to Seattle and then board a tiny prop plane that soared and dipped alarmingly over the snow-capped, hump-backed Cascade Mountains. There was no snow on the ground at Yakima's small airport and Bert Grant turned on the air conditioning in his Oldsmobile to counter the blistering summer heat. The licence plate of his car bears the name REAL ALE. Sherry, his wife, has a Porsche licensed as ALE WIFE. The commitment and a sense of history are clear. Bert is a Scot by birth but left Scotland at the age of two. He grew up in Canada where he worked as an analytical chemist for Canadian Breweries, later Carling O'Keefe. When that giant company went into terminal decline, he crossed the border and worked for Stroh's brewery in Detroit. After four years with Stroh's he moved to Yakima to rebuild a hop processing plant. The Yakima Valley, once part of French Canada, is the major hop growing region of the United States, producing Cascades and other varieties. The Yakima Valley must be one of the few areas in the world where grapes and hops grow side by side.

As he worked on hop processing, Bert Grant started to brew at home. Friends liked his beer. When production reached five hundred barrels a year, he decided it was time to go commercial. His first brewpub was in the old Yakima opera house, built in 1890. He has since moved to a greenfield site on the edge of town where he brews 12,000 barrels a year and has a capacity to grow to 25,000. He also has a new outlet in the town, Grant's Brewery Pub at 32 North Front Street, alongside the now redundant railroad station. He brews on the premises and offers some ales in cask-conditioned form, though the bulk of his draught ales are filtered. He tried selling cask versions to bars in Portland, Oregon and Seattle but the staff had no concept of living beers and they became infected. Grant has been determined to brew ales that adhered strictly to style. His Scottish Ale, which he describes without a shred of self-

ABOVE: *Sherry Grant's politically-correct licence plate.*

BELOW: *Some of Grant's labels.*

doubt as 'the best beer in the world', has the amber colour and generous nutty roastiness of dark crystal malt but is a shade too hoppy to be genuinely Scottish. But it is difficult not to end up with a hop-accented ale if you use Cascades in the kettle and Willamettes for dry-hopping. The 5.6 by volume, 4.5 by weight beer chalks up forty-five units of bitterness. It has a rich sultana fruitiness balanced by a pungent hoppiness, with more dark fruit in the mouth and a fruity and bitter finish. Grant's Celtic Ale again has too much hop character to emulate an Irish beer. The brewery's India Pale Ale is closer to style. It bursts with hop character, has fifty units of bitterness and is 4.5 per cent alcohol by volume. Bert Grant, following English precedent, uses only pale malt. For Americans puzzled by the derivation of the name, the label of the bottled version shows British soldiers in front of the Taj Mahal. Other Grant beers include a lemon and bubblegum wheat beer, a chocolatey Porter with a pronounced hint of peat smoke from imported Scottish malt, and a seven per cent by volume Imperial Stout that reaches a mouth-puckering one hundred units of bitterness. It is packed with aromas and flavours redolent of liquorice, fresh leather, coffee and hints of apple fruit. Bert Grant's ales are sold in twenty-seven states in the US, as far south as Florida. His company grew by fifty-nine per cent in 1993 but commercial success never turns his head from the enjoyment of beer. After a long day that included lunch in the brewpub, a tour of the brewery, and a long drive high into the spectacular Cascade Mountains for a memorable meal in a log-cabin restaurant overlooking a foaming river, we got back to Yakima late in the evening. Bert was heading for my hotel then 'hung a right' back to his brewpub. 'There's always time for another beer,' he said.

Dedication to beer style is taken equally seriously in Seattle by Charles Finkel. He runs a company named Merchant du Vin but his main love and commercial driving force today is the grain rather than the grape. He has a brewery museum, a bookshop and the Pike Place Brewery. The tiny brewhouse is on the site of a former brothel, a point he celebrates with a barley wine called Old Bawdy. Pike Place today is a modish, harbour-front food market interlaced with elegant restaurants. Finkel's ales include Pale Ale, East India Pale Ale — he is a stickler for history and geography as well as style — and Porter. The Pale Ale (4.5 per cent by weight) uses imported Maris Otter malt from Crisps of Norfolk, England, twenty per cent crystal malt and is hopped with East Kent Goldings. With such a generous amount of crystal, the beer is a rich amber colour. It has a peppery hop aroma, a biscuity palate, and dark hops and fruit in the finish. The East India Pale Ale (six per cent by weight) is brewed by pale, carapils and Munich malts and is hopped with Chinook, British Columbian and Goldings hops. It is tawny gold in colour, has a massive grapefruit aroma from the Chinook, more tart fruit in the mouth and a powerful hoppy finish. The Porter (five per cent by weight) has a rich coffee and chocolate aroma and palate from pale, crystal, chocolate and black malts and some dark winey fruit in a finish that becomes very bitter. Bubbling over with enthusiasm for beer in general and his brews in particular, Charles Finkel described events in the United States as a renaissance. 'We're going back beyond Prohibition and the second wave of immigrants with their lager culture to the Founding Fathers. We're going back to our roots.'

The Redhook Brewery is the biggest new wave brewery in the Northwest. It is based in a former trolley barn or tramshed in the Swedish Fremont district of Seattle. It brewed 90,000 barrels in 1994 and has built a new brewery on the edge of the city. The Trolleyman bar next to the original brewery (3400 Phinney Avenue North) offers the full range of beers and imaginative food. I tasted a spicy Wheat Hook ale, a piny, orange-fruity Extra Special Bitter hopped with Tettnang and Willamettes and brewed from pale and cara malts, a splendidly hoppy IPA with generous doses of Goldings, Northern Brewer and Willamettes, and a Blackhook Porter with black malt and roasted barley, three hop varieties and a big, bitter chocolate and coffee aroma and dark fruit finish, more of a stout than a porter. Launched in 1982, Redhook agreed in 1994 to sell fifteen per cent of its stock to Anheuser-Busch. The giant says it will market Redhook ales nationally. It is an indication of how seriously the national brewers see the rise of the micros. In the same year A-B launched an Elk Amber Ale using English ale yeast while Miller started a series of Special Reserve beers with an Amber Ale and a Velvet Stout. Let us hope their refound interest in ale does not extend to buying up independent breweries.

ABOVE: *Hooked on ale ... Redhook's tavern sign in Seattle in a former trolley car shed.*

BELOW: *Brewing giant Miller has turned to ale.*

Portland, Oregon, mirrors Seattle in its interest in good ale. The Portland Brewing Company is based in a charming brewpub in the town centre (1339 NW Flanders Street) but was due to move in 1994 to a custom-built new site on the edge of town, with German-style architecture and a copper brewhouse to rival Anchor's. Vice-president Fred Bowman was a keen home brewer who recreated a rather esoteric English ale, Bishop's Tipple from Salisbury, got the brewing bug and found partners to go commercial. The new brewery will produce 70,000

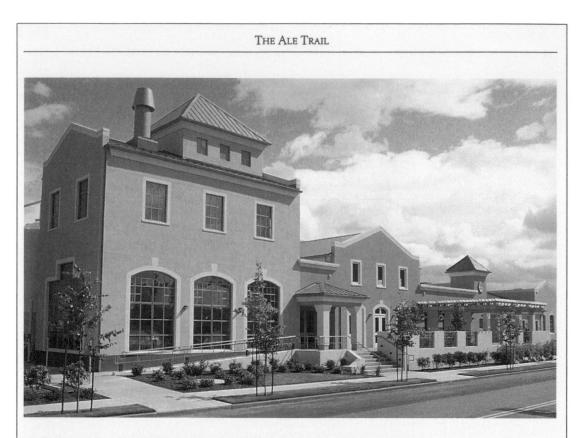

barrels a year when the new plant comes on stream. I sampled Portland Ale, around five per cent by volume, made only from pale malt, with a big citric aroma from Cascade hops, tart fruit in the mouth and a light, quenching finish. McTarnahan's Ale is a degree stronger and is named after a major shareholder in the brewery. It is made from pale and crystal malts and is hopped with Cascades. It has a rich, nutty aroma, dark sultana fruit in the mouth and a bitter-sweet finish. I also tried a Porter with English black malt that had a dark chocolate and coffee character and big hoppy finish, and a powerful Stout with a massive dark, almost burnt malt aroma, coffee and chocolate in the mouth and smooth, creamy finish.

ABOVE: 'The prettiest little brewery in the West' - Portland Brewing in Oregon

The BridgePort Brewing Company is based in Portland's oldest warehouse, a fine building decked by masses of climbing ivy. The brewery was opened in the early 1980s by the Italian-American wine-making Ponzi family who spotted a niche in the market. The large, open-spaced bar and restaurant was packed when I was there with a large crowd of mainly young people, clearly delighting in the beers and the simple, English-style pub food. Promotions manager John Forbes showed me the stainless steel brewhouse then took me through the beers, starting with a cask-conditioned ale called Coho, a dry-hopped pale beer of around 4.4 per cent alcohol by volume, brewed with Goldings and Nugget hops. It had an appealing citric aroma from the

hops, more bitter hops in the mouth and a dry and bitter finish. The 'regular' beers, filtered, served under pressure and at a lower temperature, included a peppery-hoppy BridgePort Ale, a Blue Heron Ale in honour of Portland's emblem, made from pale, crystal, black and chocolate malts with a hoppy start, soft creamy malt in the mouth and a tart and hoppy finish, and a rich Stout packed with dark malt and fruit character and a hoppy finish.

Back in northern California, Sierra Nevada Brewing Company in the university town of Chico is one of the earliest of the new wave micros, founded in 1981 by Ken Grossman and Paul Camusi. Grossman made the usual American leap from home-brewing to the real McCoy and concentrated on ales at first simply because he did not have any conditioning tanks for lager. In 1993 production passed 70,000 barrels and the company is growing by around fifty per cent a year. A new brewhouse was installed in 1987, with copper vessels gleaming inside a tiled room. The flagship ale is Pale Ale (4.2 per cent by weight, 5.3 by volume) in bottle, called Sierra Nevada Draught in keg form and slightly darker and a fraction less in alcohol. It has won four gold medals at the Great American Beer Festival. It has a spicy, citric Cascade hops aroma, malty in the mouth and with a big, dry and hoppy finish. Sierra Nevada also brews a coffeeish Porter, a six per cent volume Stout with a fine roasted malt character, and the renowned Big Foot Barley Wine, at 12.5 per volume one of the strongest beers brewed in the US. It has a rampant aroma of hops and dark malt, massive alcohol and hops in the mouth and a shatteringly rich and warming finish. The hops are Nugget for bitterness, with a late addition of Cascade for aroma, and Cascade and Centennial for more aroma during conditioning. Sierra Nevada has great faith in its beers and does not filter in bottle or keg. All the bottled beers are naturally conditioned, the ales filtered, re-seeded, primed and matured for several weeks before leaving the brewery. Sierra Nevada's ales are of outstanding quality.

Another Californian home-brewer whose business is booming is Pete Slosberg. He has ruffled a few feathers with beers called Pete's Wicked Ale and Pete's Wicked Lager on the grounds that they don't have serious-sounding names but the Ale (around five per cent by volume) has won the Great American Beer Festival's gold award in the brown ale category. It has a copper colour and distinctive chocolate and slightly vinous palate. It is made from pale, crystal and black malts and is hopped with Cascades. Slosberg, a former marketing man from the 'Silicon Valley' computer industry, first brewed his beers under contract at the Palo Alto Brewing Company. When the company went into voluntary receivership, Slosberg spent the weekend moving out his beer supplies before they could be impounded by the authorities. The beers are now brewed under contract in St Paul, Minnesota.

ABOVE: *In up to his neck ... Pete Slosberg tries a wicked bathful.*

Another award-winning brown ale comes from the Brooklyn Brewery. The famous suburb of New York City — originally settled by the Dutch — was once a powerhouse of East Coast brewing but Prohibition, Depression and the growth of national brands wiped them all out. Journalist Steve Hindy, a keen home-brewer, was dodging bullets in the Lebanon while covering the internecine strife for Associated Press when he thought there must be a safer way to make a living. Back home he joined forces with banker Tom Potter to sell beer and they secured the advice of veteran brewer Bill Moeller, who was keen to recreate pre-Prohibition Brooklyn recipes. Brooklyn Lager, with a generous amount of crystal malt and dry-hopped, almost deserves inclusion in this book as it has such a rich, fruity and ale-like quality. Brooklyn Brown (4.8 by weight, six by volume) is made from pale, crystal, chocolate and black malts, and is hopped with Cascade and Northern Brewer. It is also dry-hopped. There are chocolate and coffee on the aroma and palate with great hop character. At present both the Brooklyn beers are contract-brewed by the million-barrels-a-year F.X. Matt brewery in Utica, New York state, but Hindy and Potter were planning to open their own plant in 1995 and thus restore Brooklyn's proud brewing tradition.

The Boston Brewing Company is better known as Samuel Adams from the use of the stern face of the eighteenth-century American patriot and brewer who was a leading figure in the struggle for independence from the British. Jim Koch (pronounced Kook) is a descendant of Bavarian brewers who brought their skills to the United States but were forced out of business as a result of mergers in the 1956. Koch, Harvard-educated, gave up a business career to restore the family traditions by starting to sell beer in 1985. His Samuel Adams Boston Lager, sold door-to-door by Koch, was an almost instant success. The beer was contract-brewed, a point stressed by critics of Koch's aggressive marketing style (though face-to-face he is a charming and self-effacing person). Stung by the criticism, Koch established a small plant

on the site of the former Haffenreffer brewery in Boston's Jamaica Plain. Although several of the beers continue to be contract-brewed, the Boston plant is responsible for Samuel Adams Boston Ale, based on a now extinct English style — would Sam Adams approve? — known as stock ale, a well-matured beer that was used for blending with younger beers. Boston Ale, around five per cent alcohol by volume, has an appealing amber colour, a big hop peppery-resiny aroma from Fuggles and Saaz (the ale is hopped three times during the boil and again during conditioning), tart and fruity in the mouth and with a big malty-hoppy finish. Koch also produces a chocolatey Cream Stout, a spicy Wheat and even a Cranberry 'Lambic', though purists have pointed out that no wild yeasts are used in its production.

Perhaps the most exceptional success story in recent American brewing history is that of Pierre Celis. The man who recreated the Belgian wheat beer tradition with Hoegaarden moved to Austin in Texas when he was bought out by Belgian giant Interbrew. He now brews, with enormous success in a state where local pride runs high, Celis White, which closely resembles his original beer, a perfumy Golden, a top-fermenting Bock, and a spicy Grand Cru that faithfully replicates the Hoegaarden version. In 1995 Celis stunned his admirers by selling a controlling interest to Miller.

CANADA

Canada, like its North American neighbour, had a long period of Prohibition, running from World War One until 1932. The result was an industry controlled by a handful of giants, a situation made worse by laws banning the export of beer from one province to another. The nationals, Labatt, Molson and the now-defunct Canadian Breweries, could afford to set up plants in each province. Others lacked the capital to follow suit. Canadian Breweries had produced ales as well as lagers but with its demise, production became even more concentrated in the hands of Labatt and Molson, with their unremarkable lagers. Both companies had started as ale brewers but were converted to lager by Czech and German immigrants in the late nineteenth century and encouraged by US practice to use rice and corn syrup as adjuncts. Today's national lager brands have around ten units of bitterness, hardly enough to trouble brewing's version of the Richter scale. The situation has been compounded by both a Calvinist opposition to the pleasures of alcohol in many areas — but not French-speaking Quebec — and hostile laws that made it difficult to launch new breweries and brewpubs. It has taken a long time for the ice-floes to melt. Canada is only slowly reawakening to the joys of good beer.

I travelled to Victoria, British Columbia by fast clipper from Seattle, the boat speeding between large, wooded islands and zigzagging across the watery section of the Canadian-US border. Victoria is the most English of Canadian cities, with red London buses and a rocky coastline that resembles the remote English county of Cornwall. Spinnakers, on the outskirts of the town and with fine views over the sea, was the first licensed brewpub in Victoria. It was the dream of architect Paul Hadfield, a genuine Canadian native in an area heavy with English regional accents, and his business partner John Mitchell. Both are from Vancouver. In 1982 Mitchell returned from a trip to Britain with fourteen English ales. For Hadfield, Mitchell and friends a new world of beer tastes opened before them and determined them in their drive to open a brewpub. Bye-laws and planning regulations had to be tackled. The City of Victoria said brewpubs could not be allowed, then did a volte-face and gave planning permission as long as local people supported the plan in a referendum. Ninety-five per cent voted Yes. Even then permission to both brew and sell beer required an amendment to Federal law, which was approved just a couple of months before the pub was due to open. From opening day on 15 May 1984, Spinnakers was packed. It had to employ a man on the door to restrict entry so that no more than sixty-five people could be in the bar at any one time, to meet the requirements of the Liquor Control Board. The bar can hold 125. Mitchell lobbied the board for two years to relax this absurd rule. When he failed he resigned from the business and went back to Vancouver. Finally, seating capacity was expanded when a restaurant was added on the ground floor and the bar moved one storey up.

The small brewhouse, built by SPR of Manchester, England, has been expanded twice to meet demand. Paul Hadfield's main brew is Spinnaker Ale at 4.2 per cent alcohol by volume. It is made from pale malt and a small amount of crystal and is hopped with Cascades from Yakima and Centennial from Oregon. It has an apple fruit aroma, more tart fruit in the mouth and has a light dry finish. Mount Tolmie (4.2 per cent) has caramalt, chocolate and crystal blended with pale malt. Mount Hood hops are added in the copper and the beer is dry hopped with Cascade. It has a citric fruit aroma, dark and tart fruit in the mouth and an intensely dry and bitter finish. Doc Hadfield's Pale Ale, also 4.2 per cent, uses Mount Hood for aroma and bitterness. The ale has a resiny, piny aroma, with citric fruit in the mouth and a light, dry finish with fruit notes. Mitchell's ESB is named in honour of the other founding partner, not a distant brewery in Lancaster. It is 4.6 per cent, copper coloured, with a grapefruit aroma and palate from Chinook hops and a citric finish, with hints of sultana fruit from the generous use of crystal and chocolate malts. There is a late addition of Cascade hops. A 4.9 per cent India Pale Ale uses just Centennials hops and pale malt and is close to style. It has a resiny hop aroma, tart fruit and hops in the mouth and a citric fruit finish. A splendid 4.9 per cent Porter uses pale, crystal, chocolate and roasted malt and malted wheat, with Centennial and Hallertau hops. It is spicy, herbal, with even a slight lactic hint, and tart in the mouth. Empress Stout, with the same strength, has a pleasing bitter chocolate and hops character. Paul Hadfield now branches out with more esoteric brews, including a Hefe-Weizen and a lambic. (Spinnakers, 309 Catherine Street, Victoria BC: both bar and restaurant serve excellent food.)

Swan's hotel, restaurant and brewpub is run by Michael Williams in the heart of Victoria. He is from Shropshire and emigrated to Canada to become a sheep farmer and rancher. He moved into property, bought an old warehouse and turned it into the stylish Swan's at 506 Pandora Street. The bar is not an attempt to replicate an English pub (Spinnakers has more of a pubby feel) but is spacious and attractive with brick walls, pillars and tiled floors. Buckerfields Brewery at Swan's is large for a brewpub, with gleaming vessels. It is run for Michael Williams by Chris Johnson, a former home-brewer who graduated from the hotel kitchen. He uses pale, crystal, chocolate and roasted malts, with oatmeal in his stout, all imported from Bairds of England. Pellet hops comes from Washington state. Chris brews a five per cent Bitter with a nutty, malty aroma with good piny hops, dark raisin fruit in the mouth and a dry, bitter finish, and a 4.5 per cent Pandora Pale Gold with light citric fruit on the aroma, quenching hops in the mouth and bitter-sweet finish. His eight per cent Scotch Ale is McEwan's Export with hair on its chest. There are big winey fruit and hops on the aroma, raisin and sultana fruit in the mouth and a complex finish with malt, nuts and late hop. Appleton Brown Ale (five per cent) is named after the designer of the brewhouse, Frank Appleton. It has pronounced apple fruit and cinnamon aromas, dark fruit in the mouth, and a creamy, bitter-sweet finish. Rye Weizen, which has a four-hour run-off from the mash tun because of the sticky rye grain, is 5.7 per cent, has a dark biscuity aroma, a bready, spicy palate and a very dry finish with a late burst of fruit. Oatmeal Stout (5.4 per cent) has a rich, dark coffee and hops aroma, bitter-sweet malt and hops on the nose, chocolate and hops in the mouth, and a tart and

ABOVE: *Home from home ... Swan's Hotel and brewery in the very English town of Victoria, British Columbia.*

bitter finish. Food in the hotel is an excellent companion for the imaginative beers.

Moosehead is the largest Canadian independent. It has had a turbulent history since it began as a backyard brewery in Nova Scotia in 1867. John and Susannah Oland used recipes brought from Britain and soon went commercial. John was killed in a riding accident and Susannah's son Conrad, the brewmaster, was killed in an explosion when two boats collided in Halifax harbour. The family briefly lost control of the company during Prohibition but managed to buy it back. Its fortunes soared with the launch of Moosehead Ale in 1931, to such an extent that the brewery was also subsequently renamed Moosehead. Today Moosehead is a major exporter to the United States but the character of its ales and lagers has diminished in the quest for mass marketability. Moosehead Ale (five per cent) has a delicate malt aroma with some yeastiness, is light bodied, with a thin finish and some faint hoppiness.

The Upper Canada Brewing Company in Toronto, Ontario is a large micro specialising in ales free, as its labels proclaim, 'from adjuncts, additives and chemicals'. The beers are also unpasteurised. Dark Ale is the main brand in the style of a British ale with dark fruit, malt and hops. Its Wheat Beer (4.3 per cent) has more than thirty-five per cent wheat blended with pale malt. Hops are Northern Brewer (eighteen to twenty units of bitterness). In the brewing town of Guelph, the Wellington County brewery produces an Arkell Best Bitter to mark a connection with the Swindon brewing family of Arkell in Wiltshire. The cask-conditioned ale (four per cent) has a peppery Goldings aroma, malt and fruit in the mouth and a long, hoppy-fruity finish. The brewery also produces a fruity Wellington SPA (4.5 per cent), a hoppy County Ale (five per cent), Iron Duke (6.5 per cent), a rich and fruity strong ale, and a deep, roasty, chocolatey Imperial Stout (eight per cent).

Perhaps it is because many of the French settlers in Canada came from Normandy and the Flanders area that they have a surprising but welcome ale-brewing tradition. Les Brasseurs du Nord in St Jerôme, north of Montreal, proves the point and brews a dry Blonde, a fruity Rousse and a smooth, dark Noire. La Cervoise in the heart of Montreal has La Main, a sweetish amber ale, a golden Good Dog ale, and a dry stout called Obelix. Also in Montreal, Le Cheval Blanc offers a chocolatey Ambreé, an Espresso-like Brune and a tart Weissbier. The last word on Canadian beer goes to Unibroue, in the Montreal suburb of Chambly. As well as a bottle-conditioned, aromatic Blanche de Chambly wheat beer and a spicy Belgian-style ale called Maudite, it brews the herbal La Fin du Monde, only a shade less daunting than Belgium's Morte Subite — Sudden Death.

Chapter Eight
Australia

ABOVE: *Tyke tyro ... Thomas Cooper who went from Yorkshire to Adelaide to found a brewing dynasty. He is the great-grandfather of Bill Cooper.*

BELOW: *... and his Sparkling Ale*

The English settlers of Australia and New Zealand took an ale culture to those far-off lands. The heat and humidity of Australia in particular made a switch to lager beer inevitable, though a split personality exists to this day. Many lagers, the world-famous Castlemaine XXXX in particular, are still branded as 'bitter' in their homeland. When Castlemaine is brewed under licence in other countries, it insists on an infusion mash complete with a Steel's Masher, but fermentation is with a lager yeast. But, apart from a recent boom in brewpubs, the story of genuine ale in Australia is the story of Cooper's of Adelaide. It is now such a strong, national brand that its owners can forget the near-derision in which it was held until recent years. Cooper's Sparkling Ale was not sparkling. It tended to be a cloudy yellow-orange in the glass. Poured without due care and attention, it also attracted a heavy sediment from the bottle to the bottom of the beer. Above all, it was not a lager and was not served at the sort of jaw-jutting, near freezing temperatures used for other brands. But Cooper's has had the last laugh. It has become a cult ale, has burst from its Adelaide heartland to most parts of the continent and is available on draught as well as in bottle.

Thomas Cooper and his wife, the daughter of an innkeeper, emigrated from Yorkshire to Australia in 1852. While he worked as a shoemaker and later a dairyman, his wife brewed at home, using the skills her father had taught her. It is believed that Thomas brewed some ale to her recipe as a tonic when she was unwell. His friends were impressed and he decided to brew beer commercially. When his wife died, he remarried, producing no fewer than sixteen children, ensuring the continuation of the brewing dynasty. Thomas was a lay preacher and his staunch Methodism convinced him that pubs were places where the devil lurked. He sold beer to private customers but did not build a tied estate, which saved his company in later years when large brewers went on the takeover trail, buying up competitors that owned licensed outlets. The Coopers stuck to traditional ways and did not introduce a lager to their range until the late 1960s.

Sparkling Ale, 5.8 per cent, reminds me in its complexity, colour and fruity-hoppiness of the Orval Trappist ale from Belgium. It is brewed from local pale and crystal malts and Pride of Ringwood hops. Liquid cane sugar comprises around eighteen per cent of the grist. Units of

bitterness are twenty-five to twenty-six. Along with the other Cooper beers, Sparkling Ale used to be fermented in wood and the yeast cleansed by dropping into oak hogsheads known as puncheons. Now the ales are fermented in conicals and those who have known the products for many years say they have lost some of their character. After primary fermentation, the ale is centrifuged to remove the yeast and then primed with fermenting beer and sugar. The beer is warm-conditioned for six weeks before leaving the brewery. Sparkling Ale is fruity and intense, with a deep peppery hop aroma, citric fruit in the mouth and a tart and quenching finish with more hops and fruit.

Cooper's Stout is lesser known but is an equally impressive ale. Roasted malt is added to pale and crystal to produce a 6.8 per cent beer with an oily, coffeeish character. In recent years Cooper's has reintroduced a 'dinner ale' style beer, a lower strength version of Sparkling Ale called Original (4.5 per cent) with plenty of apple fruit and hops. Based unashamedly on the famous Welsh Brain's Dark, Cooper's is also producing a Dark (4.5 per cent) with pale, crystal and roast malt with fruity and chocolate characteristics.

The success of Cooper's has prompted other Adelaide brewers to emulate it. The Lion Brewing micro, which re-opened in 1992, brews a five per cent Sparkling Bitter Ale, less cloudy than Cooper's but with plenty of Pride of Ringwood and English Goldings character. The Kent Town Brewery in a restored Victorian maltings produces Kent Town

ABOVE: *Sepia pints ... Cooper's Brewery in Upper Kensington, Adelaide around 1911.*

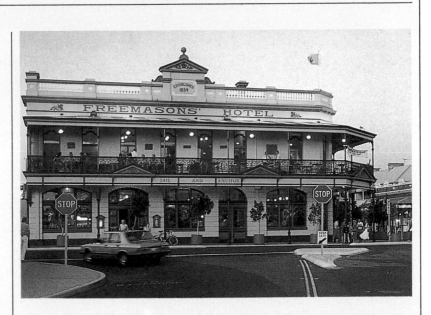

Real Ale (5.5 per cent), extremely fruity and with plenty of hop character. It manages to be even more opaque than Cooper's and was launched with the slogan 'A new cloud on the horizon'.

At the Sail and Anchor brewpub in Fremantle, Ken Duncan is brewing cask-conditioned beers that include Seven Seas Real Ale, Brass Monkey Stout and a strong Ironbrew. Seven Seas, the main beer, is 4.6 per cent alcohol based on the Burton pale ale style. It is a deep copper colour with a strong hoppy finish with thirty-five units of bitterness. Brass Monkey (six per cent) is a rich oatmeal stout with a roasted coffee aroma and mouth-filling crystal and liquorice notes with thirty-three units of bitterness. Ironbrew (seven per cent) is a deep mahogany colour with a fruity aroma, a rich crystal malt palate and well-balanced finish with thirty-three units of bitterness. Duncan also produces occasional ales, including a mild ale and a barley wine. The brewhouse has a mash mixer feeding an infusion mash tun, with boiling in a mash kettle. Late hops are added in the hop back. After primary fermentation the green beer is racked into casks where it undergoes a secondary fermentation. The beers are served by traditional English handpumps.

One of the large brewing groups, Tooths, now owned by Foster's, brews a Sheaf Stout that is genuinely top-fermenting. It is 5.7 per cent alcohol and has thirty-five units of bitterness. It has an aromatic aroma, with coffee on the palate and a good hop finish.

Chapter Nine
Odd bottles

Mackeson Stout, now something of a sideline in the mighty British Whitbread empire, was once a major brand that challenged Guinness hard in sales. And until the 1940s it was sold as 'Milk Stout', part of a breed of stouts made with lactose that were thought to be just as good for you as Guinness. A turn of the century booklet produced by Mackeson, then an independent brewery in Hythe, Kent, would cause palpitations among modern dieticians. 'Make Stout More Nourishing! That was the aim of Mackeson & Co when after a long period of exhaustive research in conjunction with one of the leading analytical food chemists, they were to produce a beverage containing nature's best food, scientifically and carefully introduced' it claims. It went on to say that milk stout gave drinkers energy, stopped distention, fullness, indigestion and headache, prevented rheumatism and was ideal for nursing mothers and invalids. Clearly, a beer that should be available on doctor's prescription. Milk had been added to beer and, in particular, porter and stout for several centuries before Mackeson in 1910 brewed a stout that used lactose, also known as milk sugar. It was thought that milk softened and sweetened beer and also added healthy properties. Lactose is a by-product of cheese making and is made up of ninety-five per cent milk sugars. It cannot be fermented by conventional brewer's yeast and leaves carbohydrates and calories in the finished beer. The first Mackeson label proclaimed: 'Each pint contains the energising carbohydrates of ten ounces of pure dairy milk'. This was later withdrawn, as was a milk churn illustration but the brand name 'milk stout' continued and was taken up with enthusiasm by rival brewers. At a time when people's diet was poor and most engaged in hard, manual labour, healthy beer was seized upon.

Mackeson was founded in 1669 during the reign of Charles II. It brewed several conventional beers, including an India Pale Ale, but milk stout soon became its main brand in the twentieth century. By a series of twists and turns — it was sold to Simonds of Reading which in turn became part of Courage and was then sold on to Jude, Hanbury in Kent in which Whitbread had a controlling interest — it became part of Whitbread. By the late 1930s, Mackeson was nationally available in bottle — a cask version disappeared — and by the 1960s it accounted for more than fifty per cent of Whitbread's output. By this time 'milk' had

RIGHT: *An early poster for Mackeson Milk Stout.* (Whitbread Archive)

MACKESONS
MILK STOUT

THE ORIGINAL & GENUINE MILK STOUT

been dropped from the title as the result of a post-war edict from the Ministry of Agriculture, Fisheries and Food on the grounds of misleading claims. Curiously, the milk churn has returned to the label in recent years without any screams from the health lobby.

As beers became paler and tastes changed, sales declined and Mackeson became a beer-on-wheels, cycling round the Whitbread empire. It ended up in the Exchange Brewery in Sheffield but that was closed in the early 1990s and the stout is now produced at the giant processed beer factory at Samlesbury in Lancashire. It is made from pale and chocolate malts, caramel and around nine per cent lactose, the lactose added as powder in the copper. The lack of fermentability of the milk sugar can be seen by the fact that while the stout has an original gravity of 1042 degrees, the finished alcohol by volume is a modest three per cent. Target hops produce twenty-six units of bitterness, destroying the belief that 'milk' stouts are sweet. The dark, almost jet-black beer has a coffee-ish aroma and palate reminiscent of post-war coffee essence. There is a gentle fruitiness and a distinct hint of those ancient sweets known as milk drops. Although Whitbread will not confirm it, there have been rumours in recent years that it may introduce Export Mackeson to Britain, with five per cent alcohol and thirty-four bitterness units. I have tasted this characterful stout and would certainly order it from the milkman if it were available.

ABOVE: *Carnegie ... Swedish Porter created by a Scot.*

A Scot named Carnegie emigrated to Sweden and started a brewery in Gothenburg, where he brewed porter. The company later merged with the state-owned Pripps and Carnegie Porter became a footnote, available at one time only on doctor's prescription. But now it is back to its former glory, brewed to the top strength permitted in Sweden of 5.6 per cent. Pripps now produces an annual vintage version of the stout. It is genuinely top-fermented and has a rich coffee, chocolate, dark raisiny fruit and hops character. Although the beer is pasteurised, it will develop slightly in bottle: I tasted several vintages in the Stockholm brewery and was fascinated by the small flavour changes from year to year. Across the Baltic, Sinebrychoff in Finland brews a Koff Porter that, with such a name, definitely should be on prescription. Again it is top-fermenting, curious in Scandinavia where many dark beers labelled porter and stout are lagers. Koff Porter is also available in an annual vintage.

In the Caribbean, old colonial traditions die hard. Two stouts of around six per cent alcohol survive, both with names heavy with promises of potency. Dragon Stout from Desnoes and Geddes is thick, sweet and syrupy, while Banks of Barbados's Stallion has an intriguing orange head and complex flavours that suggest molasses may have more than a walk-on part in the brewing process. In Kandy, high in the mountains of Sri Lanka, the Ceylon Brewery produces Lion Stout (6.2 per cent). It is fermented in wooden vessels and is brewed from English, Czech and Danish malts, Styrian hops and English yeast. The bottle-conditioned stout is superb, with rich chocolate and coffee on the aroma and palate, and great hop character. Dragon, Stallion and Lion, all beasts of beer, are available in selected outlets in Britain.

BELOW: *Imperial flourish ... Lion Stout, cask-conditioned dark beer from Sri Lanka.*

One of England's oddest beer styles is a brown ale that isn't. It is confined to the North-east where the most famous version is Newcastle Brown Ale. It is the biggest-selling bottled ale in Britain and has massive sales in the United States. It is developing a market in Russia. Newcastle Brown is a red ale though it has little in common with the red beers of Flanders. The style was developed for Newcastle Breweries by the well-

ABOVE: *Taking aim ... a range of Maxim and Double Maxim Ales in the Vaux Brewery museum.*

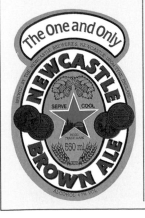

named Colonel Porter. The beer was launched in 1927 and has been a cult beer ever since. Today it is drunk by young people, many of whom have the distressing habit of drinking it straight from the bottle. It is a malty beer, made from pale and crystal malts and is blended from two different brews. The finished beer is 4.7 per cent alcohol with twenty-four units of bitterness. In spite of its impressive strength for a 'brown ale' it has a rather thin and caramelly palate. A beer in the same style but with greater character comes form Vaux — pronounced 'Vorks' — of Sunderland. Again an army man is involved. Captain Ernest Vaux lead a raid during the Boer War using the Maxim machine gun and was honoured on his return to Sunderland with a beer called Maxim. A stronger Double Maxim was introduced in 1938. It is brewed from pale and crystal malts with a touch of caramel and is primed with sugar. Only Fuggles hops are used. It is 4.2 per cent alcohol and has a superb earthy Fuggles aroma, it is rich and nutty in the mouth and becomes dry in the finish with some tart fruit. It has twenty-two units of bitterness. As a result of years of lobbying by local CAMRA members, Vaux now produces Double Maxim in cask-conditioned as well as bottled form. It's a rattling good beer.

Selected bibliography and further reading

Peter Mathias, *The Brewing Industry in England, 1700-1830* (Cambridge, 1959).

T.R. Gourvish and R.G. Wilson, *The British Brewing Industry, 1830 to 1980* (Cambridge, 1994).

H.S. Corran, *A History of Brewing* (Newton Abbot, 1975).

Michael Jackson, *Michael Jackson's Beer Companion* (London, 1993).

Michael Jackson, *The Great Beers of Belgium* (Antwerp, 1991).

Brian Glover, *Prince of Ales — the history of brewing in Wales* (Dover, 1993).

Graham Wheeler, *Home Brewing — the CAMRA Guide* (St Albans, 1993).

Dr John Harrison, *Old British Beers and How to Make Them* (Durnden Park, 1993).

LEFT: *The mash tun at Donnington's Brewery.*

Useful addresses

GREAT BRITAIN
Campaign for Real Ale, 230 Hatfield Road, St Albans, Hertfordshire AL1 4LW. Phone 01727 867201. Fax 01727 867670.

BELGIUM
OBP, c/o Peter Crombecq, Postbus 32, 2600 Berchem 5. Phone 010 323 280 1330. Fax 010 323 230 1888.

NETHERLANDS
PINT, Postbus 3757, 1001 AN Amsterdam. Fax 010 311 021 221 62.

UNITED STATES
American Homebrewers Association, PO Box 1679, Boulder, Colorado 80306-1679. Phone (303) 447 0816. Fax (303) 447 2825.

BELOW: *Hops on their way to Guinness by dray horse in days of yore.*

Index

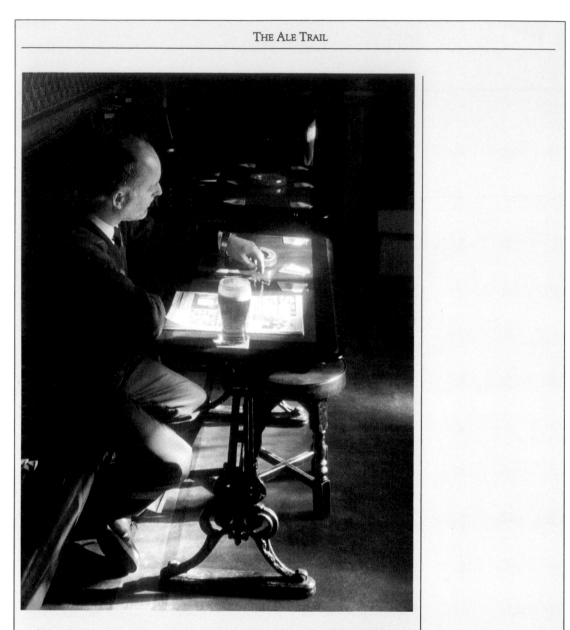

'They've been drinking beer since the time of our ancestors and our sons will go on drinking beer, and the sons of our sons until the age of ages. Lets feast, lets drink beer and lets sing when the time is right until our death. Those who drink die, those who don't drink die. We'll die, too. Let our actions live on after us, let our names remain on the lips of our children and children's children, let them live on after us as we are living now.' — Hieroglyphic inscription in the visitors' book at the famous Prague home-brew pub U Fleku, made by the Egyptologist Frantisek Lexa.